T0247938

OPENING
DOORS

ALSO BY HASIA R. DINER

OPENING DOORS

The UNLIKELY ALLIANCE
BETWEEN THE IRISH AND
THE JEWS *in* AMERICA

Hasia R. Diner

ST. MARTIN'S PRESS
NEW YORK

First published in the United States by St. Martin's Press, an imprint of
St. Martin's Publishing Group

www.stmartins.com

Library of Congress Cataloging-in-Publication Data

Names: Diner, Hasia R., author.
Title: Opening doors : the unlikely alliance between the Irish and the Jews in
    America / Hasia R. Diner.
Other titles: Unlikely alliance between the Irish and the Jews in America
Description: First edition. | New York : St. Martin's Press, 2024. | Includes
    bibliographical references and index.
Identifiers: LCCN 2023059614 | ISBN 9781250243928 (hardcover) | ISBN
    9781250243935 (ebook)
Subjects: LCSH: Irish Americans—Relations with Jews. | Jews—United States—
    History. | Irish Americans—History. | Immigrants—United States—Social
    conditions. | United States—Ethnic relations—History.
Classification: LCC E184.36.I75 D56 2024 | DDC 305.8916/2073—dc23/
    eng/20240221
LC record available at https://lccn.loc.gov/2023059614

First Edition: 2024

10 9 8 7 6 5 4 3 2 1

To Gabriella Steinberg:
Welcome to my beloved circle, as you join with your Matan,
Shira and Eugene, Hannah and Abraham, Eli and Anh, and
Emmanuel, and Steve, there from the beginning.

CONTENTS

OPENING
DOORS

Introduction

Opening Doors tells the story of two peoples who met in America. In this historical encounter, millions of women and men, had they stayed home, back in Ireland and eastern Europe, would never have spun into each other's orbit. They never knew each other before and had no real idea of the other's existence.

But America, the world's largest receiver of immigrants, with individuals streaming in from multiple places, brought them together. Here, they lived in overlapping spaces, encountering each other in apartment buildings, on streets, in schools, shops, and workplaces. American conditions shaped that meeting, and despite their differences, particularly in religion, circumstances on the ground threw them together, and they forged a singular relationship.

The Irish showed up first in the millions, starting in the late 1840s. The mass Jewish migration from eastern Europe commenced in the 1880s. Both groups gravitated to American cities, and in New York, Chicago, Boston, and elsewhere a simple reality prevailed. The Irish, already firmly planted in these places, having learned much about America and how it worked, found it in their interests to align themselves with the newly arrived Jews, assisting them as they settled down in their new homes. Jewish newcomers recognized that the Irish, so deeply entrenched and exercising so much influence in some very strategic places, namely, urban politics, public education, and the labor movement, might help them fashion their American futures. An ethnic group willing to stand up and demand rights and respect, often noisily, Irish immigrants and their children provided other newcomers, Jews included, with a model of assertiveness in an often-hostile environment.

Jews and Irish figured they needed each other. The Irish reckoned that they could keep power and serve their own interests by mentoring and guiding these relatively poor Yiddish speakers seeking to navigate the intricacies of American life. Irish politicians, for example, showed up to lead the Jews to the polls, introduce them to the American art of voting, and teach them how to become members of political clubs and then run for office. Irish women and men encouraged Jews to found unions and sustain the labor movement in which the Irish predominated, and the Irish women who made up the majority of the public-school teachers in the big cities literally taught Jewish youngsters—and by extension their parents—how to be American, providing them the skills they needed to facilitate their movement out of the working class.

The Jews, coming into an ethnically diverse society in which they, as white people, enjoyed the entitlements of citizenship and full political rights, still had to figure out who could help them with the many issues that confronted them as outsiders. Like the Irish, they came to America as permanent immigrants, not intending to go back. They had decisions to make about settling down, building families, forging communities, protecting themselves at home and abroad, and, perhaps most importantly, achieving economic stability.

Little in their premigration experience prepared them for

America. While the Jews who had migrated earlier to the United States—some of whom had become successful, affluent, and well-connected—helped out these later migrants, differences in class and outlook complicated their robust assistance. Irish Americans made up the difference.

The Irish politicians searching for the Jews' votes, Irish union activists seeking to build a broad-based labor movement, and Irish public-school teachers who stood in their classrooms and ushered immigrant children into English literacy and American culture—all paved the newly arrived Jews' paths into American life. Jews accepted this guidance, seeing in the Irish a large and powerful group that seemed to have figured out how to build ethnic communities that simultaneously preserved group solidarity and mastered American realities.

The two became partners in a very American dance, not because they admired each other or believed in abstract ideals of interfaith and interethnic outreach. They did not seek to break down communal barriers but rather needed each other, and circumstances dictated that in this choreography, the Irish led, and the Jews followed.

Both knew that a powerful force outside of their communities sought to limit them both, namely the old white American Protestant elite, which defined the nation as belonging to it. Jews and Irish understood that they had to overcome the deeply entrenched attitudes and vigorous efforts of these guardians of the nation who had erected barriers against them both. The Irish in particular referred to this group as the "Puritans," or the "Yankees," but whatever name they used, the old-stock Americans—the wealthy, those who held the top rungs of power, the sentinels of the culture—had little love for either Irish or Jews, interlopers or guests grudgingly accepted in their home. Poor white Protestants with little power, particularly in rural areas, also saw the Irish and the Jews as unwelcome aliens, bearers of traditions and cultures at odds with true American life and values.

Whether rich or struggling, these longtime Americans considered the overwhelmingly Catholic Irish as agents of the evil pope in Rome, adherents to a despised religious tradition with no rightful place in a democratic nation committed to individualism and liberty. As imagined by their foes, the drunken, lazy, stupid, lowly Irish contributed nothing to America other than their brute strength. Nearly all the social reform movements of nineteenth-century America coalesced around the project of improving the Irish, ridding them of their noxious traits, and weakening their insidiously growing influence in public life.

Jews, by definition non-Christians, challenged assertions of the United States as a Christian nation by their very presence. A treasure trove of Jewish stereotypes as too greedy, too pushy, too dishonest, too selfish, and too aggressive dogged them as they took their first steps into the American public sphere. They talked too loudly, massacred the English language with their accents, and dressed in flashy clothes. They blundered into places where many believed they did not belong. Colleges and universities, hotels and beach clubs asked, Would too many Jews drive away others, the better sort? Will they change the tone and style of our American—read Protestant—institutions?

Irish immigrants and their sons emerged within a few decades of their great migration, which commenced in the late 1840s, as prominent players in American urban politics, making policies that impacted the lives of the white Protestants of British background. By the 1870s and 1880s Irish women began to show up as schoolteachers in robust numbers, molding the minds of American children. And Irish women and men standing at the helm of the American labor movement demanded that they had the right to redefine the relationship between employers and their employees.

Neither the Jews nor the Irish had founded the nation, the discourse decried, yet now they seemed bent on changing and redefining it to serve their own interests. To many it seemed that these outsiders wanted to replace the true Americans.

Thus, Jews and Irish had some common enemies. In their efforts to undermine their detractors, Jews directly or indirectly turned to Irish women and men to help defend them and prove that Jews did belong in America. Irish writers and journalists, politicians, and community activists relished taking on their enemies, happily assuming the role of spokespersons for the Jews. By doing so, they could say that they, the Catholic Irish who had arrived as refugees from the Great Famine, had become better Americans than those who claimed to have created the nation.

For the Jews, the Irish made excellent surrogates in group defense. With their breathtaking roster of mayors, aldermen, and representatives in Congress, and their vast numbers and willingness to be outrageous and publicly demonstrative—all qualities the Jews lacked—the Irish seemed perfect defenders of a people very much, at home and abroad, in need of defense.

The scenarios re-created in this book, spanning the decades from the end of the nineteenth century into the 1930s, do not shy away from the reality that anti-Jewish sentiment flourished in Irish American communities. Nor does it deny that Jews speedily bought into the ugly prevalent American images of Irish women and men as inebriated louts, violent—if humorous—at times, fit only for domestic service and low-level manual labor.

Despite the overarching theme of Irish-Jewish mutuality that pervades this book, an ominous and negative presence hovers over it as well. The shadow of Father Charles Coughlin, the radio priest of the 1930s whose broadcasts may have been the ugliest articulation of anti-Semitism in American history, looms large as a backdrop.

He appeared on the American stage and thundered over its

airwaves simultaneously with Hitler's decision to rid Germany and then the rest of Europe of the Jews. Coughlin lavished praise on Hitler and inspired street action against Jews in the United States, causing them to question their safety in America as they also sought to aid their fellow Jews trapped within the menace of the Third Reich.

Yet his voice, however loud, and his Irish Catholic minions, however numerous, do not define the full encounter between Irish and Jews that began in the 1880s; this encounter profoundly shaped the histories of the two peoples who did not easily fit in yet managed to do so. Coughlin, for all of his toxic rhetoric, did not end Irish advocacy for Jews or stop Jews from seeing in Irish Americans able defenders of their cause. Despite Coughlin, the strategy behind the Irish-Jewish alliance persisted.

This book, as declared in the title, employs the metaphor of the opening of doors. In this, the Irish held the knobs, helping Jews to cross over so many thresholds. They might have acted differently, but they calculated that it worked for them to unfasten the locks.

The four portals that frame *Opening Doors*—public advocacy, urban politics, labor organizing, and education—did not represent the totality of the Irish-Jewish encounter in America, nor were they the only places where the one facilitated the entry of the other. But they made the biggest difference as launching pads for Jewish integration and mobility, and that makes *Opening Doors* about Irish American history.

Jews availed themselves of and sought out the Irish to help them. That they did so makes this as much a book about American Jewish history.

Their shared history points to the importance of allyship, whatever the motivation, and underscores the rarely acknowledged truth that no one, no group, makes it on their own.

1

American Meeting Places

A duo of early twentieth-century songwriters, William Jerome—born William Jerome Flannery, whose parents had emigrated from Ireland—and Jean Schwartz, a Jewish immigrant from Hungary, churned out one tune after another. Jerome wrote the words, Schwartz composed the music, and together their hefty output got sung in music halls, became incorporated into Broadway shows, was recorded for gramophone, and appeared as sheet music, making it possible for ordinary people to sing the songs in their homes, seated around living room pianos. Jerome and Schwartz did well, producing a steady stream of works and helping make New York the epicenter of the nation's popular-music industry.

Among the many tunes to their credit, one from 1912 stands out for its historic punch and its insights into the cultural underpinnings of the "little USA." "If It Wasn't for the Irish and the Jews" extolled America—"Yankee land"—for bringing together these two peoples. The United States brought them together, served as their common ground, and this, as Schwartz and Jerome depicted it, helped foster democracy. Without them in combination, "Uncle Sam would have the blues."

The phrase "If it wasn't for the Irish and the Jews" closed out each stanza, as Jerome and Schwartz ran through a list of contexts, including urban politics, popular entertainment, and quotidian life on the street, where these people met and had ample opportunity to express their "sympathetic feeling" to each other. As they sketched it out, "Hear my words and make a note / On St. Patrick's day Rosinsky / pins a shamrock on his coat."

Indeed, they mused, "I often sit and think," wondering "what would this country be" had the vast immigration from Europe to the United States, without design, not compelled Irish and Jewish women and men to encounter each other, share spaces, and change each other while they left their marks on the institutions and culture of the nation as a whole.

Those meeting places, so liltingly described by Jerome and Schwartz, caught the attention of others, perhaps less lyrically and not so consistently positively. On the whole, as contemporary observers noted, the accident of history created a complicated landscape that put the Irish and the Jews into each other's orbit. Not limited to hostile or friendly, antagonistic or appreciative, the ways in which Irish and Jews interacted reflected the reality that in urban America they had no choice but to connect, and in the main, those intersections served them both fairly well.

Robert Archey Woods, a Boston social worker, neither Irish Catholic nor Jewish, offered in his 1902 book *Americans in Process* a glimpse of the historic meeting taking place on the streets of the working-class neighborhoods of the city's North and West Ends. This same scenario occurred in other American cities where Jews and Irish shared space and learned about each other.

Woods assumed that because of the profound differences between these two peoples, they inevitably "would clash." He discovered something different. Besides the "cry of 'Christ-killer,' with which a Roman Catholic child now and then greets his Jewish fellow," Woods heard "few expressions of bigotry" and saw little marked hostility. The Jewish and Irish denizens of these gritty enclaves managed to live together. The Irish Catholic, who constantly navigated the "disadvantage on account of his religion," felt "more or less tolerant of his Jewish neighbor." The Jew, for his part, "has learned patience and long-suffering through ages of oppression," finding occasional ugliness, mostly limited to offensive epithets mouthed by youngsters, minor and fleeting, as opposed to the live-and-let-live reality of ordinary life. Woods further commented that "many Roman Catholic boys make a business of lighting and caring for the fires in Jewish homes on the days when the Jews are enjoined by their religion from engaging in manual labor." The Irish boys traversed the streets, shouting, "Fire, fire!," seeking out Jewish customers.[1]

Woods did not observe two peoples who connected with each other because of a belief in cultural pluralism. Neither did either group celebrate ethnic and religious diversity as inherently good.

His brief vignette could have described realities in most American places where Irish and Jewish people found themselves thrown together; despite the gulf that separated them, they interacted, as they had to, on a personal level, benefiting from each other's presence.

The Irish had been there first and could claim American cities as their turf. Their formal institutions, houses of worship, meeting halls, shops, and places of leisure predated those of the Jews. They already claimed informal urban spaces, streets and street corners, alleys, vacant lots, playgrounds, and parks. The Jews followed, perforce accommodating to the Irish presence on the urban landscape.

Jewish and Irish women, men, and children bumped into

each other mostly in unremarkable ways in the ethnic cauldrons simmering in American cities. Whether living in the same apartment buildings or nearby as customers and merchants, each generally entered the consciousness of the other in limited and fleeting ways, sometimes problematic, but mostly harmonious.

Memoirs have told of random street violence committed almost exclusively by Irish boys, often while uttering the ugly term "Christ-killer." In Boston, Theodore White, the son of Jewish immigrant parents, who became a noted American journalist, experienced such incidents. "We were an enclave surrounded by the Irish . . . very tough Irish—working class Irish." He recalled how "the local library lay in such an Irish district, and my first fights happened en route to the library, to get books." While "pure hellishness divided us . . . after one last bloody-nose battle, I was given safe passage by the Irish boys whenever I went to the library."

The White family and their immediate Jewish neighbors lived at the edge of several Irish neighborhoods, each with their own boy gangs who constituted an annoying fact of daily life. But in a startling turnaround, White described how "on the day my father died I climbed over the fence to call Johnny Powers . . . to come out. . . . I explained that my father had died that morning, and asked him if he could keep the kids in his street quiet for the rest of the day." In respect of the Jewish family's mourning, the Irish boys complied.[2]

Recollections like White's pepper the American Jewish immigrant-era memoir literature, written by boys about boys. Poet Harry Roskolenko encapsulated them. In *When I Was Last on Cherry Street* he described "horrifying block-fights" on the Lower East Side, where "we grew up with our fists." Unlike White, who depicted himself as the serious Jewish boy hurrying off to the library, Roskolenko described a world of generalized mayhem across many group lines, though he remembered particularly vividly how "the Jews of Cherry Street . . . fought the Irish from Front Street." In the neighborhood's violent juvenile ethnic stew, "the Micks were . . . fighting the sheenies," but we "were all cooperating against the Wops. We were obviously creating the higher values of man in boy in the comradeship of the good fight and the sharing of busted heads." The fights on Cherry Street also pitted Jews against Poles, but violence screeched to a halt on the Fourth of July and Election Day, when all the gangs put down their arms and joined together to enjoy the raucous thrill of building "six-story-high bonfires," thanks to Tammany Hall, the Irish-controlled political machine, which was always searching for the votes of others, Jews prominently among them.[3]

Sophie Ruskay, the daughter of a bourgeois Jewish family, lived a more genteel life in the New York of the late nineteenth century. But she, too, observed moments of Irish-Jewish violence. Her cousin Jack somehow broke the window of Murphy's Saloon. The owner, "a big man," came outside and, witnessing the damage to his property, confronted the vandal with "you Sheeny," to which Jack retorted unafraid, "you big Mick."[4]

These shreds of the Irish and Jewish past pointed to the reality that low-level violence, intermittent street fights, and ugly, insulting words resounded in their shared streets. Young male Jews, rather than being sad objects of Irish brutality, formed their own street gangs, challenged their Irish peers, and exchanged punches. They, like and often with Irish boys, considered other outsiders, especially Italians, fair game for the occasional beating. Labor organizer Abraham Bisno, who met America and the Irish in Chicago, told of rumbles between "Irish rowdies and our own rowdies." Slurs of "kike" and "sheeny" blended in with cries of "mick" as everyday defamations with little meaning.[5]

But neither the attacks nor the defamatory language defined the relationship, nor did they hamper the forging of more amiable connections. As a boy, David Seligson, who would become a rabbi and lead New York's Central Synagogue, lived in East Harlem, attending public school during the day and a neighborhood Talmud Torah in the evening. As he made his way home through darkened streets, "located on the fringe of the Irish neighborhood," he and his Jewish classmates sometimes "would be set upon by the 'locals,'" the Irish boys who "took it out on the 'Yid kids' most unmercifully." Painful, for sure, but the "minor pogroms," as he called these skirmishes, ground to a halt, and in public school, over time, the Jewish and Irish children "played on the teams together, got to know the 'cop of the beat,' celebrated Thanksgiving and the Fourth of July." These latter experiences he considered an expression of how "America worked its magic on all."[6]

Harry Golden, editor of *The Carolina Israelite,* offered some graphic stories of his encounters on the streets of New York's immigrant enclave, when as a child, some "Irish 'buckoes' grabbed and then 'cocktailed,'" him, that is, they derived great sport out of urinating on his circumcised penis. Yet Golden, author of *Only in America,* forged a range of positive personal relationships with Irish men and women, including his wife Genevieve Gallagher, sister of his best friend, Hubert. He explained that he had long "thought of marrying an Irish girl" because "[we] Jewish boys . . . loved the Irish." To this Lower East Side immigrant child, the Irish represented America: "they were strong. Nothing seemed more American to me than marrying an Irish Catholic."[7]

At the same time, Jewish rhetoric easily incorporated prevalent anti-Irish imagery, especially depicting the Irish as stupid. Golden had no trouble describing his brother-in-law and dear friend as "the smartest Irishman I ever knew," implying that, for the most part, Irish people lacked the intelligence and intellect that Jews claimed as theirs.

Nat Hentoff, journalist, civil-liberties defender, and jazz

critic, shared the details of his Jewish Boston boyhood in an immigrant home, like the others, retelling unsavory encounters with Irish tough boys. After a few beatings, bloodied noses, bloodied shirtfronts, and some anti-Jewish insults, he ruminated on the pain he endured and his shame at being unable to defend himself. But he knew that "we of the Yiddishe kops [Yiddish for *heads*, but more a statement about Jewish mental agility, their superior brains, as the brag went] will grow up to be served by these goyishe [non-Jewish] hooligans fattened into loutish laborers, garbage men, firemen, and cops."[8]

Observers of the Irish-Jewish encounters in those years noted how Jewish claims about their own mental prowess contrasted with statements about the low intellectual level of the Irish. Woods, who described the Irish Catholic boys selling their services to Jews unable to light fires on the Sabbath, remarked that the Jews talked about "the ignorance and stupidity of the 'firelighters,'" talk that "has passed into a proverb among Jews." These young Irish Catholic men who wanted to earn some money by helping Jews fulfill the dictates of their religion during the frigid Boston winters became the fodder for Jewish humor.[9]

The belief in Irish oafishness reflected the pervasive thinking of the era. The Irish, whether discussed in England or the United States, possessed, according to prevalent racialist thinking, inferior and degraded characteristics.

Beyond their stupidity, the Irish hated Jews, Jewish sources declared, which in turn allowed Jews to hate them. They blamed the Catholic Church, which Jewish historical memory linked to the ceaseless persecution of the Jews perpetrated by Catholicism, which had spawned nothing less than the blood libels—the accusations hurled against Jews since the Middle Ages that they killed Christian children, using their blood to make Passover matzo—as well as the ghettos, the forced conversions, and such traumatic events as the Crusades and the expulsion from Spain. Jews in their publications, sermons, and political projects pointed to popes and Catholic prelates as the sources of Jewish suffering and considered ordinary Catholics, like their Irish neighbors, too blind and lacking in intelligence to question their religious leaders.

The assumption of Irish hatred of Jews as a by-product of their irrational adherence to Catholic teachings floated around the American Jewish world as a truth. Marcus Jastrow, a distinguished scholar of rabbinical literature, speaking at New York's Jewish Ministers' Association, a forum for local rabbis, included in his address an example of this, sharing as true an unsubstantiated anecdote:

> You all know the story of the Irishman who on a Monday morning going to his quarry met a peddling Jew, and without the least warning began to pound him. His comrades, wondering at this sudden convulsive rage on one otherwise peaccably inclined, asked him, "What has this poor, inoffensive Jew done to you?" "Me," said he, "me, nothing but he killed my Savior." "Not he," said they, "but his ancestors more than eighteen hundred years ago were the perpetrators." "I do not care when it was done but I heard of it only last night."[10]

That someone as learned as Jastrow believed and reported that this had indeed happened reflected a longer political project among American Jews. One of the first Jews to serve in the United States Congress, predating by several decades the great migration from eastern Europe, Lewis Charles Levin ran for office as a Know-Nothing, the nation's virulent anti-Catholic, nativist political party. A committed temperance man, Levin joined in the political fray in 1840s Philadelphia, helping to organize protests against the decision of the local school board to allow Catholic children to leave their classrooms when lessons began using the Protestants' King James Version of the Bible. Levin attempted to give a speech against this accommodation in a heavily Irish neighborhood, Kensington. Throngs of Irish Catholic residents drove him and his fellow protestors out. He returned, leading thousands of anti-Catholic agitators, and in the tumult that followed, two Catholic churches went up in flames. Inspired by these events, in 1843 Levin decided to run for Congress, where he served three terms, zealously pursuing the Know-Nothing agenda, which focused on the perils posed by the increasingly large masses of Irish Catholic immigrants disembarking at American ports.

Anti-Irish rhetoric floated around Jewish communities. The mother in Mike Gold's classic proletarian novel, *Jews Without Money,* hated the Irish, whom, she declared, "live like pigs; they have ruined the world. And they hate and kill Jews. They may seem friendly to us to our faces, but behind our backs they laugh at us."[11]

By declaring that they "live like pigs," Gold's mother picked up on prevailing Anglo-American views of the Irish as feckless and sloppy, unmoved by middle-class standards of hygiene.

Such talk linking the Irish with dirt and contamination rampaged through American discourse. It made its way into Jewish letters and commentary. Yisroel Kopelov, like many Jewish immigrants, earned his first dollars as a street peddler in New York and noted as he wrote of his journeys around the city that "in the Irish neighborhoods the dirtiness was exceptional!" Their enclaves caused "disgust when [one looked] at them. Just the smell . . . was unbearable!"[12]

Turn-of-the-century Jews in America did not hesitate to express such sentiments. Bella Spewack grew up poor on New York's Lower East Side as the daughter of a single mother who emigrated from Transylvania, and later cowrote such Broadway musicals as *Kiss Me, Kate*. She described one of the tenements she lived in: It housed "the O'Connors, a drinking widow and her two little girls: one, a crooked-mouthed cripple, and the other of the conventional Irish type." On the fourth floor she remembered "the Murphys," who "drank spasmodically without the bacchanals Mrs. O'Connor indulged in."[13]

Jewish respondents in an early twentieth-century study undertaken by Welsh-born Protestant sociologist Thomas Jesse Jones unabashedly echoed Gold's semifictional mother and Spewack as well. "In general," Jones summarized, the New York Jews he studied saw the "Irish as thriftless and careless," and while, yes, they noted the presence of some good Irish women and men, and children who transcended the pathologies of the majority, in the main, Jews thought of the Irish in negative terms, as the "drunken Irish" who "wasted all their money in drink." And, consistent with Hentoff's juxtaposition of Jews with brains and the Irish as thugs, forever loutish and crude, Jones's Jewish informants "contrasted them with her own people, who rarely are drunkards," preferring the "vichy bottle" to the "beer-bucket" so visible in the Irish flats. One older Jewish woman whom Jones interviewed had recently moved to a neighborhood on the West Side, and somewhat reluctantly told him point-blank, "I don't like the Irish. . . . I vant to go back downtown."[14]

The Jewish antipathy toward Irish Catholics grew as many embraced socialism in the United States and defined the Catholic Church as a key obstacle to bringing about economic justice for the working class. In New York the Irish-dominated political machine, Tammany Hall, worked to block socialist electoral victories, and Jewish socialists attributed that opposition to the twinned power of Catholic conservatism and Irish parochialism. Despite the reality that some Irish did join socialist groups and turn out for socialist candidates, Jewish socialists considered Irish Catholicism an enemy to be vanquished.

Jewish immigrants imbibed these images while learning to become American. Their communal newspapers and magazines helped spread the same derogatory images of Irish people that appeared in general American publications. In the Yiddish and English-language Jewish press, Irish references popped up in jokes, amusing vignettes, and humorous sketches. Cartoons with clearly marked Irish characters—recognizable by their apelike faces, thick bodies, rude oaken sticks, cloddy oversized shoes, and ragged hats and clothes, and by the pipes hanging out of the men's prominent lips—all appeared. Irish women showed up as frowsy domestic servants with simian faces, rolling pins in hand, messy hair, and aprons draped over ample bodies.

The Irish domestic servant in particular served as an object of jokes and humorous sketches in the Jewish press, evidence that the Jewish affluent class, like many white Americans, employed Irish women in their homes. New York's *Jewish Messenger* in October 1875, for example, regaled readers with a "dialogue between a lady and an Irish servant." Asked if her mistress happened to be at home, the Irish woman replied emphatically, "Not at home!" When asked if she would inquire again, the servant goes out, then comes back to say, "She's not at home, ma'am; but she says she'll be in half an hour."[15]

The Jewish press abounded with stories about Irish maids in Jewish homes, flummoxed by kosher cooking, puzzling over Passover matzo, Jewish holidays, and the material objects of Jewish life, which they cleaned and polished. *The Jewish Messenger* told one about an Irish servant girl discussing with "her fellow servant," in Irish dialect, the odd-shaped object affixed to the door of her employer's home—a mezuzah, a ritually mandated marker for Jewish space. "Shure, Mary Ann . . . thim are the thermometers what tell you the state of the weather." Another article described some Jewish children who went to a costume party dressed as Irish servants.[16]

Jewish-Irish stories in the Jewish press often appeared as odd, funny, or incongruous, and mostly at the expense of the less-than-smart Irish, as compared to the intelligent Jews. An 1897 piece in New York's *American Hebrew* found it amusing that when the brass band of the Hebrew Orphan Asylum, its banner reading HOA, marched in the city's Washington Centennial celebration, some Irishmen misread it as AOH. According to the paper, they "presumed [it] stood for the Ancient Order of Hibernians." Not so bright and unable to speak in anything other than dialect, the Irish men declaimed, "Begorra . . . ain't thim fine Irish boys."[17]

Yet in the real world of urban America, without jokes or stereotyping, Jews and Irish found plenty of opportunities to meet, interact, and establish friendships and working relationships as they carved out shared spaces to pursue common goals.

An obvious place to look for Irish-Jewish connections might be municipal marriage-license bureaus, where city officials solemnized weddings joining Irish and Jewish partners. We cannot know how many such marriages took place, but biographies of some prominent individuals, usually Jewish men who wed Irish American women, bear witness to such matrimonial border crossings.

Harry Golden married an Irish woman, his beloved Genevieve. His mentor, Oscar Geiger, had also married an Irish woman, Nina Daly. Irving Berlin, born Israel Beilin in the czarist empire, enjoyed a long and loving relationship with Irish Catholic Ellin Mackay. Berlin's career spanned decades; he composed some of America's most popular songs, including "Easter Parade," "White Christmas," and "God Bless America," with a substantial part of the royalties he earned flowing to Jewish philanthropic causes. Few know the name of Dick Pearlstein, a Boston haberdasher who married a young working-class woman, Dolly Cushing, daughter of Irish immigrants who sold tokens at a city transit station. One of her brothers had joined the priesthood, rising to Boston's archbishop. Cardinal Richard Cushing, a prince of the church, briefly garnered a worldwide audience when he conducted the funeral mass of John F. Kennedy in 1963. But in the 1950s, prodded by his Jewish brother-in-law, Dick, he silenced an outspoken anti-Semitic priest and stump speaker, Leonard Feeney—known in Boston as "Sheeny Feeney" because of his loud outdoor rantings against the "sheenies." Cushing also played a pivotal role in rallying the American bishops as they prepared for Pope John XXIII's transformative gathering, the Second Vatican Council, which issued the *Nostra aetate* declaration disavowing the responsibility of the Jews for the sin of deicide, officially making them Christ-killers no longer. William Z. Foster, son of a Fenian from Cork and a leader of American communism, married Esther Abramowitz, a Jewish immigrant and fellow activist.

Americans of all backgrounds would have had the opportunity to think about Irish-Jewish marriages via a spate of movies and plays, the most famous of which was *Abie's Irish Rose,* first appearing as a Broadway play in 1922. Written by Anne Nichols, the play enjoyed a long life, returning in various iterations on the stage, in a radio series on NBC, and finally on film. *Abie* told the story of a very American romance between a Jew, Abie, and his Irish sweetheart, Rose. The intolerance of their fathers, steeped in stubborn hatreds, put obstacles in their path, but in the end, love conquered all. *The Cohens and Kellys,* a 1926 silent film with some spin-offs, so closely resembled *Abie's Irish Rose* that it motivated Nichols to sue Universal Pictures for copyright infringement.

These stories celebrated the power of love between two individuals who saw each other as real people, freed from the blinders of the past. They contained enough lighthearted humor, particularly at the expense of the fathers, to highlight the incongruous pairing of these two peoples, but it was done sweetly and with the humor evenly distributed between the Irish and the Jewish men.

The less amusing but also popular novel *East River* occupied a spot on the bestseller list for six months when it appeared in English in the mid-1940s. Written by the Polish-born Sholem Asch, a prolific Yiddish novelist, the book explored in vivid detail the neighborliness, casual friendship, and then highly charged courtship and marriage between Mary McCarthy and Irving Davidovsky. Asch's novel ended with a tragic denouement, warning that even love cannot withstand the primal attachments of religion and tribe.

Like the McCarthy and Davidovsky families who populated Asch's novel, Irish and Jews had ample opportunity to cross paths with each other and to foster friendships. Abraham Shuman, a successful Jewish immigrant businessman in Boston, and John Boyle O'Reilly, Irish nationalist and editor of Boston's Irish Catholic magazine *The Pilot,* socialized for decades. Shuman and O'Reilly took on each other's causes, and Shuman, who outlived O'Reilly, paid for his memorial marker, sculpted by the renowned Daniel Chester French and erected in Boston's Fenway neighborhood—a tribute to the poet, Irish patriot, journalist, and friend over decades. Edward Flynn, Tammany Hall's boss in the Bronx, recalled that "the Goldwater and Flynn families have been friends for fifty years. My two brothers were playmates of Monroe Goldwater's older brothers when they were all small boys."[18] Monroe Goldwater became Ed Flynn's law partner, gaining a prominent foothold in New York State Democratic politics. Flynn used his political prominence to support the Jewish Joint Distribution Committee in the immediate post-Holocaust era to raise money for survivors. Oscar Bernstein, a Brooklyn lawyer, hired and mentored both William and Paul O'Dwyer, 1920s immigrants from Bohola, County Mayo.

They formed a law partnership together, and the Bernsteins and the O'Dwyers as families regularly spent time together outside work.

Irish-Jewish friendships and mutual warm personal relationships grew at times out of common political and civic concerns. Jacob Billikopf, born in Vilna, Lithuania, came to Kansas City, Missouri, in 1907 to head the local Federation of Jewish Charities. The mayor appointed him along with Francis "Frank" Patrick Walsh, a lawyer whose parents had emigrated from Ireland, to a committee charged with investigating conditions in the city's workhouses. Until Walsh's death in 1939 the two remained friends, writing a steady stream of letters in which they sought out each other's counsel. The relationship between Walsh and David Lilienthal began in 1921, when the latter, then a law student, wrote to Walsh for guidance on how to build a legal practice devoted to the interest of labor rather than business.

All of these stories were a far cry from the street violence of urban boy gangs. The young Rose Schneiderman, later a labor and suffrage leader, recalled "Miss Healy," a cashier she worked with at Ridley & Sons Department Store on New York's Lower East Side. They both "read a great deal," bonding over their love of literature, and Healy, Schneiderman remembered, "would occasionally lend me some of her books," including the "risqué" novel *Camille*. Despite Miss Healy's higher position in the store's pecking order, she got to know Rose and "knew she could trust my sense of propriety."[19] Edward Walsh, a native of Kilkenny, came to Chicago in 1884 and secured work in the law firm of Salomon and Zeisler. Walsh and Moses Salomon, a leader in Chicago's Jewish community, represented the city's Central Labor Union, and according to an entry about Walsh in an 1897 book listing notable Irish men in Chicago, "the association of the two men ripened into friendship which happily still exists."[20]

Propinquity in neighborhoods made unplanned meetings ordinary and normal and laid the foundation for Irish and Jews to see each other as real people without diminishing the differences in religion, place of origin, and facility with the English language that divided them. Whether they flowered into friendships or not, these interactions fostered civility.

One writer for Chicago's Jewish paper *The Sentinel* observed this phenomenon in an article, "Patrick and Levy." He, Levy, declared that "Patrick is my next-door neighbor. We live very peacefully together, although we never exchange any visits." Levy dubbed this aptly an "American courtesy," maintaining "good terms . . . be friendly, and yet keep aloof." Beyond the "short salute once in a while or a brief conversation . . . in the hall or on the street," neither he nor Patrick ventured "one inch further than the threshold."

Cool politeness prevailed, though. "Patrick utters once in a while a foolish thing about the Jews," but Levy declared, "he soon takes it all back." Levy recalled that he, however, used at times offensive language against the "goyim" himself, calling Patrick's "son a Sheigitz—his daughter a Shiksa." While Jews lobbed these slurs broadly against all non-Jews, Levy confessed his own anti-Irish prejudices, admitting that he would "frequently ridicule the mode of their eating, especially their drinking."

However, he noted that the behavior of the Irish and Jewish men contrasted that of "our ladies," who "maintain quite a different way among themselves." The Irish and Jewish women, unlike their husbands, "are paying frequent visits to another," and as to the next generation, "the children intermingle at play."[21]

Irish Americans and Jews came in and out of each other's lives. The commercial sphere provided a place to do this. Like so many Americans, particularly working-class Americans, Irish women and men depended upon Jewish shopkeepers to procure the goods of ordinary life. Nat Hentoff celebrated his father's acumen as a clothing retailer, the proud owner of Hentoff's Men's Shop in Chelsea, a mixed Irish-Jewish neighborhood. Cy Hentoff mastered the art of the sale customer by customer, and "even goyim went out of their way to come" into his haberdashery, "including the mayor, an Irisher."[22] Hentoff emphasized his father's ability to chat with customers, flatter them, and with great skill convince them that he cared more about them than the sale itself. A good businessman, bent, like all others, on making a profit, he catered to his Irish customers by telling them what they wanted to hear. Thomas Jones, in his study of one Manhattan city street in 1904, likewise noted the easy meeting across the shop counter linking Irish customers and Jewish merchants. "This disposition," namely the jolliness, as he depicted it, "of the Irish, and the business qualities of the Jews, often make possible a degree of purely economic cooperation between" them.[23]

Utterly ordinary and ubiquitous places, like Hentoff's Men's Shop, seem to have inspired no friction between Jewish shopkeepers and Irish customers. Unlike in Polish or African American neighborhoods, Irish customers launched no boycotts against Jewish merchants, nor did they organize angry street demonstrations charging that Jews sold them shoddy goods at unfair prices or treated them rudely.

Irish and Jewish neighborhood interactions took place outside of the stores owned by Jews where Irish customers shopped. On shared city streets, Jews, rabbis and laypeople, met Catholic priests who, rather than castigating the Jews to eternal damnation as Christ-killers, extended themselves as neighbors. Father Edward McGlynn, who served New York's St. Stephen's parish from 1866 until 1887, approached the officers at the nearby Congregation Adereth El with a proposal. He pointed out that a house of worship so close to his own ought to be in a more aesthetically pleasing structure than that which currently stood. He provided funds from his church's coffers for the synagogue to replace its wooden stairs with stone ones.[24] An uncle of the New York suffrage activist Maud Malone, Father Sylvester Malone, regularly met with local rabbis in his Williamsburg neighborhood, having once attended a Purim ball. Rabbi Leopold Wintner of Brooklyn's Congregation Beth Elohim described in the Jewish press how he had "sat for more than two hours in one of the pews of Saints Peter and Paul Church" at Malone's funeral mass at his 1899 passing.[25] The father of Congressman Samuel Dickstein, a rabbi, routinely invited local Irish Catholic priests into his home and turned to them for support when his son and other Jewish boys experienced bullying by Irish young men who flung around "sheeny" and "Christ-killer" epithets. And finally, a number of young Jewish men found themselves serving during World War I in New York's "Fighting Sixty-Ninth" regiment, known also as the "Fighting Irish." They faced the rigors of battlefield combat with comfort and encouragement from Father Francis P. Duffy. Looking back to the war's horrors, the Catholic chaplain recalled shortly after the armistice that he could not "remember anything that delighted me more than when I heard" that one of the men under his care, "Sergeant Abe Blaustein was to get the Croix de Guerre," having been "recommended for it by Major Donovan and Major Stacom (the pride of our parish) and Lieutenant Cavanaugh."[26]

Nuns of Irish orders also interacted positively with Jews. Playwright S. N. Behrman grew up in a mixed Jewish-Irish neighborhood in Worcester, Massachusetts, and recalled how his chronically ill mother, an immigrant from Lithuania, spent much time at the local hospital, Saint Vincent, founded and staffed by the Sisters of Providence. He waxed eloquent about the care she got from these Irish women, about whom "she never could say enough in praise." As he told it, "Though my mother spoke very little English, she managed to become firm friends with many of them." She landed in the hospital all too often, and "whenever she came, they welcomed her. It was a charming consideration on the part of the nuns that they veiled the holy pictures on the walls—the Virgins and the Crucifixions—to spare the religious sensibilities of their orthodox Jewish patients."[27]

The sheer accumulation of such anecdotes added up, challenging the truth of the narrative of a profound clash of civilizations between Jews and Irish in America. Rather, their meetings, more benign than violent, allowed Jews to see everyday Irish women and men as exemplars of American goodness.

Some young Irish and Jewish men routinely interacted with each other in sports, in settings ranging from informal neighborhood spaces, playgrounds, and empty lots to formally constituted Irish-sponsored athletic clubs. Playing against each other this way bespoke broadly shared ideas about equality and respect in pursuit of competition, and joining the same team to vanquish a common rival required partnership and cooperation.

In this, the Irish had the upper hand; having been there first, they made up a substantial cadre of urban athletes, whether in baseball, basketball, or boxing. As athletes and fans, as managers and promoters, the Irish defined much of American sports in the latter part of the nineteenth century and into the twentieth, when in the big cities Jewish young men arrived and frankly envied Irish prowess.

Many adult Jews, communal leaders and educators, lamented the lure of sports, seeing it as a cheap distraction from the serious business of study and earning a living. But they admitted that all of their worries paled in the face of the excitement of sports. In the cities where they settled, athletics meant Irish.

American sports, from the street level to the professional, represented something new for Jewish immigrants, and Jewish commentators during the immigration era repeatedly noted how, for example, the name of John L. Sullivan—the "Boston Strong-boy," a boxer born of parents from County Kerry and County Westmeath—rolled off the tongues of Jewish boys. Jewish men seeking to enter professional boxing frequently took Irish names to sound more authentic on the posters, on the betting rosters, and in the ring. Mushy Callahan, a World Junior Welterweight Champion in the late 1920s, had been born Vincent Morris Scheer, while Benny Leonard, probably the most famous Jewish boxer of the century, began his career with the moniker "Irish" Eddie Finnegan. (Ironically, he had chosen the name Leonard on his own as his nom de guerre because his mother, Mrs. Leiner, found boxing shameful and he tried to hide his passion for the ring from her.)

Leonard might have decided on Finnegan because the Irish name sounded more athletic, or possibly because he hoped it would protect him from anti-Jewish jeers from spectators. Either way, to young Jewish men, sports meant Irish, and they availed themselves of Irish-organized athletic facilities. Nat Holman, a Basketball Hall of Fame inductee, launched his career on a New York team, the Original Celtics, founded in 1914 by Frank McCormack. This young man from the Lower East Side, a child of Jewish immigrants from the Russian Empire, dribbled his way onto the court and into national fame wearing a jersey festooned with the iconic green Irish shamrock.

Jewish entry to the world of sports through Irish routes can be seen as well in the story of Abel Kivat. Like Holman, he was the son of eastern European Jewish immigrants. An Olympian runner, Kivat belonged to the Irish-American Athletic Club (I-AAC) located in Celtic Park, founded in the late nineteenth century in New York's heavily Irish Woodside neighborhood. Irish immigrant men drawn to track racing and made unwelcome at the city's Protestant-dominated venues, particularly the New York Athletic Club, considered Celtic Park their home, with its excellent fields, well-appointed viewing stands, locker rooms for the athletes, clubhouse, dance hall, and drinking facilities, a comfortable space for themselves.

It became a comfortable space for Kivat, as well as fellow runners John Eller, Myer Prinstein, and Alvah Meyer, among other Jewish athletes. Three of the Jewish members of the I-AAC won Olympic medals.

An article in *The American Hebrew,* which generally devoted little space to sports, stated that although it was "common to find the names of the star Jewish performers on the roster of the Irish-American Athletic Club," the author wondered about Jews marching out to the field carrying the standard of the Irish club. Did it elicit "joy to thousands of Irishmen when they [saw] the colors of the IAAC brought to the fore by such loyal sons of Erin"? The tone of the piece simultaneously lauded the Jewish athletes and assumed a degree of anti-Jewish prejudice among the "thousands of Irishmen," who cheered for their club and their group, skeptical that Irish Americans could feel kinship, even if temporarily manifested from the bleachers around the track, with Jews.[28]

The Jews, by all accounts, felt utterly at home in Celtic Park, experiencing no sense of marginalization and reveling in the chance to compete in such fine facilities. No Jewish spaces could equal the Irish ones, even after Jewish agencies created the Young Men's and Young Women's Hebrew Associations in the late nineteenth century and Jewish community centers by the 1920s.

Many non-Irish athletic clubs shuttered on Sundays under the influence of blue laws, which assumed that sports and the Lord's Day did not mix. Some did hold Sunday games but banned the consumption of alcohol. Neither Irish nor Jewish athletes or spectators had any problems with Sunday sports or Sunday drinking.

This Irish-Jewish athletic meeting flourished because of the historical reality that Jews arriving in America discovered a world of sports shaped by the Irish. So, too, in the field of American entertainment: Jews bent on participating stood on the shoulders of their Irish predecessors and contemporaries who first defined the genre.

Theater, popular music, then movies, and eventually radio provided opportunities for so many Irish and Jewish immigrants and their children to fulfill their ambitions. The link between the Irish and the Jews in popular entertainment began with the highly popular, specifically urban phenomenon of vaudeville, a legacy of Irish immigrant life; the Five Points of New York was its birthplace in the 1840s. Although vaudeville had European antecedents, it came to its own among the Irish masses in New York and other American cities. Irish performers and entrepreneurs put their distinctive stamp on the form but accommodated the new immigrants, chief among them Jews, by the end of the century.

Irish vaudevillians, performers, and promoters tapped into the thirst of Jewish audiences for entertainment. The medium, with its raucousness, sentimentality, humor, and a bit of bawdiness, brought in Jews, who flocked to American popular-culture venues, not limiting their entertainment choices to purely Jewish places like the Yiddish theater or to the performances solely of other Jews. Rather, they embraced the American vernacular with gusto.

Urban Jews filled the seats of theaters and performance spaces owned and operated by Irish entrepreneurs. The Irish entrepreneurs recognized that adding Jews to the casts as singers, dancers, jugglers, comedians, and sundry others, along with weaving in Jewish-inflected songs and sketches, further brought Jews to their box offices and into the seats, adding to the profits of the promoters and managers, nearly all of them Irish.

Jewish troupers accepted the Irish entertainment styles, emulating forms of performance pioneered by Irish Americans while adding Jewish idioms, references, and character types. Jews involved with the theatrical world deployed stereotypes of their own group members, just as the Irish did. They offered images of Jews no less exaggerated and borderline offensive than that of the stage Irishman, a stock character on the American stage hated by respectable Irish community members who instead preferred dignified and refined depictions of their people.

A key element in the popular entertainment involved an assertion of the privilege of being white despite also standing outside established American culture. Jewish performers, including such greats as Sophie Tucker, Eddie Cantor, George Jessel, and Al Jolson, all donned blackface. By doing so, they entered American show business via a genre largely begun in the 1830s and 1840s by Irish performers, a reflection of the powerful racial hierarchy based on white over Black.

Just as blackface performance, a product of Irish enterprise, paved a pathway for Jewish entertainers, so, too, in the warrens of practice rooms and offices of Tin Pan Alley, Jewish lyricists, composers, and pluggers, the singers and pianists who demonstrated the songs, found opportunities in spaces founded by Irish Americans.

Irish music entrepreneurs had taken over a beehive of rooms in a few New York office buildings around Fifth Avenue and Twenty-Eighth Street, producing songs for music halls and homes in the last decades of the nineteenth century. They spewed out a mountain of works, including an inestimable number with Irish audiences in mind, like "When Irish Eyes Are Smiling" of 1912, "Too-Ra-Loo-Ra-Loo-Ral (That's an Irish Lullaby)" of 1913, "If They'd Only Move Old Ireland Here" (1913), "My Wild Irish Rose" (1899), and so many more.

Irish show business entrepreneurs understood that to keep succeeding, they had to accommodate new realities, which meant sharing space with Jews, mostly men, who knocked on their doors with their songs, lyrics, and business schemes. These Jewish newcomers sought to enter a field begun by the Irish.

The proximity of Jews and Irish in the world of American entertainment and their shared spaces led to the profusion of texts that celebrated bonds between them. The song "If It Wasn't for the Irish and the Jews" by William Jerome and Jean Schwartz, which opened this chapter, wafted through the air, along with the 1916 "Moysha Machree (They're Proud of Their Irisher, Yiddisher Boy)"; "There's a Little Bit of Irish in Sadie Cohen," written that same year by Alfred Bryan and Jack Stern; and "My Yiddisha Colleen" of 1911. "It's Tough When Izzy Rosenstein Loves Genevieve Malone," written in 1910 by Gus Kahn, fit nicely with the popular-culture fascination with Irish-Jewish marriages. Jewish performers in these decades went on stage singing Irish-marked songs that evoked a yearning for the "ould sod." Al Dubin and John J. O'Brien cowrote the theme song from the 1916 Broadway comedy *Broadway and Buttermilk*, entitling it "'Twas Only an Irishman's Dream." Al Dubin, the son of Russian Jewish immigrants, could not have written from personal experience the lament "I could hear Mother singing, the sweet Shannon bells ringin' / 'Twas only an Irishman's dream," but he wrote it anyhow, with John J. O'Brien's collaboration.

Jewish performances using Irish idioms made room for female singers as well. Sophie Tucker, who called herself the "last of the red-hot mamas," born in Ukraine, came up the entertainment ranks from vaudeville and achieved worldwide fame. She moved audiences to tears with her rendition of "Mother Machree," explaining, "you didn't have to have an old mother in Ireland to feel 'Mother Machree,'" just as she believed that anyone would be emotionally wrenched by her signature piece, "My Yiddishe Momme."[29] Nora Bayes, who sang in music halls and recorded for phonograph records, achieved stardom with her 1910 "Has Anybody Here Seen Kelly?," a song about a girl "from the Emerald Isle." Born Rachel Eleanora Goldberg and known as Dora, she sang with an Irish brogue. In one recording, she slipped in a wink to her listeners with the quick phrase, "Has anybody here seen Levi . . . I mean Kelly!"

Her Irish connections extended deeper than the one song, and the details similarly reveal the constant interactions between Jews and Irish in American entertainment. George M. Cohan, an Irish American with family roots in Cork and an exemplar of early twentieth-century American show business, enjoyed a decades-long partnership with Sam Harris, the son of Jewish immigrants. Cohan gave Dora Goldberg her stage name, the Irish-inflected Nora Bayes. He also gave her the opportunity to sing his best-known, most popular, and most enduring song, "Over There," to cheer on the American soldiers bound for the battlefields of World War I. As she belted out Cohan's words, "the Yanks are coming," they, Jews and Irish, claimed the right to be the voice of America.

Jews and Irish counted themselves among the "Yanks," despite the ambivalence and often downright hostility of other Americans, who repeatedly questioned if the two groups of outsiders truly qualified as real cultural citizens. They stood up for each other's needs and causes. Irish American politicians and others attended rallies, positioning themselves alongside Jewish luminaries, decrying the mistreatment of Jews in the Russian Empire, for example. Catholic churches and Irish charitable societies collected money for the relief of Jews suffering abroad and publicly identified themselves with the fate of Jews. In one such instance, Philadelphia's Archbishop Patrick John Ryan stood side by side with local Jewish clergy and other notables at the harbor to bless a ship carrying three thousand tons of relief supplies to Jewish famine victims in Russia. Some of the food, clothing, and medical goods came from money collected by the city's Friendly Sons of Saint Patrick. Several Boston Catholic priests and Mayor James Michael Curley attended a rally in March 1915, along with author Mary Antin, a number of local rabbis, and David Ellis, a celebrity in the Jewish community, to raise awareness and money for Jewish war sufferers in Europe. The gathering raised over $100,000, despite the fact that many Jews and even more Irish Americans expressed great ambivalence about the war "over there."

Irish community leaders stood alongside Jews in the bloody aftermath of World War I, when anti-Jewish violence rampaged across the former czarist lands during the civil war. When Boston Jews organized a march in December 1919, pegged as "Jewish Protest Day," Cardinal William O'Connell sent his personal representative, Rev. Michael J. Scanlan, to take part.

Jews acknowledged the solidarity of Irish Americans. When individual Irish Americans manifested acts of benevolence, no matter how small, Jews paid attention. Stories of loyal Irish servant women donating money to Jewish old-age homes and hospitals to honor their Jewish employers appeared often in the Jewish press. Jewish publications noted the ample gift to the Association for the Relief of Jewish Widows and Orphans of New Orleans in 1854, made by Margaret Haughery. An orphan from a young age herself, and by then a widow as well, the Leitrim-born owner of a successful bakery extended her charity to the Jews during the city's devastating yellow fever epidemic.

Providing financial aid across group lines went in the other direction, too. In the early 1880s, for example, during a devastating famine—the Gorta Beag, or "small famine"—in County Mayo in the west of Ireland, Jewish groups responded with pleas to the American public for financial help, launched by the newly formed Land League.

Rabbi Pereira Mendes of New York's Congregation Shearith Israel announced in 1880 that "the usual Purim contribution of members would be divided between the French based, Alliance Israelite and the Irish Fund," namely the Land League, founded in Castlebar, County Mayo, and led by Michael Davitt. James R. O'Beirne, a Roscommon native and a Congressional Medal of Honor awardee who had served in the Civil War, addressed a packed rally at the Washington Hebrew Congregation. O'Beirne joined other "representatives of the Irish people in Washington" at the synagogue event to "aid of the suffering Irish."[30] The campaign undertaken by the Land League inspired a trio of members of New York's Young Men's Hebrew Association (YMHA) to call a special meeting to "discuss the Irish Relief Fund," Davitt's campaign to raise money for the starving people of Mayo.

In 1877 Richard O'Gorman, a nationalist leader associated in the 1840s with the Young Ireland movement, lectured at the YMHA, and, according to one Jewish press report, he received the largest audience of the lecture season. Those assembled "evinced their appreciation of the lecture by the thorough attention which they gave to it."[31]

The event garnered ample Jewish press coverage. A reporter for *The Jewish Messenger* noted that thirty-five "gentlemen" showed up, and the group pledged one hundred dollars each and vowed to ask others to chip in the same amount. The reporter predicted that "a large contribution to the Irish Fund from the Hebrews" will help "strangle Corbinism for all times," referring to banker and railroad magnate Austin Corbin, who, as president of the Manhattan Beach Corporation, had announced the previous year that he would not allow Jews, "a detestable and vulgar people," to lodge at his exclusive Coney Island Hotel. Jews,

Corbin had opined, "are a pretentious class who expect three times as much for their money as other people."[32] *The American Hebrew* touted New York Jewry's donation to the starving in Ireland, foreseeing that it would "do three times the good in the world," feeding the hungry while showing Jews as caring and selfless.

The Irish fundraiser at the YMHA did provoke some discord. An attendee at the Mayo relief meeting declared that although he sympathized with Ireland's hungry people, the Jews, as members of a Jewish organization, should restrict their activities to Jewish causes and collect money instead for "the suffering Jews in Silesia." One letter writer to *The Jewish Messenger* put a different spin on it, saying that Jews should aid the Irish as Americans, but not as Jews. "I object," he declared, "to the Jews helping Ireland as Jews."[33]

Yet for others, heeding Ireland's call served Jews in their ceaseless quest for security and respect. The reference to Corbinism provided one such example. For an *American Hebrew* writer, enthusiastic Jewish support for the Land League work accomplished something for them. "No religion," the correspondent claimed with no evidence, "inculcated true Charity, more strongly than the Jewish," allowing American Jews to showcase their moral superiority and the falsehood of centuries-old accusations of selfishness made against them. "In no way can the prejudice against our people be more effectively eradicated than by their action in such a manner as will show that they will take the same interest in the progress of civilization . . . in the advancement of . . . the social condition of their fellow-men, as their Christian neighbors."[34]

Well-placed Jews showed up frequently at Irish protest meetings. New York judge Otto Rosalsky presided over a rally of more than one hundred thousand to honor Terence MacSwiney, the Sinn Féin mayor of Cork who died in a British prison after a seventy-four-day hunger strike in 1920. Samuel Untermyer, a prominent Zionist and corporate lawyer, donated $5,000 to the Irish Victory Fund, a campaign launched by the Friends of Irish Freedom; his gift received coverage in *The New York Times*. Philadelphia's Rabbi Joseph Krauskopf heartily accepted an invitation of the Friends to address the 1919 Irish Race Convention.

Jewish help for Irish causes and Irish praise for Jews as fellow sufferers of persecution served both well. Hanna Sheehy-Skeffington, an Irish feminist, socialist, and member of Sinn Féin, came to the United States in 1916, arriving after her husband died at the hands of the British military during the Easter Rising, the armed insurrection by Irish Republicans that had begun on April 24 that year. During her two-year lecture tour in America and in her articles, she consistently invoked the role of the Jews in the struggle for freedom. "There is something in persecution," she opined in an article in the socialist publication *The Call*, "which keeps the soul free." Writing after the Russian Revolution, she declared that "the Russian, the Jew and the Irishman love freedom so." Sheehy-Skeffington spent her American sojourn in the company of socialists and other leftists, establishing a special bond with anarchist and World War I opponent Emma Goldman.[35]

Irish nationalists like Sheehy-Skeffington included Jews as speakers at their meetings, showing the public that the cause of Irish independence mattered well beyond their own communities. Maurice Feinstone, of the United Hebrew Trades, received prominent billing at a 1919 Irish rally in New York, as did at least two rabbis. Rabbi Emil Hirsch spoke at an Irish protest meeting in Chicago that same year.

In their articles and manifestos, Irish nationalists linked the cause of Irish liberation to movements for the oppressed of the world. Speaking out for others, including Jews, gave credence to their message that their cause transcended the circumstances of that small island in the Atlantic. In 1919 Harry Boland and Liam Mellows, of the Irish Republican Brotherhood, founded the League of Oppressed Peoples, casting their net to include the many victims of imperialism, like Egyptians, Indians, Koreans, Chinese, and also the Jews of Russia. Excoriating the Great Powers, including Great Britain, for "their failure to protect the Jewish population in parts of Eastern Europe," the League linked the Irish cause to the Jewish.[36]

Jewish communal spaces, particularly Zionist gatherings, resounded with words of praise for the skill of Irish nationalists in mobilizing their masses for the homeland struggle. American Zionists consistently articulated a sense of awe and, indeed, envy of the Irish, believing that the sons and daughters of Erin in America really knew how to organize, inspire, and unify—exactly that which they themselves failed at. As they saw it, with some accuracy, most Irish Americans did identify with nationalist yearnings, while only a minority of American Jews embraced Zionism well into the 1930s. While Zionists may not have been attuned to the various and competing shadings of Irish nationalism, from their perspective, Irish community leaders could get the people out for rallies, parades, and fundraising drives.

From the late 1890s, with the founding of the Zionist movement by Theodor Herzl, American Zionists invoked the Irish as the ultimate model of diaspora nationalism. Jacob de Haas, a movement leader, addressed the women's society at Boston's Congregation Adath Israel in 1907 and sought to dispel the repeated claim that Zionism compromised the Jews' American bona fides with the argument that no one questioned the "patriotism of the Irish-American," with his "allegiance to a free Ireland." De Haas, hoping to win over the women of the Reform Jewish congregation, which as a movement within American Judaism mostly did not embrace the cause of a Jewish homeland, noted that Irish support for nationalism made them "better Americans," as "these dual patriotisms are natural."[37]

Zionists invited Irish speakers to their gatherings. Chicago's *Sentinel* reported on a talk delivered to a Zionist group by "the Hon. 'Tay Pay' O'Connor, M.P.," who declared in 1917, "Whene'er an Irishman speaks to a gathering of Israel's children he commands attention, whether he be an officer chastising a group of striking workers or a politician in the pursuit of his ballet [*sic*]," but even more "so when he addresses them on the subject of Zionism."[38]

The Lawndale Civic Center, another Chicago Jewish community gathering place, asked John P. McGoorty, judge of the superior court, to share his thoughts in 1919 on "the struggles of the Irish and the Jewish peoples, and their efforts to obtain autonomy."[39]

References to Irish pride as expressed in nationalist activity provided Jews with a yardstick by which to measure themselves, and they always found themselves wanting. Hyman L. Meites, a Chicago Zionist, offered in "Home Rule and the Jews" a contrast between Irish strength and Jewish weakness. After asserting that despite their "efforts for their mother country" and their "longing for a free Ireland," no one besmirched them with the stigma of being unpatriotic. Meites lamented the behavior of the "Reformed" Jews, who mostly rejected the movement and hoped to "thwart" it "under the cloak of patriotism to the adopted country." The Irish, on the other hand, "fortunately . . . did not have any 'Reformed Irish' and their desire and hope for home rule did not meet any opposition among their own people." This 1914 article glorified the united Irish people who together "worked and fought and the result is a glorious triumph for their cause."[40]

Endorsements of Irish nationalism as worthy of emulation by Jews emerged as a leitmotif of early twentieth-century American Zionist efforts. Louis Brandeis, who would become the first Jew to serve on the United States Supreme Court, repeatedly offered the Irish analogy to whip up Zionist sentiment. In print and on the speaker's podium, he addressed "Why I Am a Zionist," and part of his explanation looked across the Atlantic to Ireland under British domination. At Chicago's Douglas Park Auditorium in November 1914 he distilled the role of Ireland in his thinking. He began with the assertion that when "the Irish . . . lifted their heads and said they must have home rule," they got it. The Irish, Brandeis declared, wanted "the rights of a nation, of a people," and "they worked and worked for home rule . . . and American Irish helped the Irish of Ireland in their fight for home rule and their battle has been won." Speaking to his Jewish audience, he declared, "Now, ladies and gentlemen this is our time. . . . [I]f our three million Jews of America desire and will work as one we shall win, the Jewish state shall be established and the Jewish future shall be as secure as the Jewish past."[41]

Jews turned to the Irish American example to justify support for a Jewish homeland in Palestine. Even some non-Zionists believed that Jews, particularly those staring at oppression in Europe and elsewhere, should be able to move to Palestine, and they found in the Irish case a way to say that love of an ancestral home and American patriotism and integration harmonized perfectly.

Louis Marshall, a constitutional lawyer, president of the American Jewish Committee, and decidedly not a Zionist, still defended Zionism as consistent with American commitments. He echoed the idea that the Irish provided the best proof that such a synthesis worked. In a speech, attended by no less than President Calvin Coolidge, on the occasion of laying the cornerstone of Washington, DC's Jewish Community Center in 1925, Marshall declared that Jews, like others, should be able to love both America and the "home of our fathers," namely Palestine. We are, he declared, "ready to help other sons of our ancient faith to seek there the opportunities for betterment." And to prove his point, he noted that this "is the same feeling . . . which our Irish fellow-citizens have evinced for those who have remained on the old sod." Not a case of "double allegiance," the behavior of the Irish, so long in America, so deeply involved in American civic and political culture, Marshall declared, gave Jews the right to express their "love of Palestine."[42]

The Irish example worked well in American Jewish rhetoric. The Irish served as their model of an American ethnic group that could deftly balance group loyalties and agendas with securing its place in America.

As the Jews saw it, the Irish knew how to defend themselves, meeting continuous insults and vilifications, exclusions and hostilities at the hands of the dominant white Protestant native-born population with a militance and panache that the Jews could never replicate. A 1902 commentator in *The Jewish Messenger* took note of a demonstrative and highly visible boycott led by the Ancient Order of Hibernians in Baltimore of "all the theatres where Irishmen are lampooned and caricatured." Raucous Irish protests took place in the streets, and Irish women and men did not hesitate to confront the public with their anger. The city papers devoted much coverage to them because they loudly used public spaces to express their anger. The writer asked, "When will more of our co-religionists show similar pride and self-respect?"[43]

Over the course of the late nineteenth century and into the first decades of the twentieth, Jews turned to the Irish for both inspiration and for actual aid, and Irish Americans made a point of defending the Jews, showing Americans that they used power as more than just a way to gain more resources. Rather, by taking on the cause of Jews, they could demonstrate a greater level of tolerance than the Protestants who claimed such a value for themselves.

2

Defending the Jews

Mary Boyle O'Reilly, a staff correspondent for Chicago's *Day Book: An Adless Daily Newspaper,* traveled the world searching for good personality-driven stories. Her articles combined interviews with perceptive firsthand observations and carefully researched historical details, presented in crisp prose.

Her keen nose for a good story took her in 1913 to the then-Russian city of Kiev, reporting back on the "persecutions of millions of Jews in the czar's empire." O'Reilly's instinct for gripping news brought her to a local trial, which had captured the attention of Jews around the world, involving Menachem Mendel Beilis, who was accused of killing a twelve-year-old Christian child, Andrusa Yushchinsky, then using the boy's blood for Jewish ritual purposes.

This accusation—that Jews baked their matzo, or unleavened Passover bread, from the blood of Christian children—stretched back centuries to medieval European Christendom. It first began in England in the twelfth century and then spread to the continent. While such blood libels continued into the nineteenth century, the accusation against Beilis seemed particularly anachronistic, utterly out of step with the modern age of the twentieth century.

It also took place at a fraught moment, when the United States government, under political pressure from American Jews, demanded that the czarist regime mitigate its harsh treatment of Jews, as the two governments negotiated the terms of a commercial treaty.

O'Reilly's reports spared no words in their condemnation of the Russian authorities, the Russian Orthodox Church, and state officials "up to the throne" who perpetrated this "Wicked Conspiracy" against the innocent man. She snagged exclusive interviews with the chief rabbi of Kiev and the wife of the accused. Step by step, the intrepid reporter unraveled the chain of events that led to the arrest and chronicled the trial, which she declared had been marred by false testimonies by witnesses who lied on the stand.

The American reporter, daughter of the Irish-born journalist John Boyle O'Reilly, had no doubt about Beilis's innocence and was convinced that he had no hand in Andrusa's tragic fate. She took upon herself the task of informing her readers that the Kiev spectacle, the demonization of the Jews, and the accusation itself grew out of the fertile soil of Christian anti-Semitism. She appended a special section to one article that explained to the public the details of "What Ritual Murder Is" and, while noting that other non-Christians had also been blamed at times, that Jews had been overwhelmingly the victims of this oft-told lie. She declared that the "'blood accusation' is as old as the Christian era. A lie edged with ignorance and malice, it has varied to suit the passing centuries." Christians, her readers in the main, had to acknowledge their responsibility in perpetuating this travesty visited upon Jews, and she asserted that "always its appearance marked a trail of rapine and murder."[1]

Yiddish newspapers took notice of O'Reilly's reportage,

pleased yet surprised that "a famous American journalist (Christian)" chose to expose the events in Kiev, noting that she had drawn parallels at the same time between the travails of Beilis and those of Leo Frank, an American Jew who was arrested and found guilty of murdering a young white Christian girl in Georgia. *Yidishes Tageblatt,* a New York newspaper, focused mostly on what it considered the incongruity of a Christian writer taking up the cause of Beilis, a Jew.[2]

The *Tageblatt* writer should not have been so surprised. Rallies and public meetings around the country in protest of the Beilis trial featured Irish speakers, laypeople as well as Catholic priests. Illinois governor Edward F. Dunne, whose father fled to the United States in the late 1840s after the failure of the Young Ireland uprising, sent a telegram of solidarity to a massive rally in Chicago in defense of Beilis, declaring that anyone who believed in the blood libel had to be either a "malignant person or a gullible fool." Father P. J. O'Callaghan of St. Mary's parish spoke at that gathering and declared that "the greatest glory of the Catholic Church is that it is Jewish and the greatest honor any man may have is that he may say in some sense that he is of the House of Israel." O'Callaghan implored Christians in the crowd, saying "the greatest work we can do is stamp out the hatred of the Jews by men who call themselves Christians."[3] The Jews of Springfield, Massachusetts, along with some of their neighbors, held their protest meeting at Hibernian Hall, a gathering place for the local Irish community.

The newspaper also had no cause for amazement at her sympathetic reportage, since O'Reilly's father, born in County Heath, had, in his years as editor of Boston's Catholic newspaper *The Pilot,* lambasted anti-Semitism at home and in the world beyond Boston. Under John Boyle O'Reilly's editorship and that of his successor, James Jeffrey Roche, the newspaper condemned anti-Jewish actions in Russia, Germany, and

Austria, in the United States, and even at nearby Harvard University. Boston's prominent rabbi Solomon Schindler took note of O'Reilly's defense of the Jews, enlisting him to contribute to the *Illustrated Jewish Almanac,* which he edited.

Whether influenced by his deep friendship with Abraham Shulman, a local businessman and supporter of Irish freedom, or his desire to portray Irish Catholics as responsible liberal-minded Americans, O'Reilly, the former Fenian revolutionary and poet of some renown, took up the cause of the Jews. So wide did his reputation as an opponent of anti-Semitism extend that Philip Cowen, editor of *The American Hebrew,* invited him to contribute to an 1890 symposium along with Baltimore's Cardinal James Gibbons, son of immigrants from County Mayo, on the causes and nature of American anti-Semitism.

O'Reilly began his piece by flat out declaring, "I cannot find of my own experience, the reason for prejudice against the Jews as a race," and concluded with a declaration of frustration: "I do not know how to dispel the anti-Jewish prejudice except by expressing my own respect, honor and affection for the greatest race—taking its vicissitudes and its achievements, its numbers and its glories—that ever existed." He exonerated Christianity and "religious instruction in Christian schools," opining that the "least religious or Christian" bore the bulk of responsibility for hatred against the Jews, a feeling "inherited from less intelligent times." Maybe he had in mind Shulman, with whom he collaborated and socialized, when he declared, "it has been my fortune to know, long and intimately several Jewish families . . . and many individual Jews." They adhered to strict standards of conduct, and their "home life, and all its relations is the highest in the world."[4]

After O'Reilly's death in 1890, Irish Americans concerned with their group's image invoked him as a defender of the Jews, evidence of their contribution to the nation's not-yet-fulfilled promise of equality and religious pluralism. Mayor James Michael Curley, addressing a gathering of Bostonians at the unveiling of the memorial to the poet and editor, noted that a Jew had provided the funds for the historic plaque, someone "not of O'Reilly's race, but who has done more to commemorate the achievements and the deeds and the services of John Boyle O'Reilly than probably any other man in any commonwealth of New England, Mr. A. Shuman." O'Reilly, Curley declared, had been "humanity's champion."[5]

Irish American advocacy on behalf of the nation's Jews, taken on first by O'Reilly, soon shifted to Charles P. Daly, who had family roots in Galway. A Tammany Hall politician and chief justice of the New York Court of Common Pleas, Daly has the distinction of being the first individual to publicly lecture and publish on the history of the Jews of New York and the United States. His first lecture, delivered in 1872, preceded by two decades the birth of American Jewish history as a field of research and a subject of inquiry. No one, Jew or gentile, before Daly considered this topic worthy of serious concern.[6]

As Jews in the United States and elsewhere in the liberal Western world turned to their national histories to argue for inclusion in the face of rising anti-Semitism, Daly's work stood out as notable and formative. The *American Jewish Year Book,* a project of the American Jewish Committee, declared decades later that Daly's *Settlement of the Jews in North America* was one of the "hundred best books in the English language on Jewish subjects," having offered readers "the best account of the early history of the Jews in this country."[7]

The book germinated from a speech Daly gave in the early 1870s at the behest of Cowen, at a ceremony marking the golden jubilee of New York's Hebrew Orphan Asylum. The fact that Jews in New York and across America had always taken care of their own provided Daly with his core premise.

They had never let the unfortunate among them become public charges, he declared, at a time when critics of immigration claimed that defective and dependent newcomers drained public resources.

The speech evolved into a series of articles in *The Jewish Times*. Daly offered to bundle the articles together into book form, with the proceeds of sales to be earmarked for the Hebrew Fair for Mount Sinai Hospital, an institution that, like Daly's articles and the American Jewish historical project, sought to show the public how much the Jews had contributed to the common good.

The lectures focused on New York, a city in which Daly had deep connections. Cowen oversaw their publication as a book, *The Jews of New York,* published in 1883. A decade later, after Daly retired from the bench, he decided to tell the larger national Jewish history.

In this first full-length history of American Jewry, *The Settlement of the Jews in North America,* Daly praised the Jews, who he pointed out had been present in America as early as the 1650s. They were hardly strangers or newcomers, he declared, as he asserted the Jews' Americanness, but they also paid vigilant attention to the needy among themselves.

He expounded on their commitment to self-help at a crucial moment. Congress had passed in 1882 an immigration act that barred the admission of any person likely to become a public charge. Jews, Daly claimed, would never clog up the public rolls.

Both of Daly's books read like paeans to the Jews, chronicles of their good deeds. He pointed out that the first piece of evidence of their presence in North America documented "an act of benevolence on the part of a Jew to a friendless Christian stranger, and certainly the history of no people in any place can begin with an incident more creditable to them than the exercise of that charity which is limited to no sect or creed."[8]

Daly, elected to honorary membership in the American

Jewish Historical Society at its founding in 1892, had a long history with New York's Jews, stretching back decades before the orphanage speech. In his judicial capacity he had stood up for the rights of Jews to observe *their* Sabbath and keep their businesses open on that of the Christians.

In an 1857 case before the Court of Common Pleas, Daly declared that the defendants, "all of the Jewish persuasion," who "observe the seventh day of the week as their Sabbath," see the "Christian Sabbath" as a "secular day." They are, he ruled, "privileged to engage in any labor that does not disturb the rest of their fellow citizens."[9] It was a sensitive issue for Jews, as so many earned their living keeping shops, but the municipal ban on selling on Sundays hobbled the observant among them, who could not do so on Saturdays, as it violated Jewish law.

Daly became a hero to New York Jews. In 1874, as he and his wife got ready to sail off on a European vacation, a group of Jews hosted a bon voyage dinner for him at Delmonico's in honor of their "esteem and appreciation" for his "liberality, kindness and sympathy for every worthy object, without distinction as to sect or nationality."[10]

Being an activist in Irish affairs, presiding over the Saint Patrick's Society, and chairing the American Committee for Relief in Ireland added to his luster with Jews, who showered him with invitations to their gatherings and to advocate for their causes. In 1872 Daly gave the keynote address at the jubilee anniversary gala of the Hebrew Benevolent Society of New York. He delivered an expanded version of the address in 1883. In all these presentations, the invited Irish honored guest emphasized Jewish service and beneficence, declaring that rather than burdening American society, they helped their own. Jewish immigrants, in Daly's words, became useful and productive Americans. Daly maintained a lively correspondence with Rabbi Bernhard Felsenthal of Chicago, who reached out to the judge to solicit his opinions on the causes of anti-Semitism.

Daly published his two books and then agreed to their re-issue at the request of lawyer Max Kohler, a Jewish community activist and defender of immigration for Jews and others. In his introductory remarks to Daly's book, Kohler explained why the Irish judge's research mattered so much to him and to other Jews. According to Kohler, Daly directly upended the assertions of anti-Semites like Goldwin Smith, the British historian and journalist who had labeled Jews as "parasites . . . since the days of Rome who only pursued money and gain for themselves." No admirer of the Irish either, Smith smeared them as well, and according to Kohler, Daly exposed "the arrogance and effrontery to characterize the Jews" as a negative force in America. Daly, he declared, demonstrated "unceasing indignation against anti-Semitism."[11]

Upon Daly's death Kohler published a tribute to him in *The American Hebrew*. He lionized him as one who "chose to espouse so zealously the Jewish cause and so conspicuously enriched our communal life and thought by means of important contributions to Jewish history, to the extinction of anti-Semitic prejudice and the elevation and amelioration of American Jewish life."[12]

Daly's words could never be dismissed as special pleading, and as a luminary in New York's Irish community, he revealed, as the Jews saw it, the good deeds of the Jews to an influential segment of the city's politically well-connected.

A few years later the leadership of American Jewry again turned to an Irish person with a substantial American following, particularly among Irish women and men rallying around the cause of homeland nationalism. Michael Davitt's *Within the Pale: The True Story of Anti-Semitic Persecution in Russia* offered the American reading public an eyewitness account of the aftermath of the bloody attack on the Jews of Kishinev. *Within the Pale* described the events of April 19 and 20, Easter 1903, in the Moldavian city, making use of on-the-ground observers. Graphically describing how the mob had fallen on the Jewish community of Kishinev, killed some fifty souls, raped women, injured many, and destroyed Jewish homes and shops, it thrust the Russian word "pogrom," a violent riot, into the consciousness of the American public.[13]

Davitt conveyed the sights and sounds of the Jewish quarter in shambles. He talked to victims. He garnered evidence from Jews and Christians, ordinary people, clergy—both Jewish and Christian—and medical personnel, bearing witness to the "revolting deeds of mediaeval savagery in our day."[14]

A world-renowned Irish nationalist leader and globe-trotting journalist, Davitt had arrived in Kishinev at the behest of the Hearst newspapers. Subject to government censorship, which limited what he could cable out from Kishinev, he committed facts and impressions to memory, sending these to his editors after he left the czarist empire, a place, he determined, where Jews had no future.

His articles appeared in British and American newspapers, but almost immediately upon his return from Kishinev, representatives of the Jewish Publication Society of America (JPS), an enterprise dedicated to fostering Jewish culture and defending Jews worldwide, called upon Davitt, wanting to see his articles become a book. He readily agreed, and JPS published *Within the Pale* in 1903.

Jewish publications and communal leaders hailed the words of the "great Irish patriot," who "brought back scenes of the disaster." Because Davitt was an observer on the ground and a non-Jew, the *American Jewish Year Book*'s writers pointed out that his Irish Catholicism helped in "disproving the charge of Russian officials that a Jew had provoked the riot and that Jewish assailants had caused [the carnage] to be renewed on the second day." Jewish communal leaders hoped that Davitt could convince Americans about the truth of the violence and the status of Kishinev's Jews as victims, not perpetrators. Davitt's stature as a journalist and his neutrality as an Irish Catholic enhanced his credibility.[15]

JPS considered Davitt's book one of its great accomplishments. It noted a quarter century later the importance of Davitt being a "warm-hearted Irish leader," for whom "the sufferings and privations of his own people enabled [him] to appreciate and set forth in glowing language the unspeakable persecution of the Russian Jews."[16]

As they saw it, Davitt's writings on Kishinev transformed the horrific Jewish event into one that spoke broadly to Americans. It fostered sympathy for the Jews precisely because a Jew did not write it.

Davitt also made a linguistic move that bound together the Jewish and Irish experiences. Others before him had used the English word "pale" to refer to the swathe of land to which the czarist state had restricted the Jews since 1791, but the term gained greater traction with Davitt's title. The word derived from Irish history, referring to a part of Ireland near Dublin, the first region on the island to come directly under English rule in the fourteenth century. With Davitt, the word, which connoted Irish loss of their own land, transformed into a word about Jewish suffering.

Davitt's book was well received beyond Jewish circles. The convention of the New York State Democratic Party, largely controlled by New York City's Irish politicians, passed a resolution at its annual convention directly citing Davitt's book, calling upon the federal government "to exercise its influence to bring about speedy cessation of the atrocities now being committed against the Jews in Russia which have shocked the conscience of civilization."[17]

His book helped boost American Jewry in world Jewish

politics. By being the community that enabled the publication of the book that informed the Western world of Kishinev's horrors, according to *The American Hebrew,* American Jews showed "the courage and the public spirit openly to espouse the cause of their brothers as they stand ready to make the sacrifice involved in keeping open to the Jewish refugee this last asylum of the oppressed." By publishing Davitt's book, "American Jewry," for the first time, seized "hegemony of the world's Judaism."[18]

As for Davitt, serving as the mouthpiece for Jewish suffering allowed him as an Irish nationalist to align his homeland's cause with one more struggle of oppressed peoples around the world. Speaking up for the Jews fit his global vision of fighting for the oppressed against large and powerful forces, complementing his work on behalf of the Chinese against imperialism, much of it perpetrated by Britain, and of the Boers in South Africa, also casualties of British power. Davitt, a lifelong Irish nationalist, also stood up for the Jews in the Irish city of Limerick, who in 1906 endured an economic boycott and an ugly war of words, hurled at them by a local priest and his followers. Pricking America's conscience about Kishinev revealed Davitt's vision of human rights, which he firstly placed in service of the people of Ireland.

Irish Americans pointed to Davitt's powerful words of solidarity with the Jews to showcase their own broad concerns for humanity. Davitt and Daly, through their empathy for Jews, allowed Irish Americans to counter the widely held image of the Irish as narrow-minded bigots.

Other world events gave Irish Americans a chance to proclaim their support for Jews and abhorrence of anti-Semitism. In the late 1890s, as Captain Alfred Dreyfus stood accused of treason against France, Baltimore's Irish Catholic newspaper, *The Catholic Mirror,* sided with Dreyfus, chiding the anti-Dreyfusards, including the powerful French Catholic Church, for their anti-Semitism. "Look at the Jew," the paper admonished Catholics during the French trial, and see "my unbaptized friend . . . and borrow some of the light from Israel." Jews in France and the United States, the paper declared, always evinced patriotism, models of citizenship, hard work, and industry.[19]

In a different key, journalist Finley Peter Dunne, son of Irish immigrants, known through his fictional character, the very Irish Mr. Dooley, had much to say about Dreyfus. He devoted five installments of his series in *The Saturday Evening Post* to the trial, using Dooley, the bartender born in County Roscommon, to counter the anti-Semitism of his constant foil, Malachi Hennessy, both denizens of Archey Road in Chicago's Bridgeport neighborhood.

Dooley referred to "me frind Cap. Dhry-fuss" in his barroom spat with Hennessy, who mused that, surely, "he's guilty. He's a Jew." Dooley, and his creator, Dunne, came back with, "Ye don't know annything about th' case. If ye knew annything, ye'd not have an opinyon wan way or th' other."[20]

Hennessy believed that Dreyfus as a Jew had to be guilty and that all Jews were rich. Dunne spun his defense of Dreyfus into a broader defense of the Jews, as the sage of Archey Road challenged the commonly held view. The Jews are ordinary people, the saloonkeeper said, scrambling like everyone else to make a living, including "me frind Finkstein, that comes by here ivry morning hollerin' 'Rags.'" To Hennessy's assertion of Jewish wealth, Dooley opined that surely "all thim Jews that lives down in Canal street, tweinty in a room," must be counted among "the Rothschilds," and indeed, "prob'bly a great dale iv money is made by thim scared-looki'n men that stops ye at a street corner an' wants to know if ye have any ol' clothes to sell. . . . They mus' be large profits as a middleman in a thransaction involvin' a pair iv pants that cost two dollars when they were first bought an' has been worn through a picnic season an' a pollytical campaign."[21]

Dunne, through Dooley, offered a lesson on Jewish history.

He lectured Hennessy that "th' raison th'Jews is all in business is because they'se nawthin' else fr them to do. For cincheries and cincheries, Father Kelly tells me, they have been crowded out iv ivrything else. They cudden't be sojers or pollyticians or lawyers or judges. But they'sd wan pursoot where prejudice has no hand," namely business. Dooley then sketched out the implications of the Jewish concentration in business, exposing how Christian monarchs, "imprors an' kings," used the Jews, resenting them but always needing them. That Dunne made Father Kelly Dooley's source of information about Jewish history stands out and fits the moment.[22] Spokesmen for Catholics, which essentially meant Irish, understood that the nation they lived in found them a threat and that their steady growth in numbers terrified so many of the white Protestants. Anti-Irish and anti-Catholic agitation never went away. It just ebbed and flowed, even after the demise of the Know-Nothings before the Civil War. Irish Catholics in the public sphere from the late nineteenth century and into the twentieth sought to disarm their powerful antagonists to secure their own comfort. So when and where they could, they injected themselves in confrontations between Jews and old-stock Protestants, siding with the Jews as a way to take on the Protestants.

Take the case of Louis Brandeis, a heroic figure in American Jewish history. Woodrow Wilson nominated him to the Supreme Court in 1916, and the Senate took an unprecedented four months to confirm him, with twenty-two senators voting against him. While some opposed Brandeis because of his advocacy for labor, his anti-big-business stance, and his belief in state regulation of the economy, much of the antipathy arose from the fact of his being a Jew, a disability that, as his detractors saw it, disqualified him.

Among these, Senator Henry Cabot Lodge, senior senator from Brandeis's home state of Massachusetts, declared that Brandeis, a Jew, possessed an "Oriental mind." Lodge argued that "if it were not that Brandeis is a Jew, and a German Jew, he would never have been appointed." A charter member of the Immigration Restriction League, founded in 1894, Lodge considered that even Brandeis's Harvard education could not erase his inherently Jewish mind. Unable to understand the Anglo-Saxon way of life, Brandeis therefore could not understand America.

Even after the confirmation, Lodge continued to hammer away at Brandeis's shortcomings because of his Jewishness, contrasting him with the thoroughly American Justice Oliver Wendell Holmes, who had "English common law" in his blood. Holmes by nature could understand this legal system, which "evolved by the genius of a people who had built themselves the greatest nation in a thousand years." Brandeis, though descended from a "noble and ancient race," embodied his people's "unstable" nature. After all, they had "failed in all centuries to make a stable nation of itself."[23]

In this war of words, Irish Americans who had no stake in Brandeis's ordeal emerged as his advocates. They did not like Lodge, consistently citing him as the embodiment of white Protestant prejudice, the chief proponent of a narrow-minded New England derived from Puritan ancestry, which for a century and more demonized them and their forebears. They condemned the senator for purveying the myth of Anglo-Saxonism, the belief in the superiority of a race that Irish activists asserted did not exist in reality but only in the minds of bigots like Lodge.

The inaugural meeting of the American Irish Historical Society named Lodge as the exemplar of intolerance, perpetrator of an "American History It Falsified," the title of the talk delivered at the gathering. Lodge, "an amateur historian, is the high priest" of the cult of Anglo-Saxon entitlement, the society's journal declared, "the custodian and incense swinger of the deified Puritan."[24]

During the months of debate over the Brandeis nomination, Irish Americans found a perfect moment to rip into Lodge by exposing his anti-Jewish prejudices and thereby challenging and taunting the Yankee elite. Irish politicians in the Bay State had a field day. Mayor James Michael Curley, former mayor John Fitzgerald, and former governor David I. Walsh issued a barrage of words praising Brandeis and, by extension, President Wilson for boldly nominating him. They lionized the nominee, a "splendid compliment to a most able man," noting that "Mr. Brandeis believes that the law was made for man—not just that man was made to be the slave of law." While Lodge depicted Brandeis as having a mind unsuitable for the high court, these Irish politicians declared that "the nomination is admirable in every way. Mr. Brandeis is a real progressive, with a profound knowledge of law, and is certain to prove one of the greatest jurists who ever sat on the Supreme Bench."[25]

Curley, always alert to the city's Jewish voters and always eager to rattle his Protestant, old-stock enemies, Lodge among them, invited Brandeis to do something no Jew had ever done. He asked him to give the Fourth of July oration at Boston's Faneuil Hall, a sacred spot in the nation's history of independence and a sacred day on its civic calendar.

Probably, though, no individual did more to ensure Brandeis's confirmation than Montana senator Thomas Walsh, the child of Irish immigrants who had headed west upon their arrival in America. Bridget and Felix Walsh, living first in Two Rivers, Wisconsin, subscribed to John Boyle O'Reilly's *Pilot*, possibly learning about anti-Semitism in its pages, and then transmitting its ideas to their son.

When in the Senate, Walsh served on the Judiciary Committee and headed the subcommittee that recommended to the full committee and the Senate on the merits of the nominee. Walsh's zealous advocacy for Brandeis and his successful efforts to move the nomination forward stemmed from his admiration for the lawyer, who believed in "greater security, greater comfort, and better health for industrial workers," including "safety devices, factory inspection . . . the abolition of child labor—all of which threaten a reduction of dividends." Brandeis's vision of the law and society, according to Walsh, derived from the notion that "a man's a man and not a machine."

At least one Montana constituent, a miner, lauded Walsh for helping defeat "bigotry, prejudice, and hatred against a race that has been persecuted for centuries." Walsh's "magnanimity and fairness to do justice entitled you to a greatest praise and laudation, and all lovers of justice owe you a debt of gratitude," this admirer wrote.[26]

Senator Thomas Walsh, Massachusetts governor David Walsh, and Boston politicians Curley and Fitzgerald each played a part in cracking open the door, allowing Brandeis to step forward and moving the nation on a course that made room for Jews, slowly undercutting the Lodge Anglo-Saxonist view that races have minds and that the Jewish outlook did not fit American law. Through their efforts, they gave the Brandeis name visibility.

The name Israel Weinberg carries no such connotations, and most likely no one, save a few scholars of labor history, recognizes it. But his story also demonstrates the ways in which Irish Americans linked their cause to that of Jews, taking up their defense as they defended themselves.

Weinberg's story, a footnote to history, began on July 22, 1916, when a bomb exploded during San Francisco's Preparedness Day parade, a public event intended to inspire patriotism as the nation crawled toward its entry into the world war. Ten people died and forty were wounded by the blast on Steuart and Market Streets, at the entrance to the bustling Embarcadero.

Authorities swooped down on radicals, sweeping up, among others, the well-known labor and socialist organizer Tom Mooney, the son of Irish immigrants who came to America and worked in the coal mines. A committed member of the heavily Irish Knights of Labor, Mooney's father died of silicosis, the miner's disease, and Mooney entered the world of labor organizing through the Wobblies, the Industrial Workers of the World.

As the Mooney case dragged on for decades, from the first trial in 1918 onward, it served as a rallying cry for the American left. Long forgotten, though, was Israel Weinberg, a Russian-born Jewish immigrant and a jitney driver who was arrested, indicted, and set to stand trial with Mooney. No evidence then or later linked Weinberg to leftist politics or the bomb. A solid citizen and a family man, he owned his van and his home, connected to Mooney merely because his son took music lessons from Mooney's wife, Rena. He had driven the Mooney family to a strike meeting earlier that month and to an anarchist picnic on the Fourth of July.

Questioned by a police detective looking to snag Mooney, Weinberg flat out refused a bribe of $5,000 to provide "just a little circumstantial evidence" against the radical organizer. Perhaps to retaliate, the police put Weinberg's name on their list of suspects, identifying him as "Israel Weinberg, Occupation Anarchist." Indicted despite this less-than-minimal evidence, Weinberg went on trial with Mooney in October 1917. A jury acquitted him that November.

Despite his utter anonymity, the Jewish jitney driver's arrest, and his trial standing alongside Tom Mooney, gave a number of prominent Irish Americans a chance to defend the Jews while attacking anti-Irish xenophobia, antiradicalism, and the suppression of civil liberties.

New York's senator William Bourke Cockran, a conservative Democrat, Irish patriot, devout Catholic, outspoken foe of

Protestant anti-Catholicism, opponent of immigration restriction, and supporter of a homeland for the Jews in Palestine, rose to champion Weinberg. Cockran held up the government's persecution and prosecution of Weinberg as evidence of the dangerous forces at work in the late 1910s, which culminated in the passage of restrictive immigration laws and the flowering of the Ku Klux Klan (KKK). Even after the case against Weinberg ended, Cockran continued to link the Mooney case to anti-Semitism.

Cockran spoke out around the country as the legal team he headed looked for funds to defend Tom and Rena Mooney. He constantly hearkened back to what the prosecution had done to Israel Weinberg, "a man of unblemished character." Cockran told audiences that Weinberg had left czarist Russia, a "theater of frightful oppression," a regime that now, "thank God," had come to "an end forever," and that he had sought freedom in America. Cockran detailed his meetings with Weinberg, declaring that through them, "I have come to the conclusion that there could not be too many Russian Jews in America." Quite a statement from a US senator while so many Americans justified immigration restriction out of fear that those coming from Russia, mainly Jews, would bring Bolshevik revolutionary activity to America.

In the speeches Cockran delivered around the country, he drew an analogy between the Mooney case and that of Alfred Dreyfus in the 1890s. He cited both as miscarriages of justice, the latter based on "hatred of Jews," which he reminded one audience "was the cause of the memorable attempt to ruin Dreyfus, just as hatred of labor unions is now causing the pursuit of Tom Mooney." In his look back to the French trial, Cockran declared that "the motive for the Dreyfus frame-up was to discourage Jews from seeking commissions in the French army, although the whole history of France has established for the

Jewish soldier a reputation for patriotism, courage and bravery."
To another gathering he noted that he referenced the travesty
perpetrated against Dreyfus "not merely for the strong parallel
it affords to the Mooney case but for the important lesson it
teaches the people of this country in a crisis now confronting
us." That crisis, as Cockran saw it, included "the scourge of
anti-Semitism, a foul blot on Christian civilization."

Cockran and the others involved in Mooney's defense hoped
to foster Jewish support for the Mooney cause, including from
those who feared the association in American public opinion between Jews and bomb-throwing radicals, anarchists in
particular. He enlisted the help of the United Hebrew Trades;
Morris Hillquit, Socialist Party candidate for mayor of New
York; the Arbeter Ring (the Workmen's Circle); the Yiddish
newspaper *Forverts*; and the Amalgamated Clothing Workers
of America, led by Sidney Hillman, among others. These groups
might have stood up for Mooney anyhow, whether Dreyfus
was mentioned or not, but Cockran's words touched a broader
base of Jewish listeners. Rabbi Joseph Silverman of New York's
Temple Emanu-El, a bastion of Reform Judaism, participated
in Cockran's funeral rites. Silverman described Cockran as "a
loyal and devoted member of his own church, he stood above
all altars, creeds and rituals and preached justice and mercy to
all mankind."[27]

Cockran joined a long roster of Irish American officeholders
who spoke out for Jewish causes. From the late nineteenth century forward, as American Jewish communal leaders sought allies, they turned to Irish Americans to join them as they appealed
to US government officials. When Simon Wolf, Louis Marshall,
and Oscar Straus, all highly placed American-born leaders of
Jewish defense organizations, appealed to the US government in
the late nineteenth century to use its power to protest the Russian government's practice of not accepting passports of Jewish

citizens of the United States, they sought out Irish American politicians to join them. They enlisted former Boston mayor and congressman John F. Fitzgerald to add his voice to the Jewish campaign. He introduced legislation into the US House of Representatives in 1897 directing Secretary of State John Hay to demand that czarist officials grant "Hebrew American citizens" equal rights "in the matters of passports as now accorded to all other American citizens."[28]

As anti-Jewish violence flared across the former czarist lands during the civil war pitting the Soviet army against the defenders of the old regime, and in the newly established Republic of Poland as well, Boston Jews organized a march in December 1919, "Jewish Protest Day." Cardinal O'Connell's representative Rev. Michael J. Scanlan joined in. O'Connell himself put his name on a protest letter condemning Henry Ford's anti-Semitic publications in his *Dearborn Independent*. Running for eight years between 1920 and 1929, the magazine reprinted the notorious anti-Jewish forgery *The Protocols of the Elders of Zion*.

Irish Americans also embraced the cause of Zionism, speaking out in favor of the efforts of some American Jews to see the creation of a Jewish homeland in Palestine. Chicago's mayor, Irish American William Dever, announced in 1924 his plan to twin his city with a Jewish town in Palestine as a statement of solidarity with local Zionists.

The seemingly inexorable march of the United States toward immigration restriction provided a political space in which Irish Americans could come out in support of Jews. With their advocacy, Irish politicians, the Irish American press, and the leaders of Irish communal organizations could defend Jews and condemn the Protestants behind immigration restriction, particularly the New England Protestant elites who created the Immigration Restriction League in 1894. As David I. Walsh wrote in Boston's Jewish newspaper *The Jewish Advocate* in

1894, "there can be no doubt but that the foreign-born and their children, had as much right, as a descendant of the most aristocratic blue-blooded man who can trace his ancestors to the *Mayflower*."[29]

In its constant speeches and pronouncements on the subject, the American Irish Historical Society chronicled the good that immigrants did for the nation, the fitness of Jews for America, and how restrictions would hurt the Irish as well. Looking back on the work of Irish Americans on this question, the society declared one of its greatest achievements "challenging the immigration quotas based on national origin" and taking a "leading part . . . in opposing American immigration on a nebulous basis of racial origin quotas that are purely speculative and, in some cases . . . glaringly fraudulent and arbitrarily discriminatory."[30]

When Representative Emanuel Celler, a Jewish congressman from Brooklyn, tried to rally his fellow legislators to stave off passage of the Johnson-Reed Act of 1924, he turned to several other Jews in Congress but also marshaled the active assistance of William Patrick Connery Jr., James Gallivan, Robert H. Clancy, John A. Keliher, Charles Anthony Mooney, Joseph O'Connor, and Patrick O'Sullivan, with New York's Fiorello La Guardia the only non-Jewish, non-Irish representative visibly part of the failed effort.

These Irish American politicians had their own stakes in the immigration question and their own reasons to fight the imposition of national quotas and numerical limits. While Ireland did not receive as low a quota as Italy, Greece, or the countries of eastern Europe, they believed cutting the overall numbers would hurt their people back home, just as Jews feared that their friends, family, and coreligionists more generally would suffer as a result of the pending legislation. For both, it constituted a matter of disrespect by the country they lived in, contributed to, and served.

Irish Americans, in telling their immigration stories in the 1910s and 1920s, coupled their experiences with those of the Jews. One orator at the American Irish Historical Society related it graphically, declaring in 1929:

> When the Irishman . . . saw his cabin leveled to the ground, his family huddled on the roadside, the spears of the red coat making him a world outcast . . . he looked for a new start in a distant land . . . having made his last prayer over his sacred dead. . . . When the Jew in the hinterland of Russia saw the Cossack come with fire and sword, he knew that religious and racial hatred had unleashed their fury against his people, and when the storm had passed and the dead were laid to rest, he followed the path of the fugitive son of Erin and became his neighbor in the land of hope.[31]

Not surprising then that Celler, embarking on a last-ditch effort to block the 1920s restrictive legislation, turned to his Irish colleagues. They made the most sense as allies in this doomed struggle. No other ethnic group counted as many members of Congress, and none collaborated so often with Jews to counter nativism, which Jews defined as the American face of anti-Semitism. Celler could not but see their common struggle, and while Italians, Poles, Greeks, and others had a deep stake in this, too, none had stepped up more for Jews than the Irish had. None had spoken so effusively about the Jews.

In 1927 a speaker at the American Irish Historical Society, looking back on the failed fight against restriction earlier that decade, praised his fellow Irish Americans for joining up with "the Jews, who have produced some of the great types in civilization."[32]

Their struggle against restriction took on great urgency after the world war and into the 1920s, as ample opportunities arose for Irish Americans to speak out for the Jews as they battled their own foes. When, for example, Harvard University—under President A. Lawrence Lowell, a foe of Brandeis's appointment to the Supreme Court—instituted a quota system limiting the percentage of Jewish young men admitted to the college, voices within Irish Boston sounded out. Cardinal William O'Connell sent a protest letter to the university's president, Charles Eliot, and James T. Moriarty, president of the city council, condemning the new policy of the institution, "which only a few years ago discriminated against my fellow Catholics and Irish." He successfully got the Irish-dominated council to pass a resolution condemning this manifestation of anti-Semitism by the elite white Protestant New Englanders.[33]

Those years provided Irish and Jews with a powerful shared enemy. The rise and flourishing of the second Ku Klux Klan terrified them both. In their fight against the Klan, the outspoken voice of Irish Americans reached a crescendo, fighting it in its own name and that of the Jews. They took up the fight with particular energy, realizing the profoundly anti-Catholic essence of the "Secret Empire," with its klaverns spread across the country, funded by millions of donations from angry white Protestant Americans. The Klan's kleagles, highly effective recruiters, tapped into the resentments of millions of native-born Americans who believed that Blacks, Jews, and Catholics would replace them in numbers and influence.

The single most popular social movement in American history, the Klan of the early 1920s persuaded Americans in every region. It inspired them to use all means possible, violence if need be, as well as engagement in the political arena, to ensure the continued hegemony of their own, superior kind, the men who rightfully deserved to hold power. An estimated fifty thousand Klansmen, outfitted in their finest whites, marched down Pennsylvania Avenue from the home of the president to the domed Capitol in the summer of 1925.

The Irish Catholic leadership of the anti-Klan effort mirrored the reality that among its triumvirate of enemies, the KKK put Catholics and Irish people at the top. The Irish embodied the forces the Klan found most dangerous, as Catholics of immigrant heritage and purveyors of alcoholic beverages.

Not that it did not perpetrate great, and tragically familiar, violence against Black people, relying on the routine beatings, lynchings, and acts of physical intimidation that continued unabated for decades after the Klan's decline. And not that it did not unleash its vitriol on Jews, but anti-Catholicism provided the Klan with its most potent fodder for whipping up millions of white Americans, as it established vibrant chapters in Massachusetts, Illinois, New York, Michigan, New Jersey, Maine, and other places with dense Irish communities and where the large numbers of Irish Catholic government officeholders proved the point that Protestants faced a potent foe. In Chicago more than twenty chapters of the Klan operated, publishing *Dawn: A Journal for True American Patriots*. Klan chapters formed on college campuses, and Klansmen won public office around the country.

The Klan, despite waning numbers after 1925, commanded a prominent place in the life of the nation and was reinvigorated when, in 1928, the Democratic Party nominated Al Smith, a New York Irish Catholic and a "wet"—that is, an opponent of Prohibition—for president. Four years earlier the Klan had deftly blocked this Catholic, a product of the Lower East Side, once a worker at the Fulton Fish Market, from being his party's standard-bearer. When Smith campaigned in 1928, a full chorus of anti-Catholicism resounded, and Americans in every region asked if someone who took his orders directly from a foreign potentate, the pope, ought to occupy the nation's highest office.

Anti-Catholic rhetoric dominated public life, and the Klan targeted Catholic parish church buildings, planting flaming crosses outside and a few times burning these sacred spaces to the ground. Ironically, members of a local klavern firebombed the National Shrine of the Little Flower just outside of Detroit, the church from which, in the late 1930s, Father Coughlin would broadcast his anti-Semitic screeds.

Klansmen trained their sights on individual Catholic priests whom they considered especially troublesome. A local Protestant minister in Birmingham, Alabama, shot and killed Father James Coyle in 1921. Defended by Hugo Black, who in 1937 became a justice of the United States Supreme Court, the shooter wanted to punish Father Coyle for converting his daughter Ruth to Catholicism so she could marry a Catholic man. Father John Francis Conoley came to Gainesville to minister to the growing number of Catholic students at the University of Florida. He set up the first Catholic student center and established a theater group for all interested students. Father Conoley outraged the Klan in the deeply Protestant community because he promoted interfaith work and drama, something some local Protestants considered immoral. Conoley gave a lecture at a Kiwanis meeting in 1923 on the need to raise funds to help defray the educational costs of students unable to pay tuition, and on his way home, members of the Alachua Klan Number 46 kidnapped him, castrated him, and left his mutilated body on the steps of a Catholic church.

Stories like these filled the pages of American newspapers. Catholic organizations, with the Irish in the lead, fretted over how to respond. The Klan terrified them as nothing had since the Know-Nothings. The clout and respectability they had slowly amassed in the decades since then could vanish with the ascendancy of their hooded enemies.

The Catholic young men responded. Students at Notre Dame University, home of the "Fighting Irish," attacked a Klan gathering in South Bend, Indiana, while Catholics in Chicago, led by Patrick O'Donnell, formed the American Unity League, which, in answer to the *Dawn,* published *Tolerance,* printing in its pages the names and addresses of local Klansmen. Irish Catholic politicians unsparingly condemned the Klan.

Irish Catholics tackling the Klan invoked Jews, giving them high billing in their propaganda as co-victims of the Klan, despite the fact that the Klan inflicted no physical harm on Jews as it did to Blacks and Catholics. No synagogue went up in flames, no rabbi got beaten up, no crosses were burned in front of Jewish spaces. Yet Catholic rhetoric showcased the Klan's anti-Semitism to expose the organization for its evil and its violation of the American creed of inclusion and, as the Chicago publication pegged it, tolerance.

Coleman E. Kelly, a Massachusetts state legislator, introduced a bill that would expel any member of either the commonwealth's House or Senate who might propose legislation "for the purpose of injuring any religious organization" and that had been suggested by "any member of the Ku Klux Klan." The Klan, he declared, ignored the fact that "beneath the mud of Flanders many American youths are sleeping the eternal sleep—and many of them, thousands of them are Catholics, Jews and Negroes." Patrick B. O'Sullivan, a Connecticut Democrat, declared in 1924, "Let no man or woman in the grand old Commonwealth court the friendship of the Ku Klux Klan and dare to call himself a Democrat." That movement, which claims to be the defender of Christianity, denies "that the man upon whose teachings rest the dogma of every Christian Church was himself a Jew."[34]

The Knights of Columbus went to the front lines of the attack on the Klan. Predominantly Irish in membership and leadership, with individuals named Flaherty, McSweeney, McCarthy, Derry, Eagan, Moynihan, Mulligan, and Dunn at its helm, it had been founded in 1882 by Father Michael J. McGivney. This Catholic men's fraternal order gave the Klan its full attention, launching a vigorous campaign against it. The Knights had moved into the public sphere during the First World War when the War Department put it in charge of Catholic servicemen. While the Knights worked closely with the Young Men's Christian Association (YMCA), which ministered to the Protestants, it established particularly close bonds with the Jewish Welfare Board (JWB), created to serve Jewish soldiers. The Knights and the JWB recognized that they had more in common with each other than with the YMCA. The latter considered itself the nation's premier spiritual guardian, and the other two just welcomed guests. The Knights and JWB rejected that conceit, asserting their equality with the Protestants.

With the war's end, the Knights confronted the escalation of anti-Catholicism and set about attacking the newly reinvigorated Klan. It published articles, organized meetings, and presented declarations of outrage at public gatherings in opposition to the Klan. In 1921 Supreme Knight of the Knights of Columbus James Flaherty, son of Irish immigrant parents, organized some twenty-two hundred lectures around the country to combat anti-Semitism.

Knight leaders, particularly Edward F. McSweeney, a one-time union leader, an active participant in Massachusetts Democratic politics, and in the years 1893–1902, an assistant commissioner of immigration at Ellis Island, decided that the best way to confront the Klan would be to provide systematic evidence against the claim that only white Protestants of English background had built America and that the others had contributed nothing to the nation.

So, in 1922 he came up with an unprecedented historical project. He brought to the Knights the idea of commissioning a set of history books that would, "unlike any heretofore published," give "the actual history of racial contributions to the making of the United States, not from the isolated viewpoint of a single race . . . but from the viewpoint of each race." Taken together, the shelf's worth of books the Knights would commission should, McSweeney argued, convince readers that "the Negroes and Jews, but particularly . . . Catholics of all racial derivation" had made the nation.[35]

The full set of books never came out, but three did, published under the imprimatur of the Knights. Frederick Franklin Schrader, a journalist and playwright, published *The Germans in the Making of America* (1924). The author of *The Gift of Black Folk* (1924), W. E. B. Du Bois, needs no introduction. The third book, *The Jews in the Making of America* (1925) by George Cohen, brought the Irish defense of the Jews nearly full circle from the writings of Charles P. Daly in the latter part of the nineteenth century.

McSweeney introduced each book by emphasizing the gifts brought to America by all immigrants. He confronted head-on the challenges sparked by the 1921 Emergency Quota Act, which, for the first time, assigned slots to potential immigrants on the basis of place of origin, that is, nationality. (The 1882 Chinese Exclusion Act and the Immigration Act of 1917, which created the Asiatic Barred Zone, had already made racial categories part of the immigration system.)

By enacting the law, McSweeney declared, Congress and the American people had succumbed to "an organized movement which, especially since the war, is attempting to classify all aliens, except those of one special group," namely Anglo-Saxons, "as hyphenates" and "mongrels." "Haphazard, unscientific, based on unworthy prejudice," the quotas and numerical limits, McSweeney predicted, would also likely be "disastrous in their economic consequences."

McSweeney then focused on the Jews, who had long been welcome to the nation. But with the new law, the "United States has departed a long way from the policy which was recorded in 1795 by the series of coins, on which appeared the words 'A Refuge for the Oppressed of all Nations.'"[36]

Cohen repeated an argument first offered in book form by Charles P. Daly some four decades earlier, that the Jew had an American history coterminous with the European settlement of the continent. They always contributed to the nation, making it better, more prosperous, and more enlightened. They could rightfully claim their place.

A thread ran from Daly to McSweeney. Irish Americans entwined their present with that of their Jewish neighbors, as the two peoples faced common concerns about their futures in a nation that granted them, as white people, full citizenship, but littered their paths with obstacles. In their defense of the Jews, Irish Americans asserted that they could help secure their own future by serving someone else who also faced perilous realities.

They pointed with pride to what they had done, and continued to do, for the Jews. Research undertaken by the American Irish Historical Society, dedicated to showcasing Irish nobility of spirit, contribution to the common good, and commitment to using political power to enhance the lives of others, uncovered the story of Thomas Dongan, the Second Earl of Limerick, who in 1682 became the fifth colonial governor of New York. His story made its way to the society's publications and lectures, which depicted Dongan as a "gallant soldier" who made possible Jewish life and liberty in America.

That history, as told in Irish circles, noted that before Dongan, a Catholic, enunciated a robust definition of rights in the colony, "freedom of worship was circumscribed. Quakers and Jews were ostracized and driven from the pale." Dongan, however, took up his governorship with a different vision for New York, proposing "an act permitting Jews to exercise their religion." The New York Common Council, made up of Protestant Englishmen set in their intolerant English ways, "vetoed the proposition."[37]

The lesson to be derived from the twentieth-century chron-iclers of Dongan's contribution to American pluralism and the role his support of Jewish freedom played could not be clearer. His opponents, New York's English ruling class of the seven-teenth century, steeped in bigotry, stymied the birth of religious rights for Jews. An Irish Catholic, Dongan used his office to ex-tend liberty of conscience to others, including the greatest vic-tims of Christian bigotry. As Irish American writers of popular history conveyed this story, boasting of the good deeds of their forebears, they nodded to the conditions that they now faced, with anti-Jewish, anti-Irish, and anti-Catholic forces gathering steam.

Father Francis Patrick Duffy, chaplain of the "Fighting Sixty-Ninth," found much of value in the colonial-era history of New York, turning to the Earl of Limerick's deeds in a 1920 talk. The priest who had served the predominantly Irish New York National Guard, which included some number of Jewish soldiers in its ranks, considered Dongan's efforts in the colonial era illustrative of the present moment. Duffy declared, "there has recently been a lot of talk about Americanizing, but they never had to worry about Americanizing the Irish. In fact, there came along an Irishman here about two hundred and forty years ago named Dongan, who began Americanizing New York by introducing a charter of civil and religious liberties."[38]

Duffy pinned the label of first "real American" on the Irish Catholic governor; the first of his religion and national back-ground, he employed his political position to expand liberty and serve all. Being American, Duffy asserted, involved includ-ing others, not excluding. "Americanizing," the priest and so many of the other speakers at the American Irish Historical So-ciety's meetings concurred, meant enlarging religious freedom, particularly for Jews, as Dongan had hoped to do, so many centuries in the past. Dongan, they boasted, brought honor to

Irish Catholics by embodying the best and most expansive tendencies of America.

Such a claim contrasted sharply with the arguments made in the present by the critics of the Irish in America, who repeatedly described them as slavish followers of the pope served by narrow-minded, bigoted priests, opponents of liberty, and foes of tolerance, who wielded political power for their own greedy ends.

In that present, Irish Americans maintained a solid hold on urban politics. They hoped to keep it, and decided that by holding open some crucial doors for Jews, they could serve their own needs and prove, once again, their openness and liberality.

3

The Gatekeepers of American Urban Politics and the Jews Who Entered

In 1891 some Romanian Jewish men, immigrants living on New York's Lower East Side, played bit parts in a larger American political drama. Local Jewish Republicans had asked to meet them, wanting these new Americans to join their party. After the meeting these newly enfranchised men, armed with citizenship papers, decided instead to align their political club with the city's powerful Democratic machine—Tammany Hall, an Irish bastion.

The *American Jewish Year Book,* a publication associated with the Jewish elites, men primarily of central European background, in the main disdainful of Tammany and similar Irish-dominated political organizations in other cities, decried their decision to go with the Democrats. By signing up with Tammany, these immigrants, the *Year Book* claimed, had descended "to the low degree occupied by the typical political organizations that infest the entire East Side."[1]

This little story exemplifies Irish-Jewish connections in the realm of urban politics and the dynamics of the integration of Jewish immigrants. With no clearly stated ideology at stake, the Romanian Jews had rather calculated who would serve them best and would best serve their needs. Who, they likely asked themselves, could dispense the most benefits, whether jobs, material aid in times of need, contracts on municipal undertakings, or slots in the operations of the machine itself? To whom could they turn to protect their business, including semi-licit and explicitly illicit enterprises?

The Romanian story pitted two Jewish groups against each other. On the one side, the masses of Jewish immigrants having learned just enough about American political realities wondered: Who could help get a daughter a job or reduce a son's prison sentence? Whose wink would get the police to turn a blind eye to some infraction of the law, like selling goods on a Sunday or not paying the requisite fee for a peddler's license? Who could get a friendly judge to intervene on behalf of relatives detained on Ellis Island? Who stood at the apex of urban political power, controlling the most useful perks for a working-class marginal people, recently arrived to the country?

They learned that it took little to reap such rewards. They had to vote for the machine, and when called upon, give it some visible support, like knocking on doors of their neighbors and friends during the election season to drum up votes. Showing up to a rally and holding up signs seemed a small price to pay in exchange for all that the machine had to offer.

Jews, like the millions of other people from around the world who congregated in New York, Chicago, Boston, and elsewhere, newcomers and their children, pondered these matters.

The other Jews in the small Romanian story, well-off and well-meaning American Jews, many associated with the Republican Party, advocated for what they called good government. They considered the Irish-led political organizations corrupt and crude, sincerely believing that politics ought not be concentrated in the hands of men like James Michael Curley in Boston, Richard Croker in New York, Michael "Hinky Dink" Kenna in

Chicago, and so many more, who they believed neither cared about the common good nor had the ability to make rational policy choices. These Jewish notables, among them Louis Marshall, Louis Brandeis, Julius Rosenwald, Stephen Wise, the editors of the *American Jewish Year Book,* and others, argued with the Jewish immigrants that the machine politicians did not operate in their best interests.

Rather, they feared that Jewish support of these "low degree" men would exacerbate anti-Jewish sentiment among the better sorts of Americans, Protestants, who in this muckraking era spilled much ink over the evils of Irish political power, deeming its practitioners uncouth and corrupt threats to the integrity of the nation.

Like other middle-class Americans, these Jews reacted with horror to the constant stream of stories in the press about the unscrupulous behavior of these Irish "pols," with their hands in the till, trading favors, whether within the letter of the law or not, for ballot-box loyalty, and doing so with impunity. Articles about kickbacks, bribery, graft, and alliances between bosses and criminals, saloonkeepers, operators of gambling dens, and owners of brothels appeared regularly.

The Jewish elites found the idea of their own people mixed up with crooks, gangsters, gamblers, pimps, prostitutes, and dirty politicians on the take to be appalling. They fretted that the exposés splashed across the press would fuel anti-Semitism, helping to make the case for immigration restriction. Jewish good-government advocates wanted the American public to read stories of Jews as fine, respectable, good citizens in the making, not machine collaborators in cahoots with disreputable Irish bosses who treated politics and the machines of city government as their fiefdoms of greed and graft.

Yet another force at work in New York City Jewish politics— the socialists—also upset the elite Jewish leadership. But ironically the socialists, too, tried to wean the immigrant masses away from Tammany.

From the left, they preached to the newcomers about the evils of the Irish-dominated machine. Repeatedly they proclaimed that Tammany did not have the immigrant Jews' interests at heart and that Tammany did what it did for itself. The immigrants should beware of the "Tiger," Tammany's symbol.

By the 1910s socialists began to score some notable ballot-box victories, and their widely circulating daily newspaper, *Forverts* (The forward), edited by Abraham Cahan, warned its readers, election campaign after election campaign, to be suspicious of Tammany's gifts. Immigrant Jews should not be fooled by the crumbs the machine sprinkled before them.

But immigrant Jews and their immediate descendants made their own political decisions and, for the most part, rebuffed calls to abandon the ward bosses and their minions on Election Day. Despite their recent arrival to the United States and seeming lack of political clout, they did not defer to the better-off in their communities, nor, despite the attractiveness of the socialists' message of economic justice, did they choose to prioritize ideology over practicalities like work, protection, and advancement.

Taking advantage of the political freedoms America offered them, these Jews embraced what the Irish gave them, expecting with the passage of time to get more. Theodore White, for example, noted about his Boston childhood, "we voted, even my father, this Socialist, as did the Irish—a straight Democratic ticket."[2]

To immigrant Jews, the Irish politician stalking their votes, alongside the Irish policeman on his beat and the Irish schoolteacher facing her pupils, embodied America. For the most part the Jews welcomed them, and as the Jewish immigrants' first real Americans, the Irish women and men connected to the machine profoundly impacted them.

The powerful role of Irish politics in American Jewish life can be seen as the culmination of a history that had taken shape decades before the mass migration of Jews from eastern Europe. Irish immigrant men had plunged into the world of American city politics as early as the 1840s, simultaneous with their sizable arrival in the United States. Their first small victories shocked Americans profoundly and spurred the growth of the Know-Nothings and other anti-Catholic groups, Protestants exorcized by the specter of the seemingly unstoppable Irish political machine. Over time Irish immigrant men and their sons, primarily through the Democratic Party, displaced native-born Yankees, doing so by virtue of numbers and political acumen.

They essentially created a system, grounded in America's city streets, that controlled the ever-expanding activities of municipal government, including policing, firefighting, transportation, education, the provision of utilities, the courts, and more. These sources of power became theirs, and perhaps like any group with power, they wanted to hold on to it. To that end, they sought out new voters, with Jews prominent among them, who made up the great European immigration from the 1880s through the 1920s.

Irish urban politics can be seen in large measure as the politics of revenge. The Irish relished getting even with the white Protestant elite that had governed before, organized politically to lock the Irish out, and then continued to devise methods to limit Irish power.

The Irish, now in power, were bent on perpetuating their own clout, which meant more to them than just the total number of offices they held, pure and simple. They wanted to also undo the culture of the old elite. As Boston's James Michael Curley, a practitioner par excellence of the Irish political way, crowed, "the New England of the Puritans and the Boston of rum, codfish and slaves are as dead as Julius Caesar." Instead, he quipped, the region ought to be renamed "New Ireland" as a tribute to the Irish who had come there, faced poverty, dealt with adversity, and endured the disdain of those old Puritans and their progeny. Those once-reviled Irish now sat in the chambers of government, and Curley humorously mused that the time would soon come when the last Yankee would be encased in a museum exhibit, a curious relic of a dead old order. Hyperbole, for sure, but his words embodied the deep resentment against the anti-Irish, anti-Catholic nativists whose behaviors stimulated Irish politics. They envisioned that the arriving Jews would have a role to play in the continuing tug-of-war between the Irish and their antagonists from decades earlier.[3]

Irish and Irish American men like Curley intuited that Jews shared in their resentment of the Protestants, since those Protestants excluded Jews, closing the doors on them at most private colleges and universities and in housing, hotels, and places of leisure and recreation. In the 1920s Boston of Nat Hentoff, "a good many Jews also found Boston theirs when Curley made the city his." Hentoff pointed out what this sentiment of mutual loathing reflected, noting that Jews liked Curley not just because he appointed so many of them to city offices, but also because he and his Jewish peers "knew that if there was one group for whom the Brahmins," the city's Protestant elites, "had more contempt than they had for the Irish, it was the Jews." He recalled Jews like his father cheering "when Curley went up against the Brahmins," a cheer laced with the joy of revenge. "The Irish couldn't get into their clubs," as this Boston boy remembered, "and the Jews couldn't, but because of Curley the Brahmins couldn't get into City Hall."[4]

City by city the Irish had begun their political journeys in the years after the Civil War with small electoral victories at the ward level, then consolidated power with growing numbers. By century's end they occupied the top rung of so many cities, and the Irish even dominated the urban flank of the Democratic Party at the national level.

Commentators pondered the sources of Irish political success, asking how a group so despised upon arrival, so out of sync with the fundamentals of America's Protestant culture, managed to achieve such political success. No admirer of the Irish, Sir Cecil Spring-Rice, Britain's ambassador to the United States, called them "the best politicians in the country . . . with unequalled power of political organization." John Paul Bocock declared in 1894 that they had a "genius for municipal government or at least for getting municipal office."

Bocock posited the existence of an Irish "oligarchy" that "controls America's leading cities such as, New York, Brooklyn, Jersey City, Hoboken, Boston, Chicago, Buffalo, Albany, Troy, Pittsburgh, St. Louis, Kansas City, Omaha, New Orleans and San Francisco," not coincidentally places to which the newly arrived Jews flocked and carved out their new American lives. But the Irish had come to these places first and gained primacy in city government.[5]

Ensconced in city councils and city halls, the victorious Irish held sway over the basics of city life with jobs to give out, contracts to offer, personal favors to proffer, and insider information to dispense, doing so within the letter of the law, and quite often outside it as well. Those at the top of the organization handpicked those further down the ladder, deciding who would run for office, who would help operate the organization, who would lead the campaigns and on which streets—and all owed obeisance to the leaders.

Bosses, district leaders, ward workers, and street captains showed up with food and fuel to provide for the wants of the unemployed and distressed. They stood rounds in saloons and listened to the grievances and complaints of the poor and struggling people. When asked to help out, they did so, always with the understanding that the machine had to get its due in return. It gave, but the recipients had to know who had helped and that the help came with some strings attached.

They attended weddings and funerals, baptisms, and bar mitzvah ceremonies. Meetings of benevolent associations and clubs, whether conducted in Italian, Yiddish, Polish, or any other language, gave them a chance to mingle with voters. Machine politicians did not hesitate to demand payment for services rendered, essentially graft or bribery, always in amounts commensurate with the class position of the beneficiary of the aid.

To locate the origins of this in historic time, the Irish arrived and their numbers soared with the expansion of mass democracy, as property qualifications for voting ended and religious obstacles to officeholding disappeared. They showed up simultaneously with the takeoff of the nation's industrialization, which propelled millions to come to the United States, but they also found themselves often unable to make ends meet. The mercurial ups and downs of the capitalist economy meant periods of economic insecurity. Chronically in need of assistance, struggling immigrants got little from the government, as states did little to alleviate the day-to-day want. Their own families and benevolent associations provided some aid, but never enough in the worst of times. The machines stepped in to fill the void.

The Irish also moved up their political ladder as cities expanded physically, embarking on mammoth and lucrative projects, like paving roads, creating the infrastructures of public transportation, erecting bridges, digging tunnels, and laying sewer lines. They inched their way up to dominate city councils, city bureaucracies, and city halls as states extended the years of mandatory education, necessitating more school buildings and schoolteachers.

A perfect storm had gathered for them. For those who would practice urban politics, much could be gained beyond just getting a chance to shape policies. Rather, vast bounties might be had for its practitioners and, in a trickle-down dynamic, for those who would put and keep them in office.

Until about the 1880s Irish immigrants and their children constituted the largest immigrant population of most cities, and the machines almost exclusively served Irish women and men.

But after the 1880s, the new immigrants from eastern and southern Europe rendered the Irish increasingly a minority. So Irish political actors recognized the truth that to stay in power meant reckoning with the newcomers, and among them were over two million Jews, most of whom settled in New York and other large cities. These would be the new voters, and the Irish had to repackage their operations and open up their coffers to serve these new constituents with the resources at their command.

The kind of politics that machine politicians practiced, whether Tammany in New York, the various competing Irish machines in Boston, or the machines in Chicago, which changed over from one Irish faction to another, infused the lives of those new Jewish immigrants. The politicians, whether born in Ireland or the sons of those who had immigrated earlier, constituted a visible and ever-present force in the daily life of Jewish immigrant enclaves. Their leaders at the top and the lieutenants down the rungs of the ladder operated on the Jewish streets, becoming familiar beings, well-known presences to the women, men, and children who lived there. An 1898 commentator from Boston, who himself may—or may not—have liked Jews, wrote that the Irish politician "fraternizes with the Jew, eats with the Jew, drinks with the Jew," all the while talking politics.[6]

The memoirs, autobiographies, press accounts, and fiction of the Jewish immigrant quarter, whether depicting life in New York, Chicago, or Boston, abound with these Irish men of the machine who loomed large in their neighborhoods.

Twelve-year-old Eddie Cantor, living with his grandmother on Henry Street on New York's Lower East Side, who would grow up to be a wildly popular star of stage and screen, got to know his local assemblyman, Alfred E. Smith. Smith lived two blocks away on Oliver Street and reached out to Cantor and to some other neighborhood boys and grown men, asking them to stump for him in some of his early campaigns. In exchange for their work, Smith invited them all over to Bassler's Saloon, handing out rounds of schooners of beer to the older ones, and for the "kids" he "would order nothing but sarsaparilla."

Smith, the future governor of New York and first Catholic to run for president of the United States, Cantor remembered, would "lead us in song, protect the weaklings from the bullies, and add that bit of kindliness and sunshine to the dingy gloom of our lives." Cantor pinpointed an incident when an old bearded Jewish peddler fell victim to some "tough heavy-set men of the alleys," maybe actually Irish street thugs. Smith, out hunting for votes, came to the man's rescue, putting "his arm around him like a brother." Decades later as a famous performer whose name flashed on the marquees of Broadway theaters, Cantor again campaigned for Smith's run for the White House. In his autobiography, which appeared simultaneously with that race, he gushed eloquently about Smith: "I can never forget the picture of this young and handsome Mr. Al coming among the ragged, hairy, bearded people of the abyss, extending a hand of welcome and friendship to all of them, as if the lady of the Statue of Liberty had sent her own son to receive these poor, bewildered immigrants on her behalf." As a boy orator, he had climbed on the "stump" proclaiming to all who would listen, many of whom voted, "this man who is running for the Assembly is the future President, Alfred E. Smith."[7]

Smith and so many of his peers rose because they figured out who was Jewish and what the Jews wanted, and they delivered well beyond beer and sarsaparilla. Those services proved often to be lifesavers. During hard times, the machine's workers—Irish men with the Jewish men who represented them—delivered food, fuel, and other necessities to desperate families. Journalist and humorist Harry Golden recalled that "Tammany put more coal in the cellars of the poor than all of Scranton ever mined."[8] "Big Tim" Sullivan came up with the idea of providing shoes to needy children, distributing them among Jews along with other tenement dwellers. The voters, most eking out meager existences and fretting over the daily matters of getting by, surely remembered where that sturdy footwear now on the feet of their daughters and sons had come from, and they would respond appropriately. They would not forget in the depths of winter cold that the warmth in their apartments had come from the men representing the machine.

Daniel J. Riordan, who was described in his obituary in *The Journal of the American-Irish Historical Society* in 1926 as someone whose "activities were identified with the lower east side," recognized that votes would be theirs if they responded to information that a Jewish family, here or there, faced some acute crisis. Riordan's eulogist boasted that the residents of that neighborhood "have cause to bless his memory," since he, and by extension his fellow Tammany operatives, intimately knew that "section of the city much discussed but so little understood by idealists."[9]

By "idealists" he presumably meant the socialists who worked mightily to get Lower East Side votes, delivering a message to the masses that they should beware of the Irish bosses. But the ideologues from the left could never provide for the immigrants like the machine. They had no shoes, coal buckets, or bushels of food to draw upon. Indeed, no entity could respond like the machine did.

This does not dismiss the aid provided by Jewish communities themselves. They were awash in charitable societies that offered hefty amounts of emergency relief to their coreligionists in dire straits, but their embrace of bureaucratic methods based on the principles of scientific charity made the immediate help provided by the machine more personal and swifter. The machine did not care if the widows, the orphans, the sick, and the out-of-work qualified as worthy recipients according to a metric computed in the boardroom of some agency. The machine did not ask the poor to fill out forms or come to an office to plead their cases. The machine did not seek to uplift them, change their habits, or make them into new, more modern people. A sack of coal, a box of food, a pair of shoes delivered to a Jewish family—the machine calculated these as good investments, likely translatable into votes that counted.

The boss, whether Murphy, Sullivan, Riordan, or others with their distinctively Irish names and roots, organized excursions in the summer months, taking the denizens of the hot, humid, densely packed Lower East Side to cool spots along the Hudson or East Rivers. Their waterway cruises, the cool breezes, the picnics on the grass, and the hours spent away from the tenements provided relief from the crowded apartments and stifling garment shops, all courtesy of Murphy, Sullivan, Riordan, and their peers.

An 1893 report in *The New York Times* credited the Ahearn Association, a Tammany entity, with having organized "the biggest pleasure party that ever left this city by way of water." It reported how on a steamy July day, no fewer than twenty thousand "copper-lunged" East Siders enjoyed themselves mightily on a river cruise, reveling in the relief it brought them and the excitement of being part of a grand spectacle away from their apartments. The newspaper's reference to the color of their lungs reflected the high levels of respiratory diseases that plagued the Jewish neighborhood and the public discourse about its unhealthful conditions. While the outing provided no long-term cure, the Jewish poor enjoyed Tammany's day of leisure, knowing full well that ballot-box gratitude had to follow.[10]

Beyond these immediate gifts, Jews had much to get from the machine. Some Jewish voters made their meager living as vendors of pushcarts, an enterprise that required getting a license from the city. If the street merchant tried to do her business without the necessary papers, she risked a ticket and a fine. A substantial number of Jews ran small businesses, and for them Sunday closing laws cut into their chance of earning a living. Many, impossible to compute, would not work on their Sabbath, but selling on the Christians' holy day and getting caught by the police meant a fine too steep to pay. Jewish immigrants operated liquor stores and pool halls, gambling operations and liquor distilleries, places where shady characters congregated. Some took part in the business of prostitution and ran brothels, illegal enterprises in need of protection. If arrested, a friendly judge, likely handpicked by Tammany for his loyalty, might dismiss the case or impose a light sentence. Jews relied upon their Irish political connections to evade the law.

Jewish merchants made use of Irish machine contacts in pursuit of many other business ventures as well. They owned stores housed in modest structures and they owned tenement houses, both of which had to be refitted up to the changing codes, according to laws passed by city councils and state legislatures. Violating them made a shop owner or landlord liable for legal action. Under the table a friendly politician could intervene, convincing an inspector to turn a blind eye. As always, this service came with a quid pro quo.

The machine helped some enterprising Jews in the immigrant community decide to try their luck in the world of urban real estate: they went about buying up undeveloped land to erect housing at low cost in areas newly incorporated into the expanding cities and about to be served by public transportation. A friendly city operative tied to the machine could help, and such assistance surely seemed worth a vote and maybe even substantial commitment to the machine come Election Day.

Many Jewish real estate projects involved actual partnerships with Irish machine politicians. Simon Steingut, a major player in New York City real estate, whose son Irwin would follow him into Tammany headquarters in Brooklyn, forged a close connection to Tim Sullivan. Sullivan helped him with city permits, aiding him in forming a business consortium of Jewish immigrant bankers and Tammany investors in 1912 to buy up a chunk of land on New York's Second Avenue, including a lot at the corner of Houston Street. Steingut, facilitated by Sullivan, had plans for a grand venue rising there to showcase Yiddish entertainment. Steingut and Sullivan's joint efforts came to fruition, resulting in the National Theater, which helped establish New York as the world's center of the Yiddish stage.

The system worked for Jewish immigrants, mostly economically marginal, new to the country and unschooled in American ways. Political leverage came from the voting, and voting came from the machine.

The machine recognized, too, that it needed an expanding voter base, and so it used its resources to foster naturalization and make sure that immigrants actually voted. Tammany sponsored a "naturalization committee" made up of "the local captains and at times the district leader," which, according to a 1920 study focusing on Jewish immigrants specifically, "keeps tabs on the men not yet naturalized and assists them" to do so. It sponsored English and civics classes so the men could get their papers. Voters in Charley Murphy's lopsidedly Jewish assembly district received notes, handwritten by Charley himself, if by midafternoon on Election Day they had not shown up at the polls. Clearly self-serving for the machine, it worked for the Jewish immigrants as well, and what they had to do for the machine paled in the face of the services they got.[11]

Even paying bribes and protection money seemed worth it. To a Jew caught selling on Sunday or the peddler apprehended for doing business without a license, the fine mattered. Better to pay cash to the machine and not get a ticket. A 1901 report of the University Settlement, a progressive institution located on the Lower East Side, tersely stated that payment of "$5 protection money for the policeman" routinely kept the Jewish entrepreneur in business. The day's profits offset the fee, operating as just a normal part of running a business.[12]

In this and so many countless ways, Jews got much from Irish politicians. A Chicago story tells this well. James Goggin, born in County Cork, worked his way up the city's ward system, winning election to a judgeship in the late nineteenth century. Repeatedly reelected, he enjoyed machine backing and voter support.

In August 1897 he heard the case of a "Russian Jew," Louis Ruben, brought up for having set fire to his home to collect the insurance money. Jews in the United States long labored under the accusation of being "fire bugs." But when Ruben came up in front of Judge Goggin, even before his lawyer had presented his argument, the judge peremptorily dismissed the case. "Every time," he opined, a Jew has a fire, "the police start a cry of arson. That cry arson. That cry is too thin, and will not go in my court." Goggin, an Irish nationalist and machine loyalist, discharged Ruben and advised him to "Go with your friends. . . . I will not send you to penitentiary from this court." No doubt when Goggin stood election the next time he could count on Ruben's friends and other Jews to remember that when a Jew's fate lay in his hands, he stood above prejudice.[13]

Immigrant Jews and their children, lacking numbers, power, and contacts, could have done none of this on their own.

Individual by individual they turned to Irish politicians to intervene for them. The correspondence of one such machine leader, John Ahearn, provides a peek into this world of favors, asked by Jews and accommodated by an Irish American boss blessed with clout and connections.

Involved with the machine since 1882, this New York–born son of Irish immigrants occupied several political positions, including state assemblyman, then a clerkship in the city's police court, from which he went on to several terms as a state senator, and finally Borough of Manhattan president. He amassed visibility, contacts, and a good sense of what voters, Jews prominently among them, wanted. Moe Solomon in 1905 sought Ahearn's help in getting a job as a notary; Isidore Schuman wanted a position in the Tenement House Department; and Dora Rogalsky, whom he described as "a member of a family of old neighbors and dear friends," asked him to intervene with the head of the corrections department so her son Michael, incarcerated in a city facility, could get a pass for a brief family reunion. Ahearn responded to all of them, doing what they asked. He tried to get a pardon for "the Kaplan boy" from a prison sentence, a teaching job for Miss Sara Greenberg, and the voiding of a ticket for Selma Gersten, owner of a tenement house who had been found to have violated city standards. As requested by Jewish constituents, he showed up at the galas of Jewish communal and charitable societies and wrote letters of endorsement for fundraising campaigns for such institutions as the Young Folks League of the Hebrew Infant Asylum.

Examples of Ahearn's willingness to accommodate Jewish requests and their comfort in appealing to him could go on and on. Two more will have to suffice. He confirmed in a letter that he would personally support the efforts of the Kosher Poultry Dealers and Consumers' Association in its dispute with the West Washington Market poultry dealers, whom he promised to meet with, to represent the purveyors of kosher fowl. He wrote to John Pallas, the park commissioner, endorsing a proposal of Moses Selig ("I like him"), a Democratic Party stalwart, to "permit the erecting in Central Park, of some stand or pavilion in which orthodox Hebrews, during the holiday season," presumably Passover, "might obtain kosher food."[14]

Ahearn mentored promising young Jewish men to serve him in the world of politics while they advanced their own careers. Samuel Dickstein, the Lithuanian-born son of a rabbi who immigrated to New York at age two, caught the politician's eye, and while Dickstein was still in high school Ahearn convinced him to start working for the machine. After the young man graduated New York Law School, Ahearn got him a spot as a Tammany district leader. He then bumped Dickstein up the ladder, making him a special deputy attorney general for the state of New York, and then landing him a seat on the city's board of aldermen. From there he promoted Dickstein to the state assembly, and in 1922 to the US House of Representatives. Handpicked and personally groomed by Ahearn, Dickstein did the machine's bidding in every position he occupied. But he also served his Jewish constituents and Jewish interests more broadly.

While in Albany, Dickstein wrote the state's first law regulating the morass of kosher food certification, a piece of legislation that other states emulated. He pushed through legislation that allowed Jewish shopkeepers to operate their businesses on Sundays and advocated for improvements in the city's tenement-house codes, improving the living situation of so many Jews. When Dickstein took his seat in Congress, he led the fight against immigration restriction, and with Hitler's rise to power in Germany in 1933 he, more than any other congressman, took on the issue of domestic anti-Semitism, and in particular pro-fascist and pro-Nazi activity in America. Dickstein called upon his congressional colleagues in 1934 to create a special committee to investigate these threats to the Jews, to be called the House Un-American Activities Committee.

In the political drama linking the Irish machine and the Jews, the former took the lead, the latter came from behind. But both benefited. As the Jewish residents in New York, Boston, and Chicago sought entry into public life and pursued avenues for economic mobility, Irish politicians served as their agents.

Julia Richman became the first Jewish woman to be appointed as a New York City school principal and then played an important role in the city's school system. But as a young, educated woman eager to secure a teaching job, she first had to work through Tammany, which controlled personnel matters. Her father, a Tammany supporter, used his Irish contacts for her, launching her on her path toward a notable and long career. Though she would in her professional life become a passionate opponent of Tammany and a critic of its heavy-handed involvement in education, something she believed ought to be left to the professionals, the nod from Tammany got her the start she needed.

Tammany paved the way also for Nathan Burkan, a prominent entertainment lawyer who in 1914 founded ASCAP, the American Society for Composers, Authors and Publishers. His entire professional life entwined him with Tammany. It started out with low-level street work for the machine as a boy, initiated by his father, a Romanian Jewish immigrant with connections to it through his operation of some luncheonettes and pool halls in New York City's red-light district. Young Nathan attracted the attention of Martin Engel, leader of Tammany's Eighth Assembly District, put there by "Big Tim" Sullivan. Engel, with his own involvement with prostitution, mentored Burkan, getting him a job in the law firm of yet another active Tammany Jew, Julius Lehmann.

Throughout Burkan's illustrious career as legal advisor to

many of the great names of the American stage, he kept alive his Tammany ties. He became leader of the Sixteenth Assembly District and participated regularly in the activities of its heavily Jewish Wichita Club on the Upper East Side, where he developed long relationships with Al Smith and James Foley.

Despite their differences, Burkan and Richman, like so many other less well-known or less successful American Jews, moved upward through their connections to the Irish machine. Other Jews experienced steady improvements by virtue of Tammany and its sister machines in other cities. Irish-led machines had the power to give, and Jewish voters, largely shopkeepers and industrial laborers without much, surrendered their votes for services and in the recognition of what they must have considered a fair and reasonable exchange. Why should they not have done so? Taking cost little.

The Irish machine repeatedly recruited Jews to reach out to other Jews and reel them into its orbit. In his semi-autobiographical *Jews Without Money,* Mike Gold, nom de plume of Itzok Isaac Granich, highlighted a neighbor, Baruch Goldfarb, who hailed from the same Romanian town as the author's father. Goldfarb, "a successful figure on the East Side, a Tammany Hall ward politician, a Zionist leader and the owner of a big dry goods store," frequented the apartment of the protagonist's impecunious family. The novel, an indictment of American capitalism, offered a glimpse of the workings of the machine, as run by Big Tim and his Jewish intermediary, always working toward getting votes for the man at the top:

> One case I remember, Baruch came to our home and persuaded my father to vote at the elections. "It is easy. . . . Tomorrow I will make you citizen and then the next day you will vote. What could be simpler? All you do is mark a cross under the star. Under the star, remember! You will earn three

dollars and be a Democrat. It is a good thing to be a Democrat in America. . . . It brings one money and friends.

Beyond these apartment visits, Goldfarb undertook all sorts of Tammany work. He founded the Baruch Goldfarb Benevolent, Sickness, Social and Burial Society, a lodge that would "hold dances" and encourage all members to "vote Democratic at all the city elections. Best of all, the members were solemnly pledged to help each other in a business way."[15]

Hardly limited to this one example, Jews associated with machines—and conversely, the machines sought them out—and founded clubs to bring Jews together with the Irish politicos. In these clubs the party built loyalty, organized work in the heavily Jewish neighborhoods, and promoted Jews to leadership. The anointed Jewish operatives could, if they played their cards right, become leaders, run campaigns, and even run for office themselves. In turn they had to feed their Irish superiors with information about life in the Jewish enclaves, telling them what the Jews cared about and how best to deliver.

In Boston, Martin Lomasney, known as the "Mahatma," founded the Hendricks Club, which drew in those Jews of the neighborhood open to serving him and to advancing their own interests. David Mancovitz, who emigrated from the province of Posen as a child in 1884, received a thorough American education in the city's public schools and then graduated from Boston University School of Law. In a world where contacts mattered, he became the Mahatma's protégé through the Hendricks Club, and from there Mancovitz moved on to the Boston Common Council and then the Massachusetts House of Representatives.

Mancovitz knew, though, that the boss came first, and the acolyte had to defer. He sought reelection in 1916, but Lomasney decided that he, too, wanted that seat in the legislature.

Mancovitz, with no choice at all, stepped aside for the man at the top of the ladder.

All these men had either been born in Ireland or their parents had. They had been nurtured in the Irish communities with their strong belief in the importance of politics, a war they waged block by block. They declared to the Jews, We care about you, your causes matter to us, and come Election Day, remember who stood up for you, whether with a bundle of household necessities or in the halls of Congress, where we stand up against immigration restriction.

But the machine itself always remembered who helped and who did not, rewarding the former and punishing the latter. Michael Dever, a Chicago Democrat of Irish parentage, won election for mayor in 1923 with vigorous support from Jewish voters on the city's West Side. Jews in the neighborhood canvased for Dever, attended rallies, and voted for him in greater numbers than in any other immigrant wards. The city's Jewish newspapers, English and Yiddish, wrote glowing articles about him, and he rewarded many Jews with plum appointments, some near the top, including such prestigious and powerful positions as chief prosecuting attorney for the city and assistant corporation counsel.

But Jews, like any others, who had not stepped forward to do the heavy lifting during the campaign got the cold shoulder from him. Good-government advocate and Jewish local activist Jennie Purvin wanted a seat on the board of education. But she had refused to support Dever in his campaign, and according to the unwritten rules of the game, she deserved no consideration. She asked two Jewish officials of the powerful city Democratic Party and allies of Dever, S. J. Rosenblatt and Max Korshak, to intervene for her. They in turn presented her case to two other Jews with deep ties to the newly elected mayor, Henry Horner, who would become the governor of Illinois, and Judge Harry

Fisher, a mainstay of Jewish and specifically Zionist causes, asking them to plead for Purvin with Dever.

But Dever would not yield. That slot belonged to someone loyal and not to Purvin.

Her ordeal reveals in a small way the entanglement of Jews and Irish in politics. Jews got theirs, but only if they followed the rules that they themselves had not written. But if they conformed to the script set by the Irish machine, they could reap what the machine gave.

Machines devised strategies in order to bring Jews into the machine and then get them to recruit others from their neighborhoods, synagogues, and other venues of Jewish community life. Jake Arvey, for example, the son of Russian Jewish immigrants living in Chicago's political Twenty-Fourth Ward, in the Lawndale section, gravitated to the organization of Mayor Ed Kelly via Moe Rosenberg, a precinct captain. Arvey would eventually soar and become the third highest placeholder in that machine, a thank-you for his service bringing out the Jewish vote in droves for the Democrats, at a rate not equaled in any of the city's other ethnic wards.

The machine's operators went far in their quest for Jewish votes. In 1905 Tammany sank money into the publication of a Yiddish daily newspaper, *Di Varhayt* (The truth). Publishing daily until 1919, it provided news and feature articles for the Yiddish reading public while serving as Tammany's voice on the immigrant Jewish street, feeding readers favorable portraits of the machine, its leaders, and its good acts on behalf of the Jews, charging up the rhetoric in election seasons. While its subscription numbers never came close to those of *Forverts*, *Di Varhayt* cemented Tammany's hold on the masses as it fostered Yiddish culture in America. Like the other Yiddish papers, it shaped immigrant Jews' understanding of America and helped clarify their political agenda.

The Irish politicians recognized this, and beyond the personal favors they distributed, they easily understood what mattered to Jewish voters, discerning the tremendous power of symbolic efforts as tools to win over Jews, individuals keenly aware of their minority status in America and their global vulnerability.

When individuals from within the machine spoke out against anti-Semitism at home and joined in protests against violence perpetrated against Jews in the Russian Empire, when they fought immigration restriction from the floor of Congress and spoke enthusiastically about the Zionist cause, they warmed the hearts of Jewish voters. The Irish-dominated New York State Democratic Party convention in 1907, in the wake of the outbreak of pogroms in the czarist lands, resolved, "We ask the Federal Government to exercise its influence to bring about speedy cessation of the atrocities now being committed against the Jews in Russia, which have shocked the conscience of civilization," a statement that could not but satisfy the growing number of voters who had arrived from those blood-soaked towns and who still had family there.[16] Boston's Martin Lomasney, with his burgeoning Jewish constituency in the West End, testified to the state legislature in defense of *schechita*, or kosher slaughtering, opposing a bill sponsored by the American Society for the Prevention of Cruelty to Animals that proposed banning this deeply embraced Jewish practice. Irish congressmen like Boston's Patrick Kennedy and Michael Curley spoke out vociferously on the floor of the House of Representatives against immigration restriction. They failed to stave off the legislation, but these machine men made it clear to the Jews in their districts that they had championed their cause in a matter that they cared about deeply.[17]

It was irrelevant whether these actions represented sincere statements of solidarity or just strategic, no-cost ways of winning over the Jews, who would in turn vote and even work for them. They mattered for Jews who had the power to take their votes elsewhere.

Therefore, although Irish insiders held the doors, Jewish immigrants, despite their decidedly lower status in the political pecking order, never just passively received Irish largesse. They made their voices heard and expected to get some of the goodies of urban democracy. They assumed, rightly, that over time their share of those goodies would grow.

In New York's political arena, while most of the eastern European Jewish immigrants and their children voted Tammany, they showed themselves at times to act independently, causing the machine a degree of concern. The visible presence of neighborhood socialists and the booming voice of Cahan's newspaper meant that the masses, despite being Tammany voters, regularly consumed political messages different than the machine's simple script of votes for services.

Tammany realized that New York's immigrant Jewish community by the end of the nineteenth century had embraced the idea that the state needed to protect workers and provide a safety net for the poor. Even if most cast their ballots for the machine, enough of them made their voices heard on economic issues and pushed their Irish political bosses to slowly redefine themselves and step up to support calls for legislation to benefit the working class, prodding them to become more than just holders of power who traded on personal services to stay in office.

Jewish electoral support in New York in 1886 for the short-lived United Labor Party, headed by Henry George, who advocated for vigorous state intervention on behalf of labor, nudged Tammany to start tentatively talking about class and labor issues, and to call upon the state to aid the poor. In the mid-1910s, with the tragedy of the Triangle Shirtwaist Factory fire fresh on

Jewish voters' minds, Tammany emerged as a full-blooded supporter of pro-labor, pro-economic-justice issues.

As such, the Irish-Jewish political encounter moved along a two-way street, and despite Irish clout, Jews did have electoral choices, and if they felt ignored they could act on those other options. Their votes, they said, ought not be taken for granted.

Robert Woods, the Boston social worker who observed life on the ground in the city's West End, noted the Jews' sense of entitlement vis-à-vis the several competing Irish machines and declared in 1902, "The Jew is a thorn in the flesh of the Irish politicians." But, thorn or not, they had to be accommodated.[18]

The machines, despite the special place Jews held in the Irish American political calculus, had to address the needs and wants of all newcomers. Having confronted the demographic realities after the 1880s with the mass influx of immigrants from eastern and southern Europe, Irish political strategists recognized that since they no longer constituted the urban majority, they had to cater to the newer immigrants and their children if they were to retain primacy.

In Chicago, Poles and Czechs expected their due, as did Lithuanians, Ukrainians, and Swedes. In Boston, Italians arrived simultaneously with Jews, and the Irish had to accommodate them. French Canadians also found new homes there and needed to be considered. In New York, Tammany had to reckon with Italians, Poles, Norwegians, and, by the 1920s, immigrants from the West Indies.

This development presented unique challenges to the Irish, who had seized the reins of municipal power when they constituted the largest and most politically focused immigrant population, roughly in the decades right before and after the Civil War.

But some immigrants proved more difficult to win over than Jews, and the Boston, Chicago, and New York Irish machines saw them as not worth much effort. Germans had long leaned Republican, as did Norwegians and Swedes. African American men had deep ties to the party of Lincoln, transporting them on their great migration to northern cities. Decades would pass until the Democratic Party won them over, locally and nationally. White southerners, committed to principles of racial segregation, Black disenfranchisement, and the economic subjugation of the descendants of the once enslaved, still dominated the national party.

As the Irish Democrats fished around for likely supporters among the newcomers, mostly between Jews, Italians, and, in Chicago in particular, non-Jews from eastern and central Europe, they listened to them all. But the Jews mattered the most.

They naturalized and acquired citizenship faster and in larger numbers than Italians. They had little interest in returning home and defined their involvement in American politics as crucial to advancing their welfare, security, and economic mobility. They fretted constantly about the fate of their people on a global scale. Many established small businesses, making them dependent on political favors. Because so many Jewish children joined the migration, schools mattered to them. All of these considerations made the Jews an ideal constituency to cultivate. They needed the machine, and this put them above the Italians in this urban drama. One historian looking at the mosaic of New York politics in the late nineteenth century and into the middle of the twentieth described New York's Jews as "Tammany's chosen people."[19]

The Irish also had a problem with many of the other immigrant groups. Most of the non-Jews were Catholics, and Irish antipathy toward Italian and Polish immigrants, quite unlike their interactions with Jews, grew out of and paralleled ongoing struggles within the Catholic Church.

The church in America lay firmly in Irish hands. They

controlled the machinery of the faith, whether in terms of the priesthood, the hierarchy, or the institutions the church created to serve the faithful. The Irish and the new Catholic immigrants from Italy and Poland most importantly squabbled over ecclesiastical authority, ritual practice, language loyalties, and group identity, all matters in which Jews obviously had no stake. The Irish had no desire to share power with these newcomers.

Those conflicts played themselves out as Italian and Polish immigrants moved into and began to numerically dominate once-Irish neighborhoods. By dint of numbers, newly arrived Italian and eastern European Catholic immigrants took over once homogeneously Irish parishes, not just changing the makeup of the neighborhoods but also upending the character of the churches, the bedrock institutions of Irish community life. Their presence challenged Irish dominance and shook up Irish ideas about what it meant to be Catholic in America.

While this issue did not divide Irish and Jews—after all, why would Jews care who offered the mass, in which language confession could be given, which order of nuns taught in the parish school, which saints would be venerated, or if the parish should sponsor a street festival with processions, food, and music?—the Italians and Poles certainly cared.

Their cares then spilled over into politics. An Italian bootblack quoted in *The Independent* in 1902 noted, "There are some good Irishmen, but many of them insult Italians. They call us Dagoes. So I will be a Republican."[20] By 1930 Italian Republicans outnumbered Italian Democrats in Brooklyn, and in Boston's West End under the rule of Martin "Mahatma" Lomasney, Italians had to wait until 1930 to win any electoral office, while Jews two decades earlier had earned that privilege, getting to control ward committees and electing one of their own to the city council. The Irish cast their lot with Jews as the most likely allies to aid them in keeping their grip on power.

As Italians tilted Republican, the machine offered them less than it did for the Jews. Jews found themselves well served by this system of majoritarian politics, in which the party that got the most votes by definition controlled city hall, the city council, the bureaucracies, and the other apparatuses of municipal life, all of which served as seemingly bottomless conduits for all sorts of benefits. Those who voted most consistently and most correctly, as defined by the machine, perforce received the lion's share of its attention and what it could parcel out. In turn, those loyal voters made clear to the bosses that it behooved them to know who lived where, what they wanted, and what they valued, making this a genuine give-and-take in so many meanings of the phrase.

Getting chosen by the Democratic Party to either run for office, work for the machine at the street level, or secure an appointment to a nice and often lucrative position in city government constituted a real favor for Jewish immigrants and their children, mostly sons. The Jews benefited mightily from this oligarchic arrangement. With every passing year more Jewish names showed up as Democratic candidates for office, as appointees, and as operatives for the machine who did the work on the streets.

The roster of Jews who benefited from this would fill volumes, going from the lowest-level offices to some of the highest. A number of Jews had the honor of serving as editors of *The Tammany Times,* the official publication of the machine. Even the occasional Jewish woman got a chance to participate in this. Harry Golden's sister Clara, a "Tammany counter," worked year-round for the machine, but her duties became crucial on the "night before an election," when "a mysterious hand always threw a $100 bill over the transom with Clara's name written on it. Tammany sachems," the colloquial name for leaders, also gave her a ring with a setting but no stone, just a piece of charcoal. Clara used the ring to void Republican and socialist ballots.[21]

Some of those Jews chosen by one Irish machine or another have entered into the larger history of the United States and certainly into American Jewish history. Their names included prominent congressional representatives Henry Goldfogle, Samuel Dickstein, and Emanuel Celler. When it seemed like a good strategy to Irish Democratic politicos, they gave individual Jews some very prominent billing. Henry Horner's connection to Irish politicians in Chicago sent him to the governor's office in Springfield. In 1894 Tammany Hall strategized that nominating a highly respectable Jew, as opposed to an Irishman, to head the ticket might increase its odds of winning the mayoralty after some quite damning public scandals. The machine persuaded Nathan Straus, scion of a distinguished family and an honored philanthropist and businessman, to accept the offer. Straus quickly changed his mind and declined to run, claiming that his friends threatened to shun him if he ran on the Tammany ticket. But he had initially said yes, and Tammany had considered that offering him, a Jew, the nomination made good political sense. Decades later, Tammany Hall played a pivotal role in securing the nomination of Herbert Lehman to the governorship of New York.

Irish machines prioritized Jewish voters. In response, for example, to Tammany's fears of the defection of Jewish voters to Henry George in 1886, it put up Theodore Myers for comptroller, considered the second most important municipal position; Jacob Cantor to the state senate; and Ferdinand Levy for city coroner. Jews, including Henry Goldfogle, got three out of eleven slots for district judges.

Tammany not only put their names on ballots but also proclaimed to Jewish constituents that it valued them and had their interests at heart. It affirmatively lauded the Jewishness of the candidates it ran. In its campaign materials, it promoted Levy as "a truly" deserving candidate of "the Hebrew persuasion."[22] (Levy had been appointed to an earlier job by Tammany's top boss, Richard Croker.)

Levy, in turn, as an officeholder prominently associated with the Tammany "Tiger," committed himself to serving Jews and the Jewish community. When word came to him in 1891 that the newly established US Immigration Bureau had detained six Jewish families in the Barge Office (a facility used between 1890 and the end of 1891 and then again from 1897 to 1901 to process immigrants) after their Atlantic crossing from Russia, he went to his contacts to collect the money needed to post bond for them. So, too, Jake Arvey, decades later in Chicago, appeared everywhere as a vigorous patron of Jewish institutions in the neighborhood, ranging from schools, synagogues, orphanages, and clubs to social settlement houses. Every time he showed up at one of these venues, and whenever he raised impressive sums of money for them, he did so, in part, in the interests of the political machine. Not to say that Arvey did not care about these matters, but he represented and acted not just for himself but for the Democratic Party. When the Chicago Jewish paper *The Sentinel* referred to him as "an unflinching champion for Jewish education," it drew attention to the machine that the Jews voted for consistently, but this machine, like all the others, took no votes for granted, including those in the Twenty-Fourth Ward.[23]

Like Levy and Arvey, the cast of Jewish officeholders and machine operatives chosen by their Irish leaders dedicated themselves to serving local Jewish interests. They essentially had to, because the Irish bosses had chosen them in large measure to help secure the Jewish vote. In Boston, Isaac Rosnosky, born in Posen, got a spot on the ballot and was endorsed by "Smiling" Jim Donovan, a political leader of the South End neighborhood, to run for the Boston Common Council in 1878. He then went on to a seat in the state legislature, and later served as the city's assistant water commissioner. While sitting on the council, Rosnosky pulled strings to get the first Jewish policeman appointed, cracking the solid Irish monopoly on law enforcement.

More importantly, while in the state legislature in 1892 Rosnosky sponsored legislation allowing rabbis the right to perform marriages, a privilege previously reserved for Christian clergy. He rallied votes for the bill among his Irish Catholic fellow representatives and in the process helped put Judaism on an equal footing with Christianity.

Machines looped in Jews to serve as their liaisons to other Jews, all with the purpose of growing their electoral base. Theodore White, whose socialist father voted only for the Democratic ticket, associated himself with the district leader Mr. Goretsky, "a man who claimed to know Martin Lomasney," and from there to the top, since "Martin Lomasney was close to Mayor Curley," making Mr. White a Jewish link in an Irish constructed chain.[24]

Being included meant connecting the "Irishers" at the top to the Jews below them. These Jews in turn served as links to other Jewish aspirants, although the machine was always the dominant force behind Jewish intra-ethnic largesse.

These benefits came to those who wanted them with a price tag, embodying the aphorism that there is no such thing as a free lunch, or free coal, or a no-strings-attached contract for a share on a city project, or the like. The recipient who hoped to receive something from the Irish machine operatives had to declare fealty to the organization and show up at every election and cast his ballot to keep the party in power. And in the intervals between elections, individuals recognized that it behooved them to attend party meetings, join neighborhood political clubs, recruit new voters for the machine, knock on doors in their tenement buildings, or go house by house singing the praise of this politician or that. They served in whatever capacity the bosses deemed necessary. The more they served the machine, the more they could count on the machine to respond to their requests.

No doubt, the machine kept the best perquisites for itself and for its natural constituency, namely the denizens of the Irish neighborhoods, who got the most visible, most prestigious, and most lucrative positions that the organization could give out. Jews, like Italians, Poles, or others among the new immigrants who wanted something, had to wait in line until the insiders, Irish Catholics, got first dibs. But for Jews standing in that line, knowing that they would be rewarded mattered.

Machine leaders perfected the art of the balanced ticket, and while they reserved the choicest slots on the ballot—those for the most important positions, for men with Irish surnames—the fact that distinctively Jewish and later Italian ones showed up regularly demonstrated the importance these newcomers played in the machines' strategizing about how to get into and stay in power. When Jewish and subsequently Italian names appeared on ballots, even when down ticket for low-level positions, the machine, through the local Democratic Party, declared to voters, Jewish and Italian, Polish and German, Swedish and French Canadian, that they had been respected, included, and anointed by the Irish gatekeepers.

The mutual attraction between the Jews and the Irish in the political sphere coincided with the emergence of progressivism, a force dominated by Protestants and bent on wresting power away from the machines, imposing standards of efficiency on government operations, ending graft, and instilling high standards of public morality, as defined by them. Some Jews, like those who tried to convince the Romanian immigrants to go Republican, and a few Irish, too, agreed with the progressives.

But most Jewish immigrants, the vast majority of the nation's Jews, ignored the message, seeing that progressives defined them and other immigrants as problems to be solved. As Irish machine politics had done so much for them, they hardly wanted to see it destroyed.

The progressive campaign also ignited Irish-Jewish cooperation, drawing them into each other's orbit. One such issue, alcohol, considered by many Protestant progressives as a scourge, solidified the bonds between the two groups. Progressives helped pass the Prohibition amendment to ban the production and sale of alcoholic beverages in 1920, but both Jews and Irish had a stake in the liquor trade, as distillers, dealers, and saloonkeepers. Neither viewed drink as bad or immoral but rather saw it as something quotidian and a lubricant to social life.

Their common concern over restricting access to alcohol functioned as a kind of political magnet for the Irish and the Jews and manifested itself in many cities. In Baltimore, James "Jack" Pollack, a Jewish product of the tough streets of East Baltimore, entered adulthood as a boxer and then got involved in bootlegging, an activity orchestrated by the city's Irish machine. Pollack was arrested for assault, for various infractions of Prohibition, and on suspicion of the murder of a night watchman in the course of a robbery. Somehow Pollack's case never made it to trial, and he then plunged into the world of politics, mentored and endorsed by boss William Curran, a local Democratic Party operative. Deeply entwined with the Irish politico, Pollack named his son Morton Curran Pollack.

Or take the case of Leon Sanders, born in Ukraine, who came to America as a little boy. A business lawyer starting out in 1895, he specialized in handling the affairs of wholesale liquor houses and distilleries. Sanders gravitated to Tammany, which led the opposition to all bills coming up to the New York State Assembly to limit access to alcohol. Within three years of beginning his law practice, he became a Tammany leader in the Twelfth Assembly District, gave speeches for the machine, and won a seat in Albany. Tammany then elevated him to a judgeship in the city municipal court. Liquor, the law, and Tammany shaped one part of his life. He also led the Hebrew Sheltering and Immigrant Aid Society, the precursor to the world-renowned organization known as HIAS. He chaired the committee on immigration of the American Jewish Congress, held the position of grand master of the Independent Order of B'rith Abraham, and served as a board member of the Jewish Maternity Hospital as well.

When Emanuel Celler, born in Brooklyn in 1888 to immigrant parents who had made their living in the whiskey and wine business, decided to run for office in 1922, he asked Tammany for its blessing. Backed by the machine, Celler campaigned against the evils of Prohibition in his heavily Jewish district. From there and always relying on Tammany support, he proceeded to a notable career in Congress spanning half a century. He advocated for Jewish causes, and in the aftermath of the Holocaust, he spearheaded the effort to expand the number of displaced persons, particularly Jewish survivors, to be admitted to the United States. In 1965 Celler cosponsored the legislation that demolished the 1924 immigration law based on national origins.

Alcohol alone did not solidify the Irish-Jewish opposition to progressivism. When the New York City Board of Education, a pocket of Protestant native-born power, tried in 1916 to undermine the role of Tammany in selecting teachers and to shrink the political machine's involvement in school matters more broadly, the machine, zealous to maintain the status quo, organized Jews to demonstrate against the plan, imported from Gary, Indiana, and known as the Gary Plan. Tammany operatives pointed out to the Jews that the progressive plan would harm them. Progressives embraced the proposal because it emphasized efficiency and professional expertise.

The Gary Plan declared that education policy ought to be in the hands of the experts, embodying the progressive ethos that emphasized that services to the public should be based on rational procedures and devoid of politics. Without doubt the board and its allies saw this as a way to exclude machine politicians from the realm of public education.

Tammany went to work on this. It organized masses of Jewish students and their parents to come out on the streets and demonstrate. Tammany chieftains made the Gary Plan a campaign issue in the wards it controlled, warning the Jewish voters that this new educational order threatened their children's futures.

In this mayoral race, the socialists, mostly in Jewish wards, believed that they had a chance to win with their candidate, Morris Hillquit. He ran largely on his opposition to potential United States entry into the world war raging in Europe. Many predicted that the Jews would abandon Tammany for Hillquit, who also happened to be Jewish.

Tammany, however, wagered that opposition to the Gary Plan would distract Jewish voters from Hillquit. Its spokesmen, including the candidate John Hylan, appealed to Jewish visions of mobility and success, accurately assessing Jewish concerns.

The board's plan was defeated, largely because of the intensity of the Jewish reaction to it. They may never have reacted as they did, however, without Tammany's incitement and organizing. Whether it would have been good for the city's children or not, it gave New York Jews a sense of political prowess, learned under the tutelage of their Irish mentors.

Irish political action on behalf of Jews spanned the global to the local. When speaking out against anti-Jewish violence in the czarist empire, in favor of Zionism or in opposition to immigration restriction, Irish politicians did what they could to get the Jews to support them. Very locally, Tammany bosses ordered firemen, all Irish, to wash down the streets near synagogues as the Sabbath approached on Friday afternoons. On the other side of the Hudson, Jersey City's mayor Frank Hague, son of immigrants from County Cavan, deployed police to protect synagogues from hooligans and Jewish businesses from racketeers.

In city and state legislatures Jewish representatives turned to Irish politicians to help them weaken and, ultimately, they hoped, eliminate the power of Protestantism in public life, particularly in matters of welfare policy. John Ahearn engineered legislation in the New York State Assembly to ensure that Jewish and Catholic women's charitable organizations received equal state support to Protestant ones when caring for orphans and widows. Pressed by Jewish women charity activists along with Catholic nuns, Ahearn rallied his Tammany troops in Albany to pass legislation diluting the Protestants' stranglehold on public monies and enabling Jewish orphanages and other care institutions to get state resources. He likewise pushed the legislature, at the behest of rabbis, to name and pay Jewish chaplains to serve inmates of their faith in state prisons. Such efforts paralleled Irish political action to weaken Sunday closing laws. New York judge Daniel Cohalan, a militant Irish nationalist, granted a right of incorporation to the Association for the Promotion of Sabbath Observance, a boon to Orthodox Jews.

For Jews, this American drama represented a new reality, with no precedent in their history. Mostly they had lived in countries where they, and indeed most people, had no or few rights, societies where politics did not emanate from grassroots citizen participation. They arrived in America with scant experience in the rough-and-tumble of politics based on the recognition of those at the top that they had to forge ethnic coalitions with diverse peoples. After the 1870s the vast majority of Jews came from the czarist empire, hardly a bastion of democracy, in which individuals from various minority groups jostled with each other at ballot boxes and clubhouses for favors after having proved that they had voted for this party or that. The process of emancipation, which Jews experienced in Europe, usually involved Jews promising to better themselves or to become more like their neighbors.

Content to be left alone and hoping to avoid violence perpetrated against them, Jews there related to state power very differently than did their family and friends who migrated to America, where they met Richard Croker, "Silent Charlie" Murphy, John "Honey Fitz" Fitzgerald, Patrick Kennedy, "Big Tim" Sullivan, the "Mahatma," Johnny Ahearn, Michael Dever, and so many more of these Irish bosses. These men only wanted Jews to vote for them.

They had never before been players in such an elaborate game, in which non-Jews wooed, courted, and appealed to them, arose as their champions, flattered and rewarded these millennia-old pariahs for the singular and easy goal of getting their votes. They may not have immigrated to America because of the nation's robust participatory democracy for white men, but such politics shaped their lives and expanded the opportunities they could take advantage of in the land to which the majority of them flocked.

In every city to which they went—and the largest number chose New York—Jewish men met Irish politicians ranging from saloonkeepers, cops on the beat, and neighbors in tenement houses to ward bosses and those up the rungs of the political ladder, who lusted after their votes. The machine operatives, dispensers of favors, did not care about religion, ethnicity, place of origin, or mother tongue as much as loyalty on Election Day.

Much of what they wanted, a license to get a peddle on the street or operate a pool hall, a job, a good word with a judge when some case pended against them, and so much more, flowed from the machine.

And if Jewishness mattered, it did so only inasmuch as the Jewish receiver of the many favors might be counted on to bring his fellow Jews into the machine's orbit as well.

Each vote counted, and the votes of Jews, one by one, carried the same weight as those of all other men. At the ballot box what Jews did counted, and the machine valued their actions. And if they voted the right way and demonstratively embraced the machine, they could expect to get contracts for business deals, protection from crooks, jobs, insider information about real estate opportunities, and, with fairly quick turnaround after acquiring citizenship, the chance to run for low- and then higher-level offices, all on the machine ticket. Those among them who received American educations and, for example, became lawyers, could count on the machine for business and clients.

The men of the machine populated the Jewish neighborhoods, becoming familiar presences who showed their faces where they could see the voters and be seen by them. They flamboyantly dispensed their gifts and smiles in public, making sure that no act of largesse would be missed by those who mattered: the enfranchised Jewish men. And as for the Jews, the courted and the wooed, they depended on the favors, whether smaller or larger, that eased the difficulties they faced, particularly as newcomers to urban America.

The machine had much to give to the many new Jewish voters, and it had to listen not only to their personal concerns but to their communities as well to figure out what mattered. The Irish politicians took note of the strong socialist presence among the Jewish masses, women and men coming to realize that their security in America depended on fixing the conditions of their labor. So many of them clustered in low-paying, unsafe, and unstable work situations, and as they sought to make these better, they once again came into contact with Irish Americans, union organizers who, like the politicians, had much to give the Jews and had much to gain from them as well.

4

Learning for Bread and Roses

Jews and Irish Americans in
the American Labor Movement

In 1919 Leonora O'Reilly was a seasoned labor organizer and daughter of Irish immigrants—a veteran of many struggles against intransigent employers as well as reluctant male union leaders unable to conceive of women as worth organizing and an American public with little sympathy for the union cause. In that year she offered some words of advice to her sister-in-arms, Pauline Newman, a Jewish woman born in the Lithuanian province of Kovno: "To be sure, Paul dear," she penned, "'tis a topsy turvy world. But steady yourself in your seat, tuck your hat tight down on your head with one hand, hold tight to the pilot wheel of labor," and keep on struggling. O'Reilly, in her encouraging words accented with the distinctive Irish "'tis," encapsulated a bigger history of the Irish-Jewish encounter in the American labor movement.[1]

In that encounter, as in politics, the Irish who had been there first mentored Jews. They encouraged and supported the labor activists among them, like Newman, and boosted them into leadership roles, helping them to organize the Jewish working masses. As immigrant Jews positioned themselves at the "pilot wheel of labor," they encountered Irish insiders, veteran activists like O'Reilly with extensive know-how garnered over decades of struggle for workers' rights. In industry after industry, in mills, mines, shipyards, railroad depots, factories, schools, steam laundries, offices, and more, Irish immigrants and their children galvanized local and national campaigns. For decades Irish men and women had steered the movement dedicated to empowering wage earners to demand seats at bargaining tables across the country, where they pressed for fair wages, humane working conditions, and dignity. In defiance of prevailing American ideas about property and capital, they stood up for workers' rights.

They did not do this alone. German immigrants and their children had also contributed much to the movement, as did those with roots in Wales, Scotland, England, and other places in western Europe. Deep bonds developed between Jewish immigrants entering the world of industrial work with the German activists, many of them socialists. Jews—particularly those from places like Lithuania and Galicia—came with some German linguistic skills, and since Yiddish and German resembled each other enough, the two groups of workers could understand each other and organize together. Jewish immigrants in America learned Marxism from Germans who offered lessons on class and power.

But the contribution of Irish union advocates to the development of organized Jewish labor stood in a class of its own. Unlike in the German-Jewish labor encounter, the Irish-Jewish one put women into the center of action in an unparalleled way. It continued longer, had greater impact beyond the early years, involved little in the way of overt ideology, and enabled some key American Jews to use their union experience to become confidants of government officials and shapers of public policy.

Irish and Jewish women's centrality to this history makes it dramatically different from that of urban politics, a decidedly male enterprise played out in voting booths and in the smoke-filled clubrooms where brokering deals, dishing out favors, and trading acts of loyalty to the machine in exchange for jobs and protection brought men from both populations into play. In the labor story, despite pervasive gender inequality, women starred as well.

Men unquestionably dominated and held the most important positions in the union world. They sat on the national councils of the unions, met with government officials, and, for the most part, grabbed the headlines. But Irish women and their Jewish protégés profoundly shaped the movement, helping it gain important victories. In the process they developed intense and deep relationships with each other, doing so as workers, union advocates, and women with agendas of their own. Women of both backgrounds challenged the unions' male leadership and fought against Americans' strong commitment to the nearly divine rights of employers to run their businesses as they wanted. Despite the women's frustration with the unwillingness of the men in the movement to truly hear their voices, their actions transformed its progress.

Many of the Irish and Jewish women who met and worked together in the labor movement considered themselves socialists, some formally members of socialist organizations. They shared a belief that workers should have a voice in determining the conditions of their work and workplaces, and that unions should consider women's needs and listen to women's voices. They all supported women's suffrage as a human right in and of itself and as vital to achieving economic justice.

The Irish and Jewish women, represented by but hardly limited to Rose Schneiderman, Leonora O'Reilly, Mary Kenney O'Sullivan, Pauline Newman, and the millions they rallied and encouraged, subscribed to these beliefs.

But the Irish women, earlier arrivals on the scene, had

immersed themselves in the world of labor decades before the Jews, and in turn they groomed Jewish women for membership and leadership in the movement, serving as the models for those who came later.

These Irish pioneers witnessed the difficulties Jewish women endured in the unions headed by their metaphoric brothers. The unwillingness of the Jewish male organizers to include women had an unintended consequence, driving their female coworkers into the arms of the Irish women whose presence and dogged determination made them the fierce allies of the Jewish newcomers. This empowered Jewish women to rise up.

The Irish women from the labor movement aided Jewish men also, sharing their knowledge and networks to advance their unions, particularly the International Ladies' Garment Workers' Union (ILGWU), founded in 1900, and the Amalgamated Clothing Workers of America, organized in 1914. Likewise, Irish male union leaders worked with Jewish men and women also, tutoring them in the intricacies of organizing.

This mentorship of laboring, immigrant Jews served the purposes of Irish Americans. They did this to advance their own economic stability, having arrived poor and having endured some of the nation's worst work conditions; they learned, among other lessons, that they had to band together and vigilantly protect any efforts by employers to roll back victories once secured.

To do so, they had to organize other workers. The demands they made upon employers and the state required that they speak out in not only their own name but the name of all workers.

They saw in the leadership of the American labor movement a way to carve out a strategic place for themselves in American society, a power base from which to serve their own interests, while simultaneously chipping away at the hegemony of the Protestant business class, the employers who impacted the lives of the workers, commanded the nation's wealth, and shaped state policies.

Just as the men among them had plunged into the world of urban politics and made it their own, so too, by assuming the role of organizers and union leaders, Irish immigrants and their immediate descendants left their marks on American society.

The history of the Irish in the labor movement, their ascent from being the despised victims of exploitation to beneficiaries of hard-won gains through unionization, cannot be disassociated from the actions of some Irish union activists in promoting racial exclusion, of blocking Black—and in California, Chinese—workers from entering their ranks.

They did more than ignore nonwhite workers; rather, they used unions to foster overt violence and calls for state action against workers of color. Irish longshoremen on New York City's docks in the 1850s arose in armed protest against Black men who came to work alongside them. Irish workers ignited the Chinese Must Go movement in San Francisco, which, within a decade, culminated in the 1882 passage of the Chinese Exclusion Act as national policy. Many unions with Irish majorities wrote constitutions that limited membership to white people.

But when organizing white workers, regardless of from where and when in time, Irish union leaders recognized that drawing them into the unions' orbits served their own interests. Their own economic conditions depended on broad unionization. They rarely worked in all-Irish fields, and the other workers, mostly newer immigrants, needed to be included under Irish leadership in the unions they governed.

Their power in the labor movement, as shop stewards, officials of local and national unions, organizers, presidents of citywide labor federations, and the like, required that they draw in immigrants under their unions' umbrellas, adding to the numbers of workers they could represent. They had little interest in sharing power at the top, but to stay on top of the organization, they had to make room for the others in the ranks.

From the start, Irish labor activists and rank-and-file union members encountered vast opposition from fearful coworkers terrified of jeopardizing their meager wages, since employers routinely threatened to fire anyone who joined. Irish organizers confronted strikebreakers ready and willing to take any work they could, even if it meant crossing picket lines. They had to deal with an always-hostile public opinion, which considered unions anathematic to an American civic order, based on a belief in the sanctity of private property and capitalism. The press, for the most part, represented the interests of business, and it rarely had supportive words for calls to recognize workers' rights, and during organizing campaigns and strikes, unions faced police carrying clubs, thugs armed with baseball bats hired by employers ready to pummel strikers who dared to challenge their privileges, and even armed soldiers outfitted with live ammunition, called up by presidents and governors at the behest of bosses.

While Jewish labor activists and the socialist Jewish press would tell graphic stories of the police beating the striking workers on the streets and pulling Jewish women off picket lines by their hair and shoving them into police wagons, in truth Jewish immigrant labor confronted a tamer and less militarized world of opposition than that which the Irish dealt with in the latter half of the nineteenth century. Even the injuries inflicted by the *shartkers,* thugs hired by Jewish bosses against protesting Jewish workers, paled in comparison to the amassed troops of national guardsmen equipped with loaded weapons who met the Irish-born miners and railroad workers in the nineteenth century.

Perhaps because of a long tradition in Ireland of militant, often violent collective action taken up against landlords—mostly English, who exploited the poor—Irish immigrants gravitated to the idea of labor organizing when arriving in America. Despite fierce opposition, they persisted, and along with Germans and Welsh they championed the cause of labor. Much of Irish-organized labor, starting in the latter part of the nineteenth century, blended with outspoken support for Irish nationalism. This gave the workers' cause a nearly sacred significance within their ranks and in the larger Irish American polity.

While some Irish immigrants rose in America through business and the professions, most remained for a few generations in the working class. As immigration from Ireland continued into the early twentieth century, economically marginal newcomers continued to be a sizable presence in their enclaves, replenishing the ranks of Irish labor. Unions continued to visibly serve women and men and their families, and their presence remained strong. Additionally, the local political clout that Irish Americans had amassed helped their unions achieve, even before the New Deal of the 1930s, some local and state victories for the rights of workers.

Irish American labor activists were divided among themselves in changing goals and tactics. The Knights of Labor, founded in 1869 with many Irish leaders and members, appealed to workers regardless of skill or craft, reaching out to all "producers." The Knights, like many mid-nineteenth-century societies, incorporated dramatic rituals and esoteric ceremonies into meetings, but unlike the many fraternal organizations that flourished then, the Knights challenged the American class system and the prevalent ideology of laissez-faire, organizing workers and advocating for systematic political change to elevate the laboring masses. While eschewing strikes, it favored boycotts and advocated politically for the eight-hour day, the end of child and convict labor, and equal pay for women workers. As an umbrella body deemed radical by many Americans, it included individual unions with substantial Irish representation.

The Knights declined simultaneously with the founding of the American Federation of Labor in 1886, a national federation of labor unions distinguished by its emphasis on organizing skilled workers into craft unions, insisting on "pure-and-simple" unionism, and disdaining political work. Its founding and long-time president, Samuel Gompers, a Jewish cigar maker born of Polish parents in London, worked closely with Irish colleagues, particularly Peter McGuire and Peter O'Brien, who, like so many other Irish men, shaped the history of the AFL and its constituent unions nationally and locally.

Vast numbers of Irish American workers also participated in industrial unions, vertical organizations that included all workers in such industries as steel, mining, textiles, and the like, regardless of what jobs they performed. Out of this tradition would emerge in the 1930s the Congress of Industrial Organizations, or CIO.

The intense involvement of Irish women in the labor movement created a reality that later Jewish immigrant women would emulate. Kate Mullany organized the collar laundresses in Troy, New York, in the 1860s. Leonora Barry from Cork, after years working in a hosiery mill, joined the Knights of Labor, and her devotion to the cause led her to become a full-time organizer. Elizabeth Flynn Rodgers by 1886 occupied the position of master workman of District Assembly Twenty-Four of the Knights of Labor, running the organization's recruiting drives in Chicago and its environs.

The list went on, demonstrating Irish women's avid, nationwide attraction to unionization. Leonora O'Reilly, who nudged Pauline Newman with her words of encouragement, offered the following description in 1913 of Maggie Hinchey, a laundry worker who herself would collaborate with Jewish women in organizing drives in New York City and elsewhere. O'Reilly wrote:

> Margaret Hinchey is a young Irish woman, clean of thought, pure of heart, brave as truth itself. She understands that

economic justice for the workers must come through the organization of labor. When the laundry works of New York struck against inhuman conditions she threw up her position as forewoman saying, "Good God no one could be so mean as to go to work in a laundry now!" Her first strike taught her that the workers have to fight the courts as well as the employers if they want justice. When she found herself blacklisted she came to the Women's Trade Union League (WTUL) saying, "Use me in any way you can for the good of the cause. . . ." Since then her strength and her courage and big heart have been at the service of every group of girls struggling for the right to live and enjoy life.

Those "every group of girls" included Jewish women who had to learn to struggle for fair wages, better working conditions, and the chance to "enjoy life."[2]

Many native-born Protestant Americans trembled at the words "use me in any way you can." They feared that Irish labor activists would stop at nothing for the "good of the cause." They discerned an organic connection between pugnaciousness and violence, characteristics they believed inherent in the Irish and the labor activism that they read about in the press and saw around them in the streets. These, in turn, fed Americans' fears of the political gains made by Irish men, which they would use to undermine the American way of life.

The terror that gripped Americans in the 1870s over the Molly Maguires, an Irish secret society that defended, often with force, the exploited Irish coal miners in northeastern Pennsylvania, held on well after the Mollies faded. Accused of bombings, murders, and kidnappings, they inspired great fear, as did the movement of Irish labor activists into local politics. In the wake of the Molly Maguires, Irish men in the anthracite region, like Terence Powderly, a leader of the Knights of Labor born in Ireland, ran for office and won, largely supported by Irish voters. This further stoked broad worries about the Irish, their militance, and their political power grabs. Powderly became mayor of Scranton on the strength of Irish ballots, corroborating widespread fear that Irish union activity, with its tolerance of violence, went hand in hand with growing Irish political clout, stoking the image of Irish labor as dangerous to Americans and of Irish unions as terrorist groups.

The Molly Maguires gave business interests, even when far from the coal region, a bogeyman to hold up as a symbol of Irish union activity and its danger to the status quo. These interests waged vigorous campaigns to undermine victories once achieved by Irish activists, spreading the argument that unions would stop at nothing to achieve their goals and that the labor leaders, too Irish, too Catholic, and too radical in their approach, threatened the nation and the civic order.

The rise of Margaret Haley and Catherine Goggin, both daughters of Irish immigrants who had been involved with the Knights of Labor, to leadership of the Chicago Teachers' Federation in 1897 catapulted them into a storm of controversy, played out in the city press and the state legislature, which was dominated by business interests. Their detractors questioned not only why elementary-school teachers, all women and most Irish Catholic, needed a union but also why they acted so politically. Opponents of the CTF took particular aim at the union's insistence that it had a right to handle the teachers' pension funds. The union's opponents liberally used anti-Irish, anti-Catholic rhetoric, hinting that too many Catholics—read Irish—taught in the city's schools and that the CTF, by virtue of Goggin's and Haley's Irishness, resembled, in blander form, the Molly Maguires and other violent manifestations of Irish labor unionism.

The prime mover in the anti-Haley, anti-CTF forces happened to be a Jewish businessman, Jacob Loeb, president of a fire insurance firm and vice president of the Chicago Board of Education, appointed by the reform mayor Carter Harrison, himself a darling of the city's anti-machine voters. Loeb led the charge against the union, pushing through the Loeb Rule in 1915, which stipulated that teachers may not belong to any organization affiliated with a trade union. Haley declared that the policy "menaced the integrity and well-being of every teacher in the Chicago public schools" and "put in jeopardy the continued development of democracy in the United States."[3] Loeb, for his part, using language derived from the fight against the Molly Maguires, described Haley and Goggin as perpetrators of "terror" who "fight with poisoned tongues and assassinate the character of either members of the board or individual teachers." The CTF he declared as "a curse to the teachers," bent on creating "strife in the teaching force of the public schools."[4]

Obviously, Margaret Haley and Catherine Goggin did not see it that way. Strife might be a prerequisite for achieving economic justice. They believed that teachers, like other workers, had the right to a living wage and should be entitled to participate in determining the conditions of their labor.

In their work with Chicago's elementary-school teachers, Haley and Goggin joined Irish women around the country who took up the union cause, asserting that as women and as members of the working class, they deserved no less human dignity and respect than others.

Union activity hummed through Irish American life. Notable Irish American women from the labor movement played key roles in the forming of the Women's Trade Union League in 1903, creating a formal institution from which they, with their Jewish students who quickly became their peers, spread the call for women's organizing, based on the same principles that motivated the Chicago Teachers' Federation. Many of these women had been ushered into the life of organizing through their immigrant parents' involvement with the Knights of Labor.

Widely dispersed in American industry in multiple fields and places, Irish women and men carried their profound objections to such thinking to the forefront and expressed in words and deeds a belief in the rights of workers and the need for sustained collective action against employers' insistence on their entitlement to total workplace authority.

Masses of eastern European Jewish immigrants began arriving in the United States in the 1880s, making their way to the sweatshops and factories of New York, Boston, Rochester, Baltimore, Chicago, Cleveland, Philadelphia, and other large cities, where they cut, sewed, and pressed clothing, among other manual occupations. There they met up with Irish men and women standing prominently at the helm and deeply involved in union work, whether as organizers, leaders, or just the millions of rank and file who paid their dues and wore their membership pins on their shirts. They went to meetings, showed up on the picket lines when called upon, and talked union.

Firmly at the forefront of the American labor movement, particularly in New York and the other large cities, the Irish delivered a message to the Jewish newcomers, both directly and by example, declaring that only by embracing unions would the exploited Jewish workers witness any real changes in their living conditions, that they had to learn to see themselves as workers and join unions if they hoped to garner higher wages and improve the oppressive conditions of their work. That message implored them to think in class terms and, in the name of the future, to take risks in the present and stick with it. Irish unions literally inaugurated Jews into the world of organized labor.

Bernard Weinstein, a veteran of the Jewish labor movement, shared in his 1929 *Di yidishe yunyons in Amerike: Bleter geshikhte un erinerungen* (*The Jewish Unions in America: Pages*

from History and Memories) a small but graphic episode of
Irish unionists ushering a bewildered group of Jewish immigrant workers into the American movement. He quoted from
an earlier Yiddish book, *Memoirs of a Cloak Maker* by Abraham Rosenberg, who recalled how in 1885 a handful of Jewish
garment workers attended a New York meeting of the Knights
of Labor:

> We, almost all new immigrants, did not understand one
> word that the Master Workman, an Irishman, and his assis-
> tants . . . said to us. But we watched as one of them from the
> secret order took a piece of chalk, drew a big circle on the
> floor, and asked all the members to stand around it. Then an
> Irish official of the Knights put a little sword on the table
> and hung a globe on the doorway. Some of the cloak makers
> got scared thinking that they were about to be murdered.
> But one of them explained the meaning of the ceremony to
> us in German: If any of us betrayed our allegiance to the
> interests of the workers, then the sword would follow him
> everywhere because the Knights of Labor were powerful. . . .
> And that was how we became union men for the first time.[5]

Incidents like this took place, in one form or another, across
the city, and in the other places Jewish immigrant workers experienced horrendous work conditions and Irish "union men"
offered a strategy and a context to make it better.

Furthermore, Irish organizers implored Jewish workers to
challenge the authorities in their own communities. The newly
arriving eastern European Jewish immigrants routinely endured
unsafe working conditions, low pay, unpredictable hours, intense periods of work in busy times followed by bouts of unem-
ployment during the slack seasons, and, for the women, sexual
harassment and unequal wages at the hands of other Jews.

The shared Jewish bonds that held workers and employers together advantaged the latter as the former struggled to eke out a living. Bernard Weinstein shared this with his readers as well, retelling how a Mr. Messing, owner of a number of Lower East Side bakeries, forced his workers to stand over kneading boards and hot ovens "twelve to fourteen hours a night." After these long stints of arduous work, he compelled them to "go with him to the synagogue to pray and recite the Psalms as a charm to make sure that his rolls came out perfect from the oven, so that people would buy them all." Messing bitterly opposed unionization, but over time the union persisted and, "as soon as Mr. Messing's bakery became a union shop," his workers stopped going to the synagogue with him.[6]

The dense communal ties that linked Jewish workers to the Jewish businessmen who employed them can be seen in the story of the Triangle Shirtwaist Company, the most infamous factory in American history. The fire that broke out on the eighth and ninth floors of the Asch Building on March 25, 1911, killing 146 people, is still considered the nation's worst industrial accident, and it threw the conditions of Jewish labor into bold relief.

The two owners of Triangle, the "shirtwaist kings" Isaac Harris and Max Blanck—who had locked the factory doors from the outside—had, like the majority of the workers caught up in the inferno, immigrated to the United States from the Pale of Settlement. Starting out themselves as sweatshop workers, they moved up the ladder, first becoming sweatshop bosses and ultimately owners of one of the largest garment factories in New York.

Blanck and Harris had fended off organizing efforts two years earlier and remained recalcitrant even after the fire. The tragedy did nothing to shake their conviction that unionization would cut into their profits and that they should have the right to determine conditions in their own shop. After the fire, they merely moved their unorganized operation to another space a few blocks away.

Jewish industrial workers, like those who worked for Harris and Blanck, had nearly no one within their own communities who had participated in previous labor struggles that could explain to them the benefits of unionization. American Jews, whether descendants of earlier immigrants or those who had themselves arrived in the immediately preceding decades, had not planted themselves onto the American union landscape, with random exceptions, Samuel Gompers a particularly notable one.

Most of the earlier Jewish immigrants had started out as peddlers, then graduated to become owners of small businesses and proprietors of other commercial enterprises. In every city where Jews settled, untold numbers of them became the manufacturers of clothing, whether in the mid-nineteenth century producing garments in the back rooms behind their dry-goods stores, in "slop shops" where newer immigrants sewed up used clothing and then resold the garments, in small apartment-based workshops, or in sweatshops. By the 1910s larger factories, with Triangle the largest in New York, began to proliferate.

Some of the most successful among them and even leaders of their communal organizations opposed state-mandated protections of workers as proposed by unions and unionization itself. Louis Marshall, perhaps the most important architect of American Jewish defense work, the child of German-speaking Jewish immigrants from the 1850s, argued against a variety of labor laws, including one banning child labor, passed by the New York legislature in 1925. Such laws—Marshall argued, as a widely respected legal authority—violated constitutional principles.

Even more dramatically, Julius Rosenwald—president of Sears, Roebuck and Co., one of the nation's wealthiest individuals and most generous philanthropists—adamantly resisted the growth of unions in his vast business empire. The son of a former peddler, an immigrant from Franconia in the 1850s, Rosenwald began his career operating sweatshops in Chicago that employed both Jewish and non-Jewish workers who manufactured men's suits.

Rosenwald, who participated vigorously in political campaigns on behalf of progressive candidates who sought to unseat the Irish-dominated political machine in Chicago, opposed the striking workers in 1911 as they walked out of the men's clothing factory Hart, Schaffner & Marx, owned by his fellow Chicago Jews. That strike, with help from the Irish-dominated Chicago Federation of Labor (CFL), led to the creation of the Amalgamated Clothing Workers of America, which catapulted Sidney Hillman into national fame. Rosenwald's determined stand with his peers Joseph Schaffner and Harry and Max Hart put into bold relief the gap between immigrant Jews bent on organizing and Jews in the employer class dedicated to preserving their prerogative to determine the conditions of labor.

As most Jewish workers worked for Jewish employers—like Harris and Blanck, Messing, Hart, Schaffner, Marx, Louis Leiserson, and so many others—the Irish call to organize contributed to intense inner Jewish strife. Weinstein's compendium of Jewish union history repeatedly emphasized that the overwhelming masses of Jewish immigrant workers labored for Jewish bosses.

Most Jewish communal institutions depended upon affluent donors who by definition had an economic stake in suppressing unionization. Not surprisingly, they manifested little enthusiasm and indeed much antagonism toward workers' organizations. Even the National Council of Jewish Women, which exerted much energy and expressed tremendous concern for the problems faced by Jewish immigrant women since its founding in

1893, did not extend its efforts to unionization until after the 1910s.

But Irish labor activists like O'Reilly, Mary Kenney O'Sullivan, John Fitzpatrick, Agnes Nestor, Maud O'Farrell, Margaret Hinchey, Josephine Casey, and Julia O'Connor stepped in and provided inspiration and guidance to Jewish workers who increasingly chafed at the economic conditions they endured. They considered that for the sake of the larger movement, Jewish workers had to be organized.

They warned the Jewish immigrants, male and female, not to think of their bosses as their friends, even if they came from the same towns and regions in eastern Europe. O'Reilly, Hinchey, O'Sullivan, Maud Malone, John Fitzpatrick, and others came to meetings of Jewish workers to talk union. A constant presence at organizing events, they showed up, whether in New York, Chicago, Philadelphia, Baltimore, or the other large cities where Jews labored in nonunionized workplaces. They positioned themselves outside factory doors, buttonholing workers as they left for home, talking up the benefits of joining. They appeared in solidarity on picket lines set up by Jewish union women and men against their Jewish employers, emboldening Jewish industrial workers to see themselves as workers who could collectively do something about the conditions of their labor, even if their fellow Jews controlled their work lives and suppressed their efforts. They emphasized that no matter their ethnic or religious identity, a boss was nothing but a boss, bent on making a profit from the labors, literally the sweat, of his employees.

Theresa Serber Malkiel, a Jewish immigrant woman from the Ukrainian town of Bar, a shirtwaist worker in early twentieth-century New York, recalled in her semi-autobiographical *Diary of a Shirtwaist Striker* (1910) the impact of hearing a talk by Mary Harris "Mother" Jones, who convinced her that "we working people were standing by ourselves." Malkiel, who would go on to a notable career as a union organizer and a socialist activist who created National Women's Day in 1909, described how the Cork-born "Miners' Angel" "explained to us . . . that our bosses can't have any love for us, for every time we make a cent more, they get a cent less for themselves." The Jewish women who heard Mother Jones had to remember that "every time they can squeeze an extra cent from us they're that much the gainer." Only a union could change that.[7]

The work undertaken by Malkiel and the other Jewish unionists, urged on by the likes of Mother Jones, took place in an American environment in which Jews labored alongside other immigrants. Even in the densest Jewish concentration of workers, the garment factories of New York, they had Italian coworkers, and in Chicago, Cleveland, Baltimore, and elsewhere non-Jewish immigrants from central and eastern Europe. The Triangle Shirtwaist fire's grim toll included Italian women, who made up about one-third of the burnt and trampled victims. As early as the 1910s a few African American women worked in the Jewish-owned factories, and those numbers grew by the 1920s. In the 1930s, Jewish labor leaders still held on to union control, and Jewish employers still owned the factories that employed newcomers from Puerto Rico, who took their places behind sewing machines.

To secure their gains and to hold on to leadership, the Jewish men who had formed and led the Jewish unions like the ILGWU and the Amalgamated had to learn how to reach everyone. They needed a message that appealed simultaneously to Jews as Jews, and to everyone as coworkers in a common struggle against the bosses. In that outreach they modeled themselves after the Irish organizers who had brought them into the unions' folds.

Jews had come to America with little experience in doing this. Jews in the Russian Empire began to experience factory work only in the 1880s and 1890s, simultaneous with the onset of the mass exodus to America. Previously, as artisans who made and sold their own products or as peddlers and other petty businesspeople, their economic lives pivoted around a long tradition of self-employment, a model of making a living that continued to pervade the immigrants' aspirations in America. If employed, Jews worked for their fellow Jews in tailoring, shoemaking, bread baking, brush making, and the like, and their employers used communal religious power to suppress worker action.

Few among the 2.5 million Jews who immigrated to America in the last decades of the nineteenth century and into the 1910s came with a history of large-scale, sustained collective action against employers. The founding in Vilna in 1897 of the Bund, the General Union of Jewish Workers in Lithuania, Poland, and Russia, the first effort of its kind, took place in secret, and for decades this small body operated clandestinely. Czarist policies made such organizations illegal, criminalizing mass meetings; suppressing the publication of pamphlets, broadsides, and other subversive material; and prompting the arrest and imprisonment of activists. Furthermore, the Bund, dominated by intellectuals, invested more energy on ideology, Marxism, than on the practicalities of addressing bread-and-butter, here-and-now concerns, differing in this from most American unions. Even the more radical unions in America, which mixed politics with shop-floor organizing, were still built in a step-by-step process focused on winning concessions from employers and serving members in real ways.

Some sporadic union activities took place among the early eastern European Jewish immigrants in the United States in the 1880s and 1890s. But after a spate of walkouts among, for example, unorganized garment workers in New York in 1885 and in 1905–1906, labor activity fizzled out. Bernard Weinstein showed in detail chaotic outbreaks of labor actions, followed almost immediately by periods of quiescence, the formation of protean unions that quickly imploded. Most who had participated in strikes soon drifted away or lost interest, allowing employers to whittle away at the few concessions won. The field remained as unorganized as ever before.

Abraham Cahan, editor of *Forverts,* sketched out a typical cycle of Jewish labor activity in the first decade of the twentieth century, noting how "in July there is a strike. In August it is settled. . . . In October it becomes known that there are more unsettled shops than union shops. In November wage rates are reduced. . . . In December it becomes apparent that the agreements are not worth a whiff of tobacco. In January dues [union] are no longer being paid. . . . In March mass meetings are called to revive the union. In April the union ceases to exist . . . and in June they decide to strike."[8]

Observers at the time noted how Jewish workers, despite daily exploitation, yearned for self-employment and envisioned futures of proprietorship. Abraham Bisno, a onetime Jewish member of the Knights of Labor, quoted an "Irishman who worked in the same factory as me," in 1905 Chicago: "A Jew would rather earn five dollars a week doing business for himself than ten dollars a week working for someone else." Ironically, because garment making as a business venture required relatively little capital, workers could reasonably dream that they, like the successful manufacturers among them, might someday be bosses. This, too, cut down on the willingness to organize and oppose. After all, however much they may have resented their employers, they imagined themselves as bosses, too, and as such admired them.[9]

The fact that the garment industry, even after the 1910s and the drift of production from small apartment sweatshops to larger factories, still took place in relatively small workplaces scattered and independent from each other also stymied unionization. Unlike the big heavy industries—steel, rubber, machine production, and automobile—that were dominated by a few behemoth companies, relatively small numbers of workers labored together in any one place in the field of garment making. Cahan's calendar of union life highlighted the dispersed nature of immigrant Jewish work, and he aptly pointed out that at any moment in time, some shops got organized and others did not, making unionization drives difficult and piecemeal.

No wonder then that the handful of Jewish labor activists working to energize the masses in the last decades of the nineteenth century despaired of the lack of meaningful unionization among the new immigrants. Morris Hillquit, a Jewish socialist intellectual, called the immigrant Jewish workers "unorganizable," describing them as "dull, apathetic, unintelligent." In his *Loose Leaves from a Busy Life* he chronicled the "disappointments, failures and defeats" of those like himself who would organize the Jewish workers. Jewish workers, he opined, could not think beyond sporadic strikes and short-lived unions, "born in strikes . . . dead with the end of the strikes," which impeded the birth of a "Jewish labor movement . . . organized on a solid and stable basis."[10]

Despite Hillquit's efforts and those of Joseph Barondess, Meyer London, and a few other individual men, matters changed little until after the 1910s. Abraham Bisno, who after organizing the Chicago cloak makers became a deputy factory inspector for the state of Illinois, wrote, after surveying conditions in Chicago's men's clothing industry in 1905, that most Jewish factory workers "do not believe themselves to be working men for life, nor do they think that they will leave as a heritage to their children the lot of a wage worker." To Bisno such aspirational thinking limited Jewish workers' ability to recognize their daily exploitation and to see what actions needed to be taken in the present.[11]

The presence of large numbers of Jewish immigrant women workers further hampered organizing. Single young women constituted a significant part of the Jewish immigrant population, whether they had arrived with family or on their own. They made up a hefty proportion of the Jewish labor force that sewed, basted, and finished garments. Unlike heavy industries like mining, steel, construction, dock work, and so on, where many immigrant men labored with no positions open to women, the manufacturing of clothing employed both.

But Jewish male organizers considered women poor material for the long haul when it came to sustaining unions, believing that women—because they supposedly did not have to support families—worked only for pin money and did so temporarily, since surely they would quit upon marriage. Given the perceived frivolity of their labor, Jewish organizers assumed that women would not make the kinds of sacrifices that a commitment to unions demanded.

History would prove them wrong and not only because Jewish women also worked out of necessity and supported their families. Additionally, some powerful women's issues drove them to militance. They endured unequal pay, obviously earning less than men who did the same work, and they faced sexual exploitation and the dismissive reactions of their male coworkers, including the union men, to their concerns.

Jewish women tried to rise in the unions, hoping to be heard at large public gatherings. They had something to say and wanted to make an impact. Some aspired to leadership positions but found themselves silenced or ignored by men in their own community.

Few examples of this can compare in historic impact and popular memory to the mass meeting held in November 1909 at New York's Cooper Union. The meeting called by the ILGWU to bemoan the dismal conditions in the shirtwaist industry and the unsuccessful strikes at Triangle and at the Leiserson Company, another large factory, did not invite any of the striking women to address the assembly. The male leadership, including President Benjamin Feigenbaum, spent two hours gushing with sympathy for the plight of the women workers but cautioned against an industry-wide general strike, seeing it as potentially disastrous.

Clara Lemlich, a Ukrainian-born shirtwaist worker who served on the union's board, had not been invited to sit with the other leaders on the stage, demonstrating the disdain of the leadership for women. She kept raising her hand, but no one called on her since her name did not appear on the list of approved speakers. Undaunted, she got up and made her way to the dais.

Interrupting the men, Lemlich gave *the* speech of the night and perhaps of American labor history, calling out the men who had excluded her. Describing herself as a "working girl," she thundered, "I have no further patience for talk as I am one of those who feels and suffers from the things pictured. I move that we go on a general strike . . . now!"[12] The hall erupted, and over the course of the next few weeks twenty thousand—some estimates claim thirty thousand—shirtwaist workers took to the streets. The ultimately successful history of the ILGWU followed from her unwillingness to be silenced, yet had the male organizers, all Jewish immigrant men, prevailed, she would not have spoken, her words would not have been heard, the Uprising of the Twenty Thousand would not have happened, and the union's fate might have gone in a very different direction.

The story of the Uprising figures prominently in the narrative of American Jewish history, told as a celebration of the assertiveness of Jewish women and the triumph of the Jewish labor movement. As told, the tale leaves out the one woman who did sit on the platform of dignitaries, Leonora O'Reilly. Her presence made all the difference.

The Uprising of the Twenty Thousand might never have ignited without her being there. It might have fizzled and come to naught, even with Lemlich's eloquence, but for the vast time and energy O'Reilly devoted to it.

O'Reilly, who started going to union meetings as a small child in the 1880s with her widowed mother, an Irish immigrant garment worker, grew up in the movement. She took out her first membership in the Knights at sixteen when she founded the Working Women's Society, an organization dedicated to spreading trade unionism among women laborers.

Clara Lemlich's words, delivered in Yiddish, declared, "I am a working girl . . . I am tired of listening to speakers who talk in general terms. What we are here for is to decide whether we shall strike or not strike." They have come down as the battle cry of the Uprising, but O'Reilly organized the strike itself.[13]

Words and oaths of solidarity would never have gotten the twenty thousand and more out on the streets and shut down the shirtwaist industry, leading to recognition of the union by most of the manufacturers. Lemlich's stirring rhetoric galvanized the workers, but creating a union infrastructure took strategy, coordination, and funding.

Credit for that must go to O'Reilly, who hustled from picket line to picket line, talking with the striking women, encouraging them to keep going. She worked with city officials and used her Irish insider contacts to spur Tammany Hall to inch toward support of the workers. She also brought in the considerable financial resources of the well-connected, well-intentioned, and importantly well-funded upper-middle-class women who had never seen the inside of a factory but with whom she worked in the suffrage movement and the Women's Trade Union League, which she had founded in 1903, to provide crucial money, legitimacy, and increasingly positive public relations to the striking women. She convinced Gompers to support the women, and she shuttled back and forth between the striking women and the male leadership of the ILGWU.

Irish female labor activists—O'Reilly a key player among them but hardly alone—recognized the dynamic of Jewish male organizers paying little attention to the needs of women, ignoring their complaints, downplaying their calls to action, and dismissing their aspirations for leadership. O'Reilly pointed this out to Rose Schneiderman, born in Russian Poland in the town of Saven in 1882. Schneiderman, who immigrated as a child to the United States, emerged as probably the most important and well-known of the Jewish women labor activists. O'Reilly drummed into her that the men of the International Ladies' Garment Workers' Union operated according to their gender interests, which stripped the women of dignity and authority. "Remember, Rose," she wrote, "that no matter how much you are with the Jewish people, you are still more with the people of the League," referring to the Women's Trade Union League, where the two worked together with so many other women of their "people" and supported each other.[14]

Schneiderman would have a decades-long love-hate relationship with the ILGWU and its leaders, quitting several times when she found that the men in charge silenced her and gave her few options for real leadership. But she never turned away from the Irish women she met in the League. They remained her lifelong partners and allies.

Over the course of her life in the labor movement, Schneiderman, like Pauline Newman and the others, worked with the Irish women who offered guidance on how to achieve their goals. They met with each other when they found themselves in the same places at the same time. The Irish and Jewish women jointly attended labor seminars at settings like the Brookwood Labor College in Katonah, New York, and the Bryn Mawr Summer School for Women Workers in Industry in Pennsylvania. Their meetings and collaborations blossomed into real friendships.

In the 1920s they spent time together in New York's Hyde Park at gatherings hosted by Eleanor Roosevelt, whom the Irish women of the League knew first and then introduced to Newman and Schneiderman.

A small but poignant testimony to this relationship across group lines, welded together by the bonds of labor activism, can be read in the tributes paid by Schneiderman and Newman to one of their Irish mentors, Maud O'Farrell, on her sudden death in 1936.

Born in County Kildare, O'Farrell (who had a brief marriage to a Swiss man named Swartz and often went by the name of Maud O'Farrell Swartz) held leadership positions in the Women's Trade Union League. Her particularly close friendship with Schneiderman proved propitious. It was O'Farrell who introduced Schneiderman to Eleanor Roosevelt, who in turn made it possible for the once-impoverished garment worker, ignored by her male colleagues in the ILGWU, to rise to national prominence.

Upon O'Farrell's death, Schneiderman wrote to President Franklin Roosevelt, "I shall miss Maud terribly." She recalled that "we had been pals for twenty-three years. . . . Her loss is an irreparable one." To Newman, also close to O'Farrell, Schneiderman made note of her mentorship as she described O'Farrell as "logical, often brilliant, and always convincing," testifying to the degree to which the Irish-born activist took on the teacher role. "Convincing" conveyed in no uncertain terms that when the two differed on strategy, O'Farrell's position won the day. And O'Farrell's introduction of Schneiderman to the Roosevelts meant that she made it possible for the Jewish immigrant working woman to walk in some important circles.[15]

The efforts of O'Reilly and the others had borne fruit in

the 1910s after the Uprising of the Twenty Thousand. By that time other conditions on the ground facilitated the beginnings of systematic unionization among Jewish workers. New, larger, and more centralized factories replaced the small scattered shops where bosses and workers had labored together in close proximity. Now in these bigger workplaces groups of workers gathered, shared their common concerns, and could talk about strategies to make matters better, unions prominent among them. The 1897 launch of *Forverts*, an avowedly socialist Yiddish daily edited by Louis Miller and Abraham Cahan, began to feed the immigrant reading public a steady diet of news about labor conditions, with constant critiques of the bosses and their powerful presence in the Jewish community, inspiring the readers to start thinking step-by-step about the connection between class, work, and the need for concerted and thoughtful action. The arrival from the czarist empire after 1905 of veterans of the Bund played a role as well, as did the 1910 founding of the Arbeter Ring, or Workmen's Circle, which, although not a union, helped shape a Jewish immigrant culture in the United States and honored unions and celebrated class consciousness. It functioned independently of the conservative, employer-inflected, religious ethos that hampered earlier union drives.

Beginning in the 1910s Jewish unions flourished. The masses of Jewish workers joined, linking up with the American labor movement. The once-tottering ILGWU, an organization that had stood on the brink of dissolution in 1908, experienced a burst of activity in 1909, in large measure invigorated by the Uprising of the Twenty Thousand, and went on to gain much ground, while the Amalgamated Clothing Workers of America, founded in 1914 and made up of workers who sewed men's clothing, took off, despite not belonging to the American Federation of Labor.

These unions, although riven in the 1920s by bitter fights

between communists and non-communists, beset by charges of racketeering, always vulnerable to employer efforts to undermine union gains, and certainly impacted by the Great Depression, became part and parcel of Jewish life.

Jewish elites, men like Louis Marshall, despite his cool stance toward unions, and Louis Brandeis, future justice of the US Supreme Court, concluded by 1909—after the pivotal shirtwaist makers' strike, the Uprising with a capital letter—that stability in the garment trade and some semblance of harmony between Jewish workers and Jewish employers served critical Jewish interests. Despite their distance from the world of labor, these Jewish communal leaders came out on the side of the workers who clamored for recognition by the factory owners. Marshall and Brandeis, along with a few other high-status Jewish notables, nearly all sons of Jewish entrepreneurs who had emigrated from central Europe in the mid-nineteenth century, went in 1910 to the owners of the garment factories, their fellow Jews, cajoling them to sign the Protocol of Peace and recognize the ILGWU, fix a fifty-hour workweek, offer time-and-a-half wages for overtime, pay a minimum wage, provide a dozen paid holidays, and more.

Increasingly, Jewish communal bodies started including representatives of labor into decision-making. Jewish labor groups and the Arbeter Ring got seats on the newly formed Jewish community councils, which sprang up around the country in the late 1920s. Arbeter Ring schools, which taught Yiddish and celebrated Jewish labor, participated in communal boards of Jewish education, their class-conscious ideology and programming notwithstanding. Some Jewish parents, many no longer factory workers, enrolled their children in these schools, which in turn spread among the rising generation of youngsters a heroic view of labor unions and their organic connection to Jewish culture.

The success of the unions mattered. Once they gained traction, wages went up, conditions improved, and, despite constant disagreements between employers and employees, Jewish laborers began to enjoy better lives, like most unionized workers. Their salaries crawled up steadily, allowing them, family by family, to move out of cramped tenement apartments to somewhat more commodious ones, fretting less about empty larders and bare tables. Fewer of their children had to abandon school to go to work.

Unions made a tremendous difference to their members. The Jewish unions created a robust infrastructure of institutions and activities, including health centers, cooperative housing projects, life-insurance programs, classes, and clubs. In 1919 the ILGWU opened a summer resort in Pennsylvania's Pocono Mountains, Unity House, where union members and their families could hike, boat, swim, eat sumptuous meals prepared either in the eastern European Jewish or the Italian style, hear lectures, and be entertained, all thanks to their union's ability to win concessions from employers. They got, through the union, the opportunity to taste the pleasures of middle-class life.

The growth of the Jewish unions mattered nationally. They gave organized Jewish workers a chance to prove their American progressive bona fides not just by serving as members and improving their own lives but also by ameliorating the conditions of other Americans. The Amalgamated in 1919, a mere half decade after its founding, donated $100,000 to aid the United Mine Workers of America, a labor union with no Jewish presence. When the Amalgamated opened its bank in 1923, it used its resources not only to finance its own housing and health projects but also to provide funds to support unionization drives in other industries, far removed from the Jewish working class. Its money helped finance the National Association for the Advancement of Colored People as it struggled for civil rights.

The ILGWU, like the Amalgamated, lent support and money in the 1920s to A. Philip Randolph, who organized the largest union of African American workers, the Brotherhood of Sleeping Car Porters. The Jewish unions as well as the Arbeter Ring invited Randolph to address their annual conventions, and all three placed advertisements in the Brotherhood's magazine, *The Messenger,* expressing the solidarity felt by the Jewish working class to "our exploited Negro brothers" and to "our Black Fellow Workers." In the 1930s, the ILGWU and the Amalgamated helped create the Harlem Labor Council, an effort to spread unionization among Black women and men, who only recently had been allowed to take factory jobs. Indeed, the Jewish labor unions stood up for the cause of civil rights decades before the other Jewish organizations or the Jewish religious denominations did. The Jewish unions, the leadership and members, secured a place for Jews in the liberal coalition that in the 1930s helped shape the New Deal and which offered Jews a place from which to present themselves as the best of Americans.[16]

In the 1930s these Jewish unions, along with other unions, participated in an effort to promote the idea that unions legitimately belonged in American life. As one small but dramatic—literally—example: in 1937 the ILGWU staged a Broadway play, *Pins and Needles,* which ran for over eleven hundred days, including a special performance at the White House for Franklin and Eleanor Roosevelt. A theater sensation, *Pins and Needles* celebrated with music and dance the humanity of the working class and the dignity its members had won by fighting employers. Its rousing opening number, "One Big Union for Two," set the tone, with a courting couple crooning to each other, singing that they should "take a hint from the A.F. of L. and the C.I.O." and get married, as they proclaimed to audiences that "Fifty million union members can't be wrong."[17]

Jewish labor leaders, despite representing small unions in a very specific corner of the economy, gained the respect of their peers in the bigger movement, playing increasingly prominent roles in its broad efforts to reshape American society. David Dubinsky of the ILGWU won election to the AFL Executive Council in 1934, and two years later he helped found the rival CIO, the Congress of Industrial Organizations. He, along with Sidney Hillman representing the Amalgamated, made Jewish labor a key element in the emergence of a new era in American labor history and played a hand in shaping New Deal policy.

Jewish labor activists in the 1920s and 1930s, unlike those who had come before them, earned the respect of government officials, at the state and even federal levels. Policymakers and officeholders began to consider Jewish activists from the garment unions expert insiders who could advise on matters dealing with labor, work, and gender as they affected all Americans. Pauline Newman, whom Leonora O'Reilly felt obliged to encourage to stay strong and keep up her union work, found herself by the 1930s advising New York State officials and others in Washington in regard to the needs of women workers. A frequent visitor to the White House during the New Deal, Newman gained much from her close association with Eleanor Roosevelt, whom she had met through the Women's Trade Union League (WTUL). This access translated into some highly visible appointments. She served on the United States Women's Bureau, and after World War II, on the United Nations Subcommittee on the Status of Women. Her colleague Rose Schneiderman, who had gone to work in a garment shop at thirteen and joined a union at twenty-one, by the mid-1930s served as the only woman on the newly formed National Recovery Administration's Labor Advisory Board. Roosevelt turned to her on labor matters in the drafting of the Social Security Act.

The flourishing of the Jewish unions enhanced the group's

visibility and prestige in American society. It provided them with allies in their hour of need. During World War I, John Fitz-patrick of the Chicago Federation of Labor spoke at a number of rallies on behalf of the People's Relief Committee for Jewish War Sufferers, dedicated to raising money for Jews trapped between the warring armies of central and eastern Europe. The Jewish Labor Committee (JLC), founded in 1934 in response to the rise of Nazism, had no trouble convincing the AFL to endorse a boycott of German goods at its convention later that year. The AFL, responding to suggestions made by the Jewish unions, created the Labor Chest, its monies used to fund JLC rescue efforts to spirit Jews and other labor leaders away from Hitler's clutches in Germany and bring them to the United States.

These Jewish unions made a profound difference then, for those who joined, for their children, for Jews as a community, and for American society as a whole. American Jews, whether organized workers or not, pointed to the service that their people had rendered to American labor, considering it one of their contributions to the United States, and conversely, as one key factor that had enabled them to partake of the comfort and security of America.

But this sea change in the status and fortunes of American Jewry did not just happen because of what Jews did. It also came about because Irish American labor organizers, beginning in the 1890s, started to work for the unionization of Jewish workers, considering it one of their projects.

They showed up where Jewish workers congregated and talked union. They provided advice on how to transform sporadic and disorganized walkouts into effective campaigns to win recognition, as O'Reilly had done in 1909, and introduced them to well-placed, well-meaning Americans, neither Jewish nor Irish, who could help out with funds during strikes. Irish unionists mentored the Jews, stimulating class consciousness, offering models of activism, providing leadership opportunities—for Jewish women in particular—and as such brokering for them in the "topsy-turvy" world, as O'Reilly had described it to Newman.

Irish labor leaders reached out to Jews, whether those in the working class in need of organizing or those with means and influence who in turn could embrace the cause of labor. The case of Louis Brandeis can be illustrative.

By 1916, when he ascended to the US Supreme Court, Brandeis had become widely known as a champion of labor. His critics used that against him in the nomination process, since he not only defended the rights of workers to organize but also had declared that the creation of a just and equitable society depended upon worker empowerment.

But he did not come to this on his own. It took the daughter of Irish immigrants, a former dressmaker with a fourth-grade education, Mary Kenney, to educate the Harvard-trained lawyer on the realities of workplace exploitation.

Kenney, who got her start in organizing through the Woman's Bindery Union in Chicago, moved up the ranks in the city and then to the national level as a labor official, traveling the country investigating conditions and shaping union campaigns. She purposely reached out to affluent and well-connected Jewish women in the progressive movement, seeking to bring them over to the side of labor, even if their husbands owned factories.

In 1896 while on a national tour, she spoke at a parlor meeting at the home of Josephine Goldmark, a prominent Boston reformer, Jew, and sister-in-law of Brandeis. Kenney, who would later marry Jack O'Sullivan, another labor organizer, and be known by her married name, described in graphic terms what she had witnessed during the recent brutal strikes in Homestead, Pennsylvania, and in Haverhill and Lawrence, Massachusetts.

She shared with these comfortable and well-placed Bostonians, including Brandeis, who would soon become known as the "People's Lawyer," the hardships faced by the workers and the ruthless, militarized responses of the employers. After hearing Kenney, Brandeis recalled, "I saw at once that the common law, built up under simpler conditions of things gave an inadequate basis for the adjustment of the complex relations of the modern factory system." Confronted with the logic of Kenney's message, he admitted, "I threw away my notes and approached my theme from new angles." Those "new angles" shaped his career as an attorney and advocate for unions and working women and then manifested themselves in the decisions he rendered from the nation's highest court.[18]

Brandeis remembered the lessons he had gotten from Mary Kenney and connected them to another one imparted to him by John F. Tobin, president of the Boot and Shoe Workers Union. Brandeis actually represented the employer in a lawsuit filed by the union, but Tobin's descriptions of life in the working class moved him. Despite his professional obligation to provide his client with a zealous defense, Brandeis learned from Tobin about the many techniques employers used to limit the rights of workers, even those already organized. This all came as a surprise to Brandeis, who had never had access to such knowledge, but conversations with the Irish-born shoemaker led Brandeis to admit, "Your policy in this, as in so many other respects, appears to me to be eminently wise." As in response to his encounters with Kenney, he embraced a new understanding of the world of workers and bosses, something he would take with him to the US Supreme Court.[19]

Brandeis's conversion to the cause of organized labor, facilitated by Mary Kenney, her future husband Jack O'Sullivan, and Tobin, had an impact on American Jews. His pivotal role in negotiating the Protocol of Peace, which ended the great strikes of 1909, opened the doors to the growth of the ILGWU and made unions active elements in Jewish community life, reflected in large measure in the lessons he had derived from his teachers, not those at Harvard, but the Irish women and men who knew labor and knew the bosses far better than he.

An Irish teacher–Jewish student relationship also brought Agnes Nestor and Sidney Hillman together, and it equally transformed American labor and American Jewish history. Nestor's parents, like O'Sullivan's and O'Reilly's, had emigrated from Ireland, and she, too, spent time as an industrial laborer in a glove-making factory in Chicago. As a young woman, Nestor had joined a union, became active in her local, and then transitioned from the shop-room floor to serving as a full-time labor organizer, working closely in this case with John Fitzpatrick, head of the Chicago Federation of Labor.

And like her counterparts, Nestor also worked often with Jewish women through the Women's Trade Union League in organizing campaigns in New York, Chicago, Philadelphia, and elsewhere, and helped form the Chicago locals of the ILGWU.

Before working with Hillman, Nestor had helped a number of young Jewish woman, like Hannah Shapiro, a worker in a men's clothing factory, teaching her how to speak to large crowds, a crucial skill at meetings and on picket lines. She became particularly friendly with one Jewish woman, Bessie Abramowitz, who reached out to Nestor during the bitter 1909 strike that convulsed the garment industry in many cities. Abramowitz, frustrated with her own attempts at organizing, figured that Nestor, already prominent in Chicago as a skilled union organizer, could help her. Nestor, Abramowitz believed, could aid her in overcoming the tough resistance she had been encountering among the women pants makers she was trying to organize.

Nestor came to Abramowitz's rescue, and together they

successfully brought the workers out onto the streets and into the union. But Nestor's greatest impact on the Jewish labor movement came not from her connection to Shapiro or Abramowitz but from her relationship with the latter's future husband, Sidney Hillman, arguably the most important figure in the American Jewish labor movement.

Hillman, born in Lithuania, would found in 1914, and then preside over until his death in 1946, the Amalgamated Clothing Workers of America. During the 1930s he served on the Labor Advisory Board of the National Recovery Administration. He assisted Senator Robert Wagner in drafting the National Labor Relations Act and advised Secretary of Labor Frances Perkins in authoring the Fair Labor Standards Act. Indeed, word around Washington during the New Deal purported that anytime a labor issue came up, FDR quipped, "Clear it with Sidney."

These achievements lay in their future. First Agnes Nestor had to teach Hillman how to organize. They met in Chicago in 1910 during a turbulent set of strikes that rippled through the men's clothing industry. As president of Local Number 39 of the United Garment Workers (UGW), Hillman believed he could accomplish little, and the local organizers wondered if Hillman in truth had the skills it took to narrow the chasm between the striking workers and the employers. They suggested that Hillman seek out help, advising that he meet with Nestor. Only she, they told a frustrated Hillman, could demonstrate to the fledgling organizer "how you make agreements and negotiate them."

Nestor did just that. As she recalled in her autobiography, "It is amusing now to remember that I gave Sidney Hillman his first lesson in collective bargaining."[20]

Whether bragging or not, Nestor made an apt observation. She and so many other Irish labor activists shared their knowledge and insights about organizing with Jewish men and women, drawing them into the union cause. When in 1914

Hillman challenged the leadership of the United Garment Workers and declared the birth of a new, socialist-inspired union—the Amalgamated—he again relied upon her expertise and on that of John Fitzpatrick, president of the Chicago Federation of Labor. He also sought out the assistance of Leonora O'Reilly to help him launch his open rebellion against the older, conservative, craft-oriented union.

The three Irish labor leaders indeed sat on the dais at the organizing meeting, positioned just behind Hillman, who addressed the crowd as the assembled workers agreed to form this new union, giving the newly born Amalgamated a stamp of legitimacy. Bucking the might of the United Garment Workers and the American Federation of Labor to which it belonged, Hillman, with their input, garnered visibility, influence, and a place in American history.

Despite the successful launch of the Amalgamated, Hillman continued to fret over attacks by the UGW, which repeatedly claimed that the new union lacked the right to organize workers and represent them, constituting, as it did, a case of dual unionism, or the existence of two competing unions in the same industry, something the American Federation of Labor considered illegitimate. Hillman again sought Fitzpatrick's counsel, who advised Hillman to continue on the path he had laid out and not be deterred by the older union's sanctions. Fitzpatrick would claim that he considered his mentoring of Hillman one of his greatest achievements.

Fitzpatrick, Irish-born and a lifelong zealot for Irish nationalism, interacted on a constant basis with many Jewish labor activists from the 1910s onward. He boosted the leadership role taken by Lillian Herstein, daughter of a Chicago seller of Jewish books. Herstein, a high school teacher, had gotten involved with the Federation of Women High School Teachers in 1914 and met Fitzpatrick when her union elected her to the executive board of the CFL. As the only woman board member, Herstein caught Fitzpatrick's attention, and he turned to her when organizing campaigns or when strikes seemed to need a female voice. He sent her, for example, to Peoria to address a group of striking miners. Her success there cemented the relationship with Fitzpatrick, who, recognizing her effectiveness, provided her with increasingly visible roles in the labor world. A long friendship developed between the two of them, and in 1920 the pair served on the national committee of the Farmer-Labor Party, from which Herstein ran for Congress for a seat from Illinois.

Herstein's long career in the labor movement, which extended into the New Deal and beyond, began under Fitzpatrick's patronage. President Roosevelt named her the US representative to the International Labour Organization, which met in Geneva, Switzerland, and in 1936 the weekly magazine *Life* named her the most important woman in American organized labor.

Fitzpatrick groomed Jewish men and women, preparing the best of them to move up the ranks of the organization. Mollie Levitas began as an office worker in the CFL headquarters in the mid-1920s and under Fitzpatrick's tutelage became a public speaker and organizer in Chicago and beyond.

Irish union insiders helped situate the Jewish unions into the formal apparatus of the labor movement. Workers in the fur industry, for example, tended to be overwhelmingly Jewish, and they lagged behind the Jewish shirtwaist workers and cloak makers in organizing efforts. The United Hebrew Trades (UHT), founded in 1888, actively supported efforts by the fur workers to organize, but as it lacked any formal connection to a national body, its aid could do little beyond the symbolic. What the UHT and its leadership could not do, Hugh Frayne—the son of Irish immigrants, a onetime Knight of Labor, and by then an official of the AFL—could. He engineered the process by which the

Jewish New York furriers got admitted to the national organization, which could support striking workers.

Irish American unionists activated their larger political and press networks on behalf of Jewish labor. O'Reilly, as an Irish American, enjoyed numerous connections to Tammany politicians, and despite her commitment to socialism, deployed her Irish insider relationships in the 1910s, after the Uprising and after Triangle, to get the machine men like Charlie Murphy and Al Smith to support the progressive legislation championed by the unions then stalled in Albany's legislative halls.

They deployed their connections in local newspapers to benefit the predominantly Jewish unions and their Jewish leaders, reaching out to sympathetic, usually Irish, reporters and writers. In 1925 Mollie Friedman, an ILGWU staff member, came to Chicago to help out with the dressmakers' union, an organization damaged by a brutal strike the year before; she sought out Agnes Nestor for help. Rather than turning to Chicago's Jewish communal leaders, she considered Nestor her best ally, someone who would, without a doubt, come to her aid. As Nestor recalled, "Mollie came to see me and said that she would like to begin by building up good public relations regarding the union." To accomplish this, Nestor wrote, "I took her around the newspapers and they offered their cooperation."[21]

Much of this Irish-Jewish labor collaboration took place in specific unions, the International Ladies' Garment Workers' Union the most frequent, and the Amalgamated. But working together, with women the key actors, also occurred outside of the specific unions, controlled as they were by male leadership.

Rather, Irish and Jewish women joined in the cause of labor had to find ways to work together in supportive settings independent of the male-controlled unions. No organization proved more important in this project than the Women's Trade Union

League, and in no place did Irish and Jewish activists work more closely together.

In this cross-class coalition that brought together working women, mostly Irish and Jewish, with wealthier women smitten by the progressive rhetoric of the era, the Irish women entered first. Indeed, they founded the organization, with O'Reilly and O'Sullivan chief among them, in 1904. They then brought the Jewish women, Schneiderman and Newman most importantly, into the League.

The working women in this always-shaky alliance educated the better-off, native-born, mostly Protestant women reformers about unionization, getting them out of their comfortable homes to come out for strikes and join working women on picket lines in New York, Chicago, Boston, Cleveland, Rochester, and elsewhere.

The Irish women—Mary Kenney O'Sullivan, Leonora O'Reilly, Josephine Casey, Julia O'Connor, Agnes Nestor, Maud O'Farrell Swartz, all except Swartz once industrial laborers—played a role in stimulating better public support for the women on strike and raising money for them as they lost their wages when refusing to work. The WTUL, among its other accomplishments, got the AFL, always hostile to women workers, to support women's suffrage.

The Irish women labor activists took the lead in the formation of the WTUL. Mostly American-born of immigrant parents, they had a fine command of the English language, better than that of any of the Jewish women, all immigrants. The Irish women had some American education and deep family roots in the labor movement, and they knew some important male labor leaders to whom they could turn.

They specifically targeted Jewish working women as potential recruits to the organization, seeing them as excellent candidates for the struggle. They likewise reached out to men involved in Jewish communal work to participate in the League's efforts. In Boston, O'Sullivan, for example, cultivated Jewish social worker Meyer Bloomfield and Philip Davis, a Jewish immigrant from Russia and onetime textile worker, successfully transforming them into male allies. She courted the Goldmark sisters, Josephine and Pauline, already active reformers, to get them to include the League among their progressive causes.

To achieve its ends, the League recognized that the working-class women who worked for it had to extend beyond its Irish base. Nestor, O'Connor, O'Sullivan, O'Farrell, O'Reilly, and the others self-consciously took on the Jewish women and helped them learn the ropes, preparing them for roles as potential League leaders. The organization incubated Rose Schneiderman, Pauline Newman, Fania Cohen, Rose Pesotta, Theresa Malkiel, and dozens more on local levels, who in turn gained knowledge about organizing in general and forged networks of support for their campaigns. They trusted the Irish women, and even if they did not always agree, differences on strategy did not fall along Irish-Jewish lines.

The Jewish working women found in the Irish actual allies who provided the practical support they needed and which they had rarely gotten from Jewish male labor leaders or affluent Jewish women. Jewish women expressed awe at Irish women's skills and appreciated how they boosted the Jewish women into prominence.

Malkiel described how O'Reilly literally took her by the hand to meet the upper-middle-class women allies in "that swell hotel." Malkiel marveled at the aplomb with which O'Reilly "gets so many of them"—the rich women—to listen. O'Reilly addressed the well-off women first as they gathered in the reception room, "telling . . . the sad story of the shirt made by her mother and grandmother in Ireland and by herself in New York. A story of work, suffering, privation and self-denial; a story of love of kin as strong as death." And, when O'Reilly finished her remarks, she turned over the podium to Clara Lemlich, the garment worker whose fiery words had launched the Uprising of the Twenty Thousand in 1909. As Malkiel remembered the event, when "little Clara rose . . . I felt mighty proud for that simple Jew girl."[22]

Throughout the history of the League, tensions between the working-class women and their comfortable allies, often dubbed the "Mink Brigade," threatened the alliance. The affluent women considered that since they gave the money, they could give out advice. They tended to counsel caution rather than militancy.

The Jewish and the Irish women felt uncomfortable with their economic betters, who had never seen the inside of a sweatshop or been on a factory floor, but the Irish women felt the tension most sharply. Suspicious of the Protestant American women who claimed to be supporters, the Irish women repeatedly articulated to their Jewish peers the dangers of working too closely with them. Irish women in the League implored the Jewish women to not be fooled by the upper-class women's claims of solidarity. O'Reilly warned Schneiderman that "Contact with the Lady does harm in the long run. It gives the wrong standard," and imparted to Newman that "the 'cultured' ladies may be very sincere. . . . O! don't doubt their sincereity [sic] but because their views are narrow and their knowledge of social conditions limited, they cannot do as well as some of us can," with the "some" being Jews and Irish together.[23]

Perhaps, and it can only be speculation, their skepticism grew out of the reality that women like O'Reilly and O'Sullivan, products of Irish enclaves, must have known legions of Irish women who had once been domestic servants who cleaned the homes of the "'cultured' ladies." As servants, Irish women since the 1850s had lived with these well-off women, cooking, cleaning, laundering, caring for their children, being at their beck and call, and deriving intimate insider knowledge of the lives and attitudes of the white Protestant American women. These millions of Irish servants, all called "Bridget," had endured mistreatment, insults, humiliation, deprecation, and condescension by their employers, a recipe for unease when their daughters, literal and figurative, met the allies in the League.

Neither Newman, Schneiderman, Malkiel, nor the other Jewish women activists would have carried such memories into the WTUL, spared as they and their mothers had been from such firsthand overexposure to the women they had to depend upon now in their union work.

In this WTUL labor encounter, Irish women came in with greater knowledge of America more broadly than the Jewish neophytes. The Irish women had greater command of the language and greater familiarity with Americans. They therefore took the lead, teaching the Jewish women how to do their common work. Jewish women in the WTUL expressed awe at the way the Irish knew how to speak in public, using their words to get the wealthy women to be good allies and the working women to join. Newman marveled at how O'Reilly's "voice alone would get you," how they seemed to be "on the verge of tears," and by that, "caught the attention of the strikers."[24]

When Josephine Casey and Pauline Newman went to Kalamazoo, Michigan, in 1912 to organize the workers at the Kalamazoo Corset Factory on behalf of the ILGWU, Newman found herself befuddled as to how to address "an entirely American element." In a city and in an industry with no Jewish workers, Newman felt adrift.

Casey however seemed quite comfortable with that "element" and took the lead, explaining to the public the goals of the strike. She told the readers of *The Detroit Times* that the time had come "to purify the factory." She also intuited, unlike Newman, that the public would be outraged to learn about the sexual exploitation going on in the factories. Casey saw no reason to hide the issue and thought details of the physical mistreatment of women would nudge the public to their side. Newman, on the other hand, preferred that the issue be kept under wraps, but Casey made a point of calling for the dismissal of the foreman who had been preying on the female workers, "dragging not a few of them down to ruin."[25]

Although Newman felt ill at ease inserting the issue of sexual harassment into the rhetoric of the strike, her relationship with Casey and the other Irish women shaped her life in the movement. In the main, the Irish women had come first to the labor project, bringing with them their longer and greater knowledge about how America worked, and from that base, Jewish women found friends for themselves and gained access to the larger world beyond their own communities.[26]

Organizing efforts by telephone operators in Boston also involved Irish women teaching Jewish women how to unionize and opening doors for them into positions of leadership. Julia O'Connor and Rose Sullivan, both founders of the Boston Telephone Operators' Union, organized the WTUL branch there in 1916. These two daughters of Irish immigrants then mentored Rose Finkelstein, born in Ukraine, one of the few Jewish young women to be employed by the telephone company, encouraging her to join and learn to lead. The two Irish American women transformed the small union that they had created to become part of a larger national organization, and by 1918 they presided over the more substantial Local 1A. O'Connor and Sullivan brought Finkelstein with them onto the board of Local 1A and encouraged her to participate in the work of the League as well. Finkelstein quickly rose up there too and soon served as a board member and then president of that body. After learning to unionize from the ground up, Finkelstein launched into a notable career as an organizer, which spanned the 1930s and 1940s and would send her across Massachusetts, Maine, Pennsylvania, and New Hampshire to organize countless workers, male and female.

Finkelstein's entry into union work, guided by O'Connor and Sullivan, reflected the higher position occupied by Irish women in the labor market and in labor organizing. By the 1910s certain kinds of jobs came to them because of language and the other advantages of American birth. Ironically, telephone companies in the big cities like New York, Boston, and Chicago, which were overwhelmingly owned and managed by white Protestant natives, tended to hire Irish Catholic young women as telephone operators. They did not have audibly foreign accents and often had graduated from high school. As high school graduates, standard American diction would have been drummed into them as teachers, whether nuns in parochial schools or those in public schools, emphasized the imperative for students to speak clearly and devoid of working-class, Irish-inflected accents. Companies like the New England Telephone Company believed that girls like O'Connor and Sullivan, who had graduated from Catholic parochial schools, not only would have been drilled in neat penmanship, spelling, and arithmetic but also would passively defer to authority and steer clear of unions.

However, O'Connor and Sullivan, who grew up in Irish communities, knew the power of labor unions to transform lives and accepted the truth that workers should have the right to organize. They passed this on to Finkelstein, as they also conveyed the message of the WTUL that women workers had special needs that were unmet by the larger male-dominated unions.

The strikes that wracked the garment industry in 1909 and 1910 in New York, Chicago, Cleveland, Boston, Rochester,

Philadelphia, and elsewhere and that revived the International Ladies' Garment Workers' Union involved few Irish women as workers but drew some of the most energetic and skillful activists among them to work directly with the Jewish women. O'Reilly, Hinchey, Nestor, and O'Sullivan spent weeks meeting with Jewish women who refused to go out on strike, trying to convince them that the union would truly change their lives. They showed up on the picket lines, worked with the upper-middle-class allies, but most importantly spoke in small and large venues to groups of women workers, expounding on the long-run benefits of unionization.

In those years when the industry roiled in turmoil in many cities, the Women's Trade Union League sent out squadrons of organizers to the places where women sewing garments needed help in organizing. They showed up in larger cities like Boston and smaller ones as well. During that trip to Kalamazoo, Newman, Casey, and O'Reilly got themselves arrested and spent over a month in jail.

Casey, originally from Boston, came to Cleveland in 1911 during an ILGWU strike and met the local women workers. She implored them to see that their interests lay with the union and that only organizing would change their situation. She reached out to all of the women, including the Italians and Bohemians who made up much of the female workforce, but focused her efforts first on the Jewish women, considering them both more organizable and more prepared to assume leadership on their own.

Looking back on her Cleveland organizing campaign, Casey recalled that she had declared to them:

Oh you girls of Cleveland! You who a short time ago wept instead of protesting when you were unjustly treated, will in the future fight instead of weeping. The Bosses did not think you could fight. The men who worked alongside of you did not count on you. The only ones who knew you would make good were the women throughout the country, who had been on the fighting line some time themselves! You have justified their faith in you and it is because through the fight you have found out how fine and strong you are that the Garment Workers' Union is going to stay in Cleveland.[27]

Jewish women responded to Casey's words. A young woman named Becky Fisher joined the picket line, got herself arrested no fewer than thirty-nine times, and as a result the Cleveland chapter of the National Council of Jewish Women came out in support of labor for the very first time. Despite the unfavorable press, the condemnations of the strikers by local businesses, and the expected hostile reactions of the Jewish employers, the union planted itself in the city. Casey's work proved pivotal: Jewish women got organized and convinced more middle-class Jewish women to join the struggle.

The 1909 strike also brought Nestor from Chicago to Philadelphia at the request of Abe Rosenberg, president of the city's ILGWU. He asked for her explicitly, and when she arrived, "Mr. Rosenberg . . . expressed great relief" at her arrival. Nestor remembered that Rosenberg had been smeared in the press, accused of living "extravagantly" while "the poor strikers were starving." Nestor sprang into action, "aware of the tactics of the reporter" and his newspaper's goal of "discrediting the strike" at the behest of the employer. Knowing of Rosenberg's impecunious circumstances, she went to the editor and the reporter to straighten out the true record.[28]

The end of that strike—which achieved some victories, although never as many as the women wanted—did not represent the last journeys Irish women would make to sites of Jewish union agitation. When the Children's Dressmakers' Union in New York, mostly Jewish and female in membership, went out on strike in 1916, Maggie Hinchey, a former laundry worker, showed up and urged them to keep up the fight. All in all, the Women's Trade Union League functioned as an extremely effective organizing space for Irish and Jewish women.

The Jewish and the Irish women who met and worked together in the trade union movement for the most part shared a commitment to socialism, understanding that the American system inherently favored employers and put the dictates of capital ahead of anything else. But as they saw it, the existing socialist movement in the United States, despite its rhetoric, had no place for women to be heard and to lead.

They also coalesced around the cause of women's suffrage. Women's lack of a vote mattered greatly to them, but as they saw it, major players in the suffrage movement, like the National American Woman Suffrage Association, had no room for working women and certainly no vision of the connection between class and disenfranchisement.

In response to this oversight, Irish women created the Wage Earners' Suffrage League, which, while not a union per se, provided a political space to advance working women while pushing for the vote. Formed in 1911 by O'Reilly, who quickly recruited Rose Schneiderman, the group attracted an array of Irish and Jewish women to its ranks. Margaret Hinchey joined O'Reilly on the Irish flank, while Schneiderman brought in Rose Pastor Stokes, Clara Lemlich, and Mollie Schepps. The women voted for O'Reilly as the first president and Clara Lemlich the founding vice president.

The Jewish women, shepherded by the Irish women, made the connection between economic inequality and the need for women's suffrage. Together they declared that all women deserved robust paychecks, earned with dignity as women. But they would never secure their economic rights without political rights; they were both essential rights to which they were entitled, and one could not be separated from the other.

Rose Schneiderman said it most clearly and eloquently in 1911: "The woman worker," she proclaimed in the pages of *Life and Labor,* the official publication of the Women's Trade Union League, founded by O'Reilly, "needs bread, but she needs roses too."[29]

Schneiderman, along with Newman, Lemlich, and Malkiel, taught by O'Reilly, Hinchey, O'Sullivan, Casey, Nestor, and the others, issued a call to arms, imploring "working women to understand the necessity for the vote, to agitate for the vote and to study how to use the vote when it has been acquired," while they emphasized to well-off women that the vote would have massive economic consequences for the working class.[30]

The Irish women who flocked to the labor movement proved to be steadfast partisans of the cause. They not only formed unions where they had not existed and joined those that did, they also knew from life experience that political participation did much more than just elect this one or that one to office. These women used their unions to press for women's suffrage in order to simultaneously enhance their livelihoods and get a chance to become political actors with voices that had to be heard.

Jewish women immigrants to the United States arrived at a time when Irish women involved in the labor world spoke out, wrote, and organized around issues of worker exploitation, the hardships endured by the poor, and their rights to respect and power. Jewish women had come with long histories of work but had no histories of organizing and fighting for their entitlements as workers and as women.

Irish women labor activists, seeing the hundreds of thousands of Jewish women streaming into the sweatshops and factories, decided that their Jewish counterparts—the sewing-machine operators, buttonhole makers, stitchers, and more—needed to understand how they might mitigate the wretchedness of their conditions (often meted out by the men from their own communities). Irish women unionists showed Jewish women laborers that they could secure their rights once they recognized their untapped power.

It worked. Jewish women gravitated to the movement. They took the message to their shops and to their organizations and came to constitute a disproportionate number of the organized women in America. By the 1920s Jewish women made up almost one-quarter of all women who belonged to unions in America, and this despite their gradual movement out of the working class and into white-collar occupations and their tendency to leave the paid labor force upon marriage. Even if they, as rank and file, belonged to unions for just a few years, they acquired a worldview from their experiences that they carried into their families and communities about women's worth and women's work.

The rise of Jewish labor depended on the tutelage and guidance of the Irish who met them. Sidney Hillman achieved what he did in part because of the guidance of John Fitzpatrick and Agnes Nestor. Louis Brandeis experienced his conversion to labor through the efforts of Mary and Jack O'Sullivan and John Tobin. Rose Schneiderman and Pauline Newman, who prominently participated in shaping the nation's labor policy during the New Deal, got where they did because Irish activists opened doors for them. They moved from unorganized immigrants to labor zealots. A handful of them were called upon by governors, cabinet secretaries, policymakers, and presidents. And ordinary immigrant Jewish workers, once unionized, had good reason to believe that their children would have futures beyond the working class.

They achieved all this in part because of the invaluable

lessons they learned from their Irish mentors, who considered it important to invest in teaching the Jews. This Irish teaching and Jewish learning enhanced and expanded the rights of all American workers, men and women, far beyond the confines of these two communities.

5

Classroom Lessons

Irish Teachers, Jewish Students

In an interview in the 1980s Leah Boroff, the daughter of eastern European Jewish immigrants, described her decades-long career as a New York City public-school teacher. She recalled that as a woman she had always dreamed of becoming a schoolteacher, recounting how she trained to be able to achieve her goal.

Her story differed little from that of her peers, the thousands who in the 1920s and 1930s, fueled by those same aspirations, made that same choice. Collectively, this first American-born generation of the great Jewish migration became the majority of the women and men who instructed the city's children.

In other cities, large numbers of Jewish women of immigrant families also opted for schoolteaching as their profession of choice and their gateway into the middle class.

But regardless of location, the mobility of young Jewish women into teaching grew out of a particular historic dynamic: as children, they had been taught by Irish American women in the public schools. When they trained to become teachers themselves, they learned again from Irish American women. When they entered the schools as qualified teachers, they once again benefited from opportunities first pursued by their Irish women predecessors.

Thousands in New York, like Boroff, enrolled in Brooklyn's Maxwell Training School, where they received the education and credentials they needed. The school, founded in 1885 and in operation until 1933, by the early twentieth century had started hiring a largely Irish American female teaching staff, most of them seasoned public-school teachers, to instruct young women, like Boroff, who aspired to the challenge, income, and respectability of the profession.

In this, Maxwell reflected New York's on-the-ground educational reality. In the public schools, particularly at the elementary level, the American-born daughters of Irish immigrant women made up the largest ethnic group of teachers by the last decades of the nineteenth century. They served on the front lines of educating the youngsters from around the world—Jews among them—who immigrated to the United States after the 1880s.

Similar normal schools in Chicago and Boston, places with large Irish and Jewish populations, mixed these two populations together, one as teachers and the other as students. In the process of coming together that way, they shaped the larger histories of Irish Americans and American Jews. Circumstances of time and place threw them together, and Boroff and her Irish teachers played minor parts in a larger historic drama.

When Boroff reminisced about these experiences, she wove in one particularly revealing detail. Her Maxwell teachers, like herself, had come from humble roots. The immediate descendants of Irish women who had started their American lives as domestic servants in the homes of well-off employers, the mothers of Boroff's teachers had worked in some of the "finest homes," and the teachers, as Boroff saw it, carried with them standards of American bourgeois comportment. From their mothers, her teachers had "learned the oh-so-proper manners," which they now hoped to model to their aspiring Jewish pupils.

They, she remarked, "tried to teach us the same. In the spirit of *noblesse oblige* . . . we were forever invited to their genteel tea parties." Those get-togethers exposed some gaps between the Jewish students and Irish teachers, and she painted a vivid portrait, rendered either with humor or consternation—whether felt at the time or only in retrospect—of herself and her Jewish classmates "who drank tea from a glass at home, trying" in front of their mentors "to lift our pinkies like our teachers" while sipping from the delicate china. The Irish teachers insisted that "to be a teacher meant one was a lady," and that "we should learn how to be ladies by emulating them . . . implying that we Jewish women had no idea what being a lady meant and needed their help in this way."[1]

This cameo portrait of the Irish American women who exposed the Jewish students at the Maxwell School to both the nuts and bolts of pedagogy and refined tea drinking with raised pinkies reflects a tiny element of the benefits that Jewish immigrants and, most importantly, their children received. Irish Americans like the women at the Brooklyn school had come on the scene first and seized opportunities to enhance their incomes and status by gravitating to the profession of schoolteaching. By their sheer presence and by the actions they undertook as teachers, they paved the way for American Jews to do the same while learning to be American.

More than just another example of ethnic succession in America—a constant process in which a new immigrant group arrives and an earlier, settled, and already somewhat better-off population departs—the story of Irish teachers and Jewish students involved a complex dynamic through which the former and the latter, in the decades of transition, met and served each other's needs. By arriving when they did, Jews encountered Irish

American teachers, and both benefited from that unplanned interaction. Sheer circumstances brought them together.

The history of the Jews' movement from immigrant steerage, cramped apartments barely paid for by the meager earnings of families laboring in sweatshops and ramshackle stores, into the American middle class cannot be told without giving a nod to the Irish Americans whose presence facilitated this transition. The involvement of Irish American teachers, ranging from the women who greeted kindergarteners on their first days at public school through the professors who taught law, medicine, pharmacy, and business at the professional schools housed in Catholic universities that were founded and run by Irish American clergy and laymen, certainly does not diminish the efforts of Jewish parents to educate their children and launch them into American society as literate, competent citizens. Nor does it take away from the young people's own agency, but they did not do this on their own.

Jewish parents did not seek out Irish teachers for their children. Jewish applicants to Maxwell and to other professional schools embedded in Catholic universities with Irish roots did not want to attend these institutions for the sake of experiencing cultural or religious diversity. Rather, those schools provided the instruction Jews wanted and needed to get ahead. Similarly, Irish teachers did not intentionally gravitate to Jewish students. They did not specifically yearn to teach Jewish students, but in teaching them, they benefited as well.

From the youngest grades through the institutions for professional training, Irish Americans occupied crucial spaces that drew in Jewish immigrants and their offspring. In New York, Boston, Chicago, and other large cities, schoolteaching had become an Irish female niche. Like Boroff's teachers at Maxwell, the daughters of Irish immigrants, many of whose mothers had labored in domestic service, flocked to schoolteaching, becoming in some cities the majority.

Political machines, so firmly in Irish control, also had a heavy hand in staffing the public schools at both elementary and secondary levels, and loyal machine men could turn to their bosses to secure jobs for their American daughters and some sons. Irish girls from the 1880s on lived in a world where the brightest of them aspired to teaching, seeing such work as their ticket to self-sufficiency and material comfort, measured by the standards of their working-class communities. Along with nursing, Irish American women's professional attainment laid a firm basis for economic and social mobility.

Similarly, in large cities various Catholic religious orders, nearly all Irish in composition, founded universities like St. John's in Brooklyn, Fordham in New York, DePaul and Loyola in Chicago, Providence College in Rhode Island, and so many more offering professional education for the sons, mostly, of Irish immigrants. They created these institutions, governed them, and staffed them in order to shape a rising generation drawn from their own aspiring Irish Catholic working class.

By the time the Jewish immigrants from eastern Europe arrived, settled down, and focused on the fate of their next generation, these Irish teachers, whether in public-school classrooms or in the lecture halls of Catholic universities, stood ready to provide the tools for Jewish mobility. Few left any words at all about those experiences, and even fewer shared their reactions to the students whom they taught. Did they empathize with the children of immigrants who, like they had, considered education a pathway to better lives? Did they feel a kinship with the children of the newcomers who understood that their communities endured disrespect by the larger society and suffered from discrimination? Did they viscerally intuit what it meant to be strangers in a new land?

Likewise, only a few of their former Jewish students expressed in writing their reactions, whether in childhood or looking back from the vantage point of adulthood, to their teachers. Did they feel any bond with these women who had once been just like themselves, only a generation removed from impoverished immigrant neighborhoods, crowded apartments, and stigmatized immigrant parents?

Ultimately, it does not matter; simply by doing their jobs, these teachers provided Jews with the keys needed for entry into American society. They took enthusiastic advantage of the educational opportunities provided by Irish Americans. In turn, by teaching the new immigrants, Irish American community leaders could boast about their service to the nation, which fretted over what so many considered the stubborn resistance of the newcomers to the English language and American ways. Irish Americans had, in the face of continuing animosity against them, a point of proof. We serve America by Americanizing the immigrants.

Surviving stories of these encounters do not all brim with the theme of love beamed from teacher to student or from student to teacher. Not all show examples of Irish American teachers who went out of their way to understand the world of the Jewish children, to appreciate Judaism, or to look with sensitivity upon the culture of their students' homes. Not all reminiscences offer evidence of teachers advocating for the Jewish youngsters, the products of Yiddish-speaking families who by dint of circumstances had come under their tutelage in English-speaking America. Likewise, not all documents from this era convey Jewish respect or affection for the Catholic women, the non-Jews of Irish ancestry, who stood in front of them as the sentinels of American culture, so strict in their standards of comportment, so emphatic about classroom discipline, and so sure of their right to be teaching the children sitting in front of them.

But in truth the historic evidence points to a mutually positive on-the-ground encounter in the big-city schools where Jewish children learned from their Irish American teachers. So too material drawn from many of the professional schools at numerous Irish Catholic universities points to open doors for Jewish students. Memoirs, reminiscences, and autobiographies show few examples of Jewish students or parents resenting teachers for hostility. Rather, the details of actual behavior of students and faculty reveal that in the main the Irish American teachers taught these students well and did so with consideration, believing that by teaching these students they contributed to American society.

The absence of heated condemnation of Irish teachers as insensitive bigots in the Yiddish press pushes the equation in that direction as well. These periodicals, and the documents produced by Jewish defense bodies and the English-language Jewish publications of the time, spared no words when it came to anti-Semitism and ill will toward Jews wherever it was encountered. They did not hesitate to call out Americans who harmed Jews in words and deeds, and the classroom teachers escaped pretty much unscathed.

Indeed, at times some Jewish communal leaders worried that the positive bond between teachers and students and the teachers' powerful image as dignified, refined Americans—and speakers of crisp proper English—might cause Jewish children to become ashamed and distance themselves from their immigrant, Yiddish-speaking parents and communities. A lawyer and Jewish community activist, Harold Riegelman, offered what read more like fiction than factual reporting in a 1917 piece in *The Menorah Journal*. He described the experiences of two youngsters, David and Sarah, whose parents "came from a little village in Russian Poland." Hardworking, long-suffering, they could not compete with the public-school "teacher . . . well-appearing, light-haired, neatly dressed. . . . She spoke an excellent English and encouraged a like quality in her scholars." Their mother, by contrast, "short of stature and very broad . . . wore a wig, 'a sheitel,'" and alienated the children from their new American environment as represented by the teacher. Their shame pushed them onto the streets. David became a juvenile delinquent, in short order landing behind bars in Sing Sing, and "Sarah is now in an institution designed to reclaim her kind and make useful, respected women of them." While not accusing her of any malice, Riegelman did in this rare, discordant article ponder the downside of the immigrants' rush to public education and the seductive power of the teacher as representative of a new and more attractive world.[2]

However extreme his story, Riegelman did make a point that the teacher encouraged all sorts of American behaviors in her students. She may have resembled Leah Boroff's teachers, who took time out of their schedules to cultivate the proper etiquette of middle-class life. Pointedly, in recounting the tea-drinking incident, Boroff emphasized how often the teachers reached out to them, evincing a sense of duty, even sympathy for the rising crop of Jewish young women, grooming them for success by showcasing outward signs of respectability befitting teachers.

Her experiences, more typical than David and Sarah's, reflected the reality that American classrooms brought Jews and Irish into each other's orbits, with the teachers occupying positions of authority and the immigrants' children at the receiving end of the educational process.

This historical encounter took place against another reality: since the vast majority of Jewish children attended public school, their communities decided not to invest in parochial or all-Jewish private schools. A few Jewish traditionalists pointedly created a handful of such institutions, like New York's Yeshiva Eitz Chaim, which was founded in 1886, but few followed the example of these outliers. The masses opted for what America provided.

Catholics had done the opposite, as many—although far from a majority—influenced by their religious leaders, turned their backs on public education, opting for parish and other Catholic-run schools ranging from kindergarten through university. Catholic clergy vigorously advocated for Catholic schools as the only way to educate the young, avoid Protestant influences, and keep successive generations attached to faith and community.

But Jews did not do that. Rather, boys and girls alike from immigrant homes attended public schools in robust numbers, with the majority going on to acquire high school educations, which in turn equipped them to experience American mobility. While their numbers might have been too small in most places to have created an elementary and high school system of their own, they could have done so in New York, Chicago, Philadelphia, and a few other large cities, but they did not, choosing instead to embrace free public education.

It may be no exaggeration to say that most of the immigrant youngsters and the American-born children of immigrant households, not just Jews, who settled in the big cities after the 1880s and 1890s met America most intensely and directly through their Irish women teachers, who loomed large as the newcomers' most obvious model of what an American looked and sounded like. Often the first Americans with whom they had close contact, these Irish daughters of immigrant parents conveyed to most recent immigrants the authority of American society. They stood for the new place, imparting insider knowledge to children whose parents spoke little or no English, lacked much exposure to the intricacies of getting around and getting ahead, and labored at the bottom of the economic ladder. Irish Americans represented America to them.

The parents of these children likely could not sing "My Country, 'Tis of Thee," "America the Beautiful," or "The

Star-Spangled Banner." They probably could not recite the Pledge of Allegiance, or understand words like "republic" or "indivisible." They would have been unable to recite Longfellow's poem celebrating the ride of Paul Revere, and would have thought of the idea of eating a turkey with stuffing, sweet potatoes, cranberries, and pie on the last Thursday of November as an odd practice that did not speak to them, having grown up in so many villages and towns spread across the European continent.

The students acquired from these teachers not only the key idioms of American patriotism but, of equal or greater significance, their facility with the English language. They learned to read, write, spell, and handle numbers, mastering all the skills that prepared them to move ahead in America.

Despite the reality that Irish Americans in the late nineteenth century still experienced the sting of prejudice, enduring widespread hatred of their religion meted out to them by Protestants claiming to be "true" Americans by virtue of their English ancestry, these teachers offered their immigrant students history lessons celebrating the nation's founding and, as such, its decidedly non-Catholic, or non-Jewish, origins. As one Jewish memoirist, recounting his education in the New York public schools of the early twentieth century, stated, "American holidays and our Puritan roots were emphasized." He, Harry Leibowitz, did not hesitate to adopt this story as his own, employing the possessive "our" as he continued: "We had a textbook about Puritans, pictures of Puritans with the big hats and Thanksgiving and so on, and then about the Revolutionary War and the Fourth of July and Betsy Ross and George Washington, and those things we *learned*," with the emphasis in his original text. With no retrospective resentment, he declared that the teachers "brought out beautifully with dates" America's mythic story.

Leibowitz did not name his teacher or provide her ethnicity, but statistics make it likely that an Irish American woman, following the city's curriculum, drew the boy into American cultural citizenship.[3]

Irish American women, standing in front of students, with their well-coiffed hair, clean dresses, and speaking a refined English, exposed them to all these novelties and more. They also imparted basic skills while attending to the emotional needs of the children.

For Jewish immigrants, particularly those who came before World War I, the American educational world represented a new reality. In the Pale of Settlement from which most came, certain patterns predominated. Few girls received formal educations; most boys learned exclusively in Jewish communal settings, such as in the nearly ubiquitous *cheder*, which only slowly began to include some limited secular subjects, and men taught them, not women. Material extraneous to the Judaic system entered the curriculum at a trickle and tended to be practical rather than intellectual. Jewish children did not sit in classrooms with non-Jewish children, nor did they learn from non-Jews. In large cities, some more-modernized Jews sought out other educational options for their children in the latter part of the nineteenth century, but most of the immigrants to America came from smaller communities, particularly the masses arriving before the second decade of the twentieth century, where long-standing educational patterns continued.

Innovations in the teaching of Jewish children flourished during and after World War I with the creation of the Bais Ya'akov schools for girls, which spread out from Krakow; the Tarbut schools in Poland, which emphasized Hebrew; and, most decisively, after 1918 the creation of both the Second Polish Republic and the Soviet Union, where Jewish children entered en masse into the state-run public schools open to all.

But decades before that, the Jews who opted for America, if they came with children, immediately confronted the novelties of the public schools in the cities to which they went. The children born to them in the United States likewise moved into those schools, entering into a brand-new world of learning. Curricula might have differed in minor ways state by state, and forms of school governance varied city by city, but everywhere, schools mixed boys and girls in the same classrooms; taught arithmetic, history, literature, science, and citizenship—perhaps more accurately, patriotism; emphasized hygiene; provided time for physical education; included some art and music in the daily schedule; and attended a bit to the emotional well-being of the children. They did not cater to Jews only; and women, many of them Irish, stood facing the children, guiding them through their lessons and into American adulthood.

The teachers, with women far outnumbering men in the classrooms, did not design their own curricula, and each city and state developed its own mandate as to what they should do when, and how. The late nineteenth century, simultaneous with Irish American women's entry in large numbers into the teaching profession, saw increased centralization of authority over curricular matters into the hands of local and state boards of education. Progressives of that era wanted teachers to be more accountable for what they taught, but depending on place and time, teachers enjoyed some leeway in terms of how they might add to or embellish the guidelines. The teachers alone greeted the children each day, with or without a smile or a hug, disciplined them when unruly, or comforted them when upset. They had direct contact with the students, and they conveyed the material with their own styles and tones. Despite their official lack of autonomy, they dominated the schools by their sheer presence.

The Irish presence can also be seen in percentages and

numbers. In 1870, less than three decades after the famine exodus, Irish women made up over 20 percent of New York's teachers, and by 1900 they constituted the largest group, with more than two thousand out of a city teaching force of seven thousand. In some New York wards, particularly those where the new immigrants settled, Irish women made up four-fifths of the teachers. In 1908, they were 26.2 percent of the teachers in Buffalo; 38 percent in Scranton, Pennsylvania; 26.4 percent in Fall River, Massachusetts; 49.6 percent in Worcester; and so on. Irish Catholic women made up over half of the students who attended Boston's Normal School in the late nineteenth century, and in Chicago by 1902, two-thirds had come from Catholic high schools (by inference, they were Irish). The 1911 Dillingham Commission, surveying immigration as a factor in the life of the nation, calculated that Irish-born or daughters of Irish immigrant mothers made up 23.8 percent of all teachers in the United States, a figure that does not encompass the third-generation Irish, the grandchildren of the immigrants.[4]

Their dominance could not be missed. A study of a small industrial town in New England in the 1920s declared that "with the exception of one young woman who is straight Yankee, all the teachers in the grammar school today, including the principal, come from this [Irish] stock."[5] The mainline Protestant magazine *The Christian Century* noted in 1933 that "a study of the records of the Chicago normal college shows that in proportion to enrolment, the Catholic high schools furnish about ten times as many graduates of that college as do the public high schools. . . . The Catholic schools continue to furnish more normal school graduates than the public schools by a ratio of ten to one, in proportion to the total enrolment in each class." The ethnic realities of Chicago, with the more recent arrival and smaller numbers of Italians and Poles, made "Catholic" synonymous with "Irish."[6]

While very few Americans saw this as a good thing, E. A. Ross, a sociologist well-known at the time for his dislike and fear of the arriving eastern and southern European immigrants, considered Irish women "swift climbers," who made the best teachers. He claimed in his popular book *The Old World in the New* that "a city school superintendent" told him that if he had "two applicants . . . I take the teacher with an Irish name because she will have less trouble in discipline, and hits it off better with the parents and the neighborhood."[7]

Irish communal notables took pride in the educational contribution of their women and encouraged Irish young women to pursue teaching. Despite the insistence of Catholic priests and prelates on educating their children in their own institutions, they encouraged Irish Catholic girls to go into secular teaching as a practical way to achieve respectability and financial security, and to help the Irish to dispel the prevalent myths that depicted them as lazy, stupid, drunken louts. St. James High School in Chicago, nested in a thoroughly Irish parish, insisted that all female seniors take the entrance exam for the Chicago Normal School as a prerequisite for graduating. A 1907 booklet in praise of Irish Catholic girls asserted that "thousands of Catholic girls . . . had graduated from being pupils of public schools," and when "becoming teachers," they brought "credit alike on the race that produced them, the church to which they belong, and the country which afforded them and their Irish-Catholic parents the splendid opportunities which culminated in their education."[8] The keynote speaker at the American Irish Historical Society annual gathering that same year declared, after complaining that "there are few races, if any, which have been so persistently misunderstood and undervalued," that in the matter of "public schools, it would be a sin of omission . . . not to mention the thousands of young women of Irish birth or parentage who are doing faithful work as schoolteachers in all parts of the United States." Their work gave the lie to what the speaker and so many others saw as the widespread deprecation of the Irish in America.[9]

Yet a ceaseless rhetoric projected the Irish as incompetent, their politics as corrupt, and Catholics as dangerous. The 1880s saw the birth and flourishing of the American Protective Association, which occupied a comfortable berth in the Republican Party until its demise in 1896. Dedicated to minimizing what it considered the inordinate presence of Catholics in public-school teaching, the APA enrolled many more members than the Know-Nothings had before the Civil War. It linked Irish political power to the many Irish schoolteachers who it claimed polluted the minds of America's children, poisoning them with Catholic propaganda.

Over a million Americans subscribed to *The Menace,* a weekly that began publication in 1911, churning out its propaganda for a decade before changing its name in 1920 to *The New Menace.* Whether new or not, both publications identified the menace as Catholicism and claimed it wielded undue power over American life, spread largely by Irish Catholic teachers. These women covertly used their classrooms to convert unsuspecting American children.

Respected and respectable Americans joined this chorus. President Theodore Roosevelt declared at a gathering of Methodists, "I would rather address a Methodist audience than any other. . . . You know for one thing that every one there is an American." And, he claimed, "The Catholic Church is no way suited to this country. . . . Its thought is Latin and entirely at variance with the dominant thought of our country and institutions."[10]

No wonder they worried so much about the women who taught America's children. From the days of the APA on, the specter of the Irish Catholic female schoolteacher, who got her job through the nefarious interventions of Irish Catholic politicians, swirled around in nativist rhetoric. Partisans of this position advised Americans, as Protestants, to protect themselves and their children from the Catholic menace by persuading boards of education to limit the number of Catholics whom they hired. American parents ought to be aware of the dangers lurking in their classrooms, as legions of Irish Catholic women were likely to spread Rome's propaganda and undermine American values.

Thomas Beer, an American writer from Iowa, recalled in his memoir, *The Mauve Decade,* how a young Irish woman, an applicant for a teaching job in the town of Council Bluffs, "had to take an oath that she was a Unitarian in order to teach." Beer described how, as she made her way back, humiliated, "to her lodging, she found a gang of Christian women rifling her trunk in search of a nun's veil or penitential emblems."[11] The *Chicago Tribune* reported on the presence of Irish teachers in the city's schools in 1891 with a banner headline, ROMANISM'S POWER . . . AND THE PUBLIC SCHOOLS, citing the frantic remarks of a member of that very Protestant bastion, the Woman's Christian Temperance Union, who warned that "the situation is becoming alarming. . . . Our school teachers are 70 percent Catholic."[12]

Less overtly progressive educators like Chicago's Ella Flagg Young considered that the problems plaguing urban education stemmed in large part from the power that lay with the men of the political machine, who, despite no expertise, dispensed jobs as partisan favors. She, too, considered the teachers' unions, like that founded by Margaret Haley and Catherine Goggin, threats to quality education. That the founders, leaders, and many members of the union happened to be Irish and Catholic cannot have been incidental to the venom with which she and the city's Protestant elites fought the union.

Young's bias against Catholic teachers revealed itself in the kinds of reforms she sought to institute in the matter of standards for certification. Aware that two-thirds of the candidates who passed the Normal School entrance examination in 1902 came from Catholic girls' high schools, and indeed 25 percent had graduated from St. James alone, she unsuccessfully proposed a limit to the number of students who could be accepted from any single school.[13] In 1904 she successfully enacted an order stipulating that graduates of nonpublic high schools—clearly the Catholic high schools—would have to take an extra test to qualify for admission, while exempting public high school graduates.

No matter the rhetoric or the incessant political action aiming to eliminate the problem of too many Catholic or Irish teachers, Jewish immigrants still sent their offspring to these schools without a moment's hesitation. For them, as immigrants who came to America with no goal of returning to their home communities, school mattered greatly. Casting their lot with the United States meant that they believed that they and, more importantly, their children needed to acquire skills for economic mobility and meaningful citizenship.

While Jewish immigrants may have gravitated to American schools because of their own long tradition of widespread male literacy, the extensive immersion in text study that took place in their communities, and their centuries-long reverence for the educated among them, American public education represented something else in their history and served other purposes.

As working-class people, industrial laborers, and the proprietors of small shops, they had no desire for their children to replicate their occupations. They saw public schools as an avenue to get up and out.

That goal of economic security had propelled their migrations, and they recognized that their children had to learn the language and master the skills of English literacy, numeracy, and American culture in order to seize the opportunities that might await them. Some hoped that Yiddish would survive as a vibrant co-language in monolingual America, and they built supplementary schools to teach it when the public school, sometimes referred to as the "English school," day ended, but none on record resisted English acquisition as a universal desideratum.

Most immigrant families expected their sons to learn basic Judaic skills, including some Hebrew, develop some familiarity with the prayer book, acquire a knowledge of canonical texts, and so on, but not at the expense of what they needed to navigate their new American homes. Only the public schools could teach that.

Those schools shaped the lives of adults and children alike. David Blaustein, director of the Educational Alliance, one of the anchor voluntary institutions of the Lower East Side serving the Jewish immigrant population, noted that "the public schools are the first free institutions with which the immigrant makes acquaintance and often remains the chief tie between him and his adopted country." In the neighborhood "the immigrant appreciates perhaps more than native Americans, the benefits of free education. . . . No sooner are they landed in this country, than they send their children to school."[14]

Their educational history reflected the permanence of the Jews' migration and the fact that children made up a large percentage of the immigrant pool. According to US immigration records, those younger than fourteen constituted about one-quarter of Jewish immigrants after the 1890s, making education an immediate issue. While many older immigrant Jewish children headed straight for factories and family businesses, younger ones and those born in the United States went off to the classrooms. The vast majority of both boys and girls went to school, most stayed on through high school, and outsized numbers went on to college as well.

American Jews during the immigration era and long beyond invoked with pride that swift movement from immigrant homes to the middle class, facilitated by their parents' investment in education. Books have been filled with assertions extolling high rates of Jewish school attendance and achievement. The American Jewish narrative has zeroed in on the achievers, the learners, the lovers of school, and their headlong rush to the professions.

Indeed, so widespread was the brag among Jews about the educational attainment of the children of the immigrants that historians and sociologists have even devoted books to dismantling what they considered to be mythic rather than real. Sherry Gorelick's *City College and the Jewish Poor* of 1981 and Stephen Steinberg's *The Ethnic Myth* of the same year challenged what they considered an inaccurate history told widely among American Jews that claimed that the children of the poor, immigrant Jews seized American educational opportunities, excelled, and within a generation launched themselves out of poverty.[15]

Whether hyperbole or not, schools mattered, and Jewish immigrant families valued them greatly. J. K. Paulding wrote in 1905 that teachers "confirm the prevailing impression that these pupils—the children, for the most part, of poor Jewish immigrants from Russia—are among the brightest in attendance at the public schools" and that "they ran high in all examinations for advancement of the secondary institutions of learning."[16]

Jewish community leaders joined a loud chorus praising the schools, the children, and their parents. Mordecai Soltes, a Jewish educator, declared in the mid-1920s that the Yiddish newspapers all "express pride in the American Public School System" and "in the sacrifices which poor Jewish parents and widows are prepared to make for the sake of their children's education, and in the achievements of the Jewish pupils in the various schools and colleges." Written against the backdrop of escalating anti-Jewish rhetoric of the 1920s from the Ku Klux Klan, Henry Ford, and the restrictionists in Congress, Soltes asserted that "the Jews' age-long thirst for knowledge" and "their zeal for education" have "evoked the admiration of their neighbors."[17]

Jewish immigrant students won the admiration of a variety of commentators, from professional educators and government officials to journalists and others, like Kate Holladay Claghorn, a sociologist and staff member of the US Industrial Commission, which issued its multivolume report in 1901. As to New York, she noted in her volume, "one of the most striking social phenomena . . . is the way in which the Jews have taken possession of the public schools, in the highest as well as the lowest grades." Claghorn asserted that Jewish children were not only present in large numbers but were "the delight of their teachers."[18] Where teachers' voices appeared in reports and journalistic pieces, they echoed Claghorn's assessment, and as one teacher told Pauline Young for an article in *Social Forces* in 1928, "They are mentally alert, colorful, intelligent. . . . The Jewish children are the backbone of my class."[19]

Behind and alongside these celebrations of the educational accomplishments of Jewish immigrant youngsters stood Irish women. Sources do not consistently label teachers by ethnicity, but given the percentages of Irish teachers in big cities, Irishness can be assumed. Last names also provide a good clue. Invocations in a memoir or an article to a Miss Murphy, a Miss Sullivan, a Miss O'Brien, and the like make it quite clear that Irish women taught the children.

Nat Hentoff, born in 1925 in Boston, gained a national reputation as a journalist, novelist, jazz and country music critic, and passionate advocate for civil liberties. As a youngster he started out, according to his own account, as a desultory student at the William Lloyd Garrison Elementary School in the Jewish enclave of Dorchester, but somehow he gained admission to the prestigious Boston Latin School, where he joined an illustrious roster of alumni, including, as he noted in his autobiography, "Cotton Mather, Sam Adams, Charles Sumner, Ralph Waldo Emerson," among others.

But Hentoff did not miraculously get in. Rather, he gained admission to this incubator of American prestige through the actions of Miss Fitzgerald, his elementary-school teacher. She

> marched . . . all the long way down Elm Hill Avenue, turned into Howland Street, and proceeded to knock firmly on the door of our apartment. Accepting a glass of the usual scalding tea, which she polished off without a blink, Miss Fitzgerald told—actually commanded—my mother to allow me to take the entrance examination for the Boston Latin School. If I applied myself, Miss Fitzgerald glared at me, I could do the work. And unlike the local high school . . . Boston Latin School led to sure success in later life. Success for those—she glared at me again—who had the stick-to-it-iveness to stay the course.

The determined Miss Fitzgerald took Hentoff's mother's silence for consent, since the teacher "could not imagine any immigrant parent holding a child back from so bounding a head start on the ladder." The future award-winning journalist's father later that evening agreed to try for the Latin School; Hentoff, a lifelong radical, noted that no one had asked what he wanted, but "I would never have thought of crossing Miss Fitzgerald."[20]

Born a decade earlier and also a product of Boston's immigrant

Jewish neighborhood, journalist Theodore White developed supreme command of the English language, ably demonstrated by his admission to Harvard College, and pursued a lengthy career as a journalist and prizewinning book author. He paid homage to not just one Irish teacher but a number, including "Miss Phelan, Miss Brennan, Miss Murray, Miss Kelly," all of whom taught "us to read, write . . . and add. They made us memorize poetry, and poetry was all New England—Henry Wadsworth Longfellow, James Russell Lowell, John Greenleaf Whittier. But memory was essential, as it was in Hebrew school, where we memorized the Bible."

White's connection to Irish schoolteachers extended back, in fact, a generation earlier to his mother, who had immigrated as a child to Boston and attended a city public school. She had been plagued by poor eyesight, and "would never have been fitted with eye-glasses if the public-school teacher had not summoned my immigrant grandfather to school and indignantly insisted on it."

That teacher essentially gave the girl the gift of sight. All in all, he concluded that the "Irish schoolteachers dried our tears, kissed and coddled us, and taught us what their Yankee overlords in the Boston public-school system directed them to teach."[21]

One more American Jewish journalist offered readers of his memoir a no-less-sweet and compassionate account of his Irish American teacher. Harry Golden, editor of *The Carolina Israelite,* raised in New York's immigrant East Side, paid tribute to Miss O'Day, who had proclaimed to his mother, "You have such a smart boy in Harry," a comment that no doubt swelled her heart with pride and validated him. He depicted how she ushered him into American life, recalling decades later that she chose him to recite Henry Wadsworth Longfellow's "The Building of the Ship." He declared the teachers at P.S. 20, like O'Day, "the first Christians" he had met in America, and pointed out that they differed radically from "the Christians of whom one's parents talked, the European peasants who used every Easter . . . to assault the ghetto." He remembered his first Christians, these schoolteachers, as "kind, gentle, and generous. They thought of Jews only as students and knew they were poor." And to launch them into success, his one male teacher, Mr. Ryan, "our Irishman," suggested that those going to high school might consider anglicizing their first names.[22]

Fragments such as these crop up repeatedly. Mike Gold wove into his *Jews Without Money,* the classic proletarian work of the 1930s, a "Miss Barry, the English teacher," who encouraged the recalcitrant novel's protagonist, as a teenager not interested in continuing his education, to go on to high school. "She tried to persuade me," he wrote, remembering that "she was fond of me. She stared at me out of wistful blue eyes, with her old maid's earnestness," reflecting the reality of the unmarried status of most of these Irish teachers.[23]

Some Irish American men opted for schoolteaching as well, almost exclusively at the high school level. Joseph Freeman, editor of *New Masses* in the late 1920s and early 1930s, learned some important lessons from "the principal of our public school . . . an Irishman," who taught him that true education lay beyond the books, that life in the city itself offered "the best way to Americanize immigrant children."[24]

Far less known than White or Gold or Golden or Freeman, Morton Kaciff came as an eleven-year-old to Chicago from the Soviet Union in the mid-1920s, settling in the heavily Jewish Douglas Park neighborhood, where many members of his extended family already lived. They had as a group changed their name from Katziv to Kite, and urged the boy's father, Abraham, immediately upon arrival, to do so as well. They counseled that Mordecai, or its diminutive, Mottel, would not make it in

America and pushed for Mike as a better, more American first name. His aunt took him to public school and, following the family's wishes, registered him as "Mike Kite."

Decades later in a family history, he still remembered how the boys in the class mocked him as "Mike Kike," and "although, I wasn't versed enough in the English language," it "didn't take me long to realize what had happened." Mike, or better Mordecai, and his father, Abraham, took the matter to the principal, Miss Reilly. Introducing the boy to Miss Reilly as Mordecai, she suggested they consider Morton as a compromise name, one that incorporated the first syllable of the Hebrew name into an English one.

So just as an Irish American teacher gave Theodore White's mother clear vision, and Nat Hentoff's teacher gave him the wherewithal to follow in the footsteps of the Yankee elite, in his own way, Morton Kaciff's Miss Reilly offered the Jewish immigrant child a name that served as a pathway to America, one that did not wander too far from tradition but did not stigmatize him as too foreign in an unforgiving land.[25]

She encouraged him, as did the Irish American teachers of the others who have left stories of their immigrant school days. Even Freeman and Gold, who grew up to become implacable critics of American capitalism, emphasized their teachers' support and influence. They claimed school as a special and positive place, an oasis from the turmoil of the streets around them, a window onto a bigger world. Labor leader Rose Schneiderman regretted the brevity of the time she spent at P.S. 13 on Houston Street, time she dearly enjoyed before circumstances forced her into the world of work, where she found socialism and union organizing. Rather than seeing school, with no doubt Irish American teachers, as a tool of capitalism, she recalled those years as formative and decidedly pleasant.

Few sources, whether written at the time or looking backward, expressed resentment at teachers, who held up American standards of speech and decorum. None found fault with the compulsory immersion in American culture, delivered through the poetry and imagery of the nation's founding fathers. None seethed with anger or claimed that the teachers deprecated their Jewish and immigrant families.

Probably the best-known Irish schoolteacher, and for sure the one who left the longest paper trail and who came in contact with Jewish students, happened to be someone who taught only briefly. But by turning to fiction she immortalized the world of Irish teachers and Jewish immigrant children in early twentieth-century America. Myra Kelly, born in Dublin in 1875, came to New York with her father, a physician who opened a medical practice in the Jewish immigrant neighborhood on the East Side. After graduating from Teachers College, Columbia University, in 1899, Kelly headed downtown and taught at P.S. 147 on Houston Street for three years.

A few years later she took up fiction writing and left three volumes of short stories drawn from her teaching years, told through the adventures of a Miss Constance Bailey, who day after day taught mostly Jewish and some Irish first graders not yet initiated into American culture. In *Little Citizens: the Humors of School Life* (1904), *Wards of Liberty* (1907), and *Little Aliens* (1910), she offered kind portraits of the children, describing their stumbling steps into the English language, their first forays into American idioms, and the lovely Miss Bailey, who charmed them and whom they charmed with their sincere efforts to learn. Kelly, as Bailey, defended her children, Morris Mogilewsky, Isidore Belchatosky, Eva Gonorowsky, Yetta Aaronsohn, sometimes standing up for them against callous school administrators. In one notable scene in *Little Citizens,* the heroine-teacher stood up to the Irish associate superintendent, Timothy O'Shea, on behalf of her charges. When he demanded that she "stamp out the dialect" in the children, she came back at him with an appropriate retort that he stemmed from immigrant antecedents himself and spoke "not" with "an English voice, nor is O'Shea distinctively an English name."[26]

Jewish publications took note of Kelly's writings, considering that her stories projected a positive portrait of Jewish children as delightful, avid learners, standing on the threshold of Americanization through education. At a time when much public discourse in the daily press and in popular magazines painted decidedly negative scenes of Jewish immigrant life, her vignettes stood as endearing contrasts. They bubbled with warmth and promised a rosy American future for the children. The *American Jewish Year Book* considered her 1906 story, "A Soul Above Buttons," in *McClure's Magazine's* August issue a noteworthy event worth including among the year's important happenings for Jews.[27]

Kelly touched a broad range of American readers, neither Irish nor Jewish, who may have from these volumes developed some sympathy and warmth for both the Jewish immigrant youngsters and their Irish teachers. *McClure's* included as part of the foreword for *Wards of Liberty* a letter of endorsement from President Theodore Roosevelt, who in praising the book revealed not only that "Mrs. Roosevelt and I and most of the children know your very amusing and very pathetic accounts of East Side school-children almost by heart" but also that when serving as New York City's police commissioner he visited the very school on Houston Street where the fictional Miss Bailey taught. "I was immensely interested and impressed by what I saw there. I thought that there were a good many Miss Bailies [*sic*] there, and the work they were doing among their scholars (who were so largely of Russian-Jewish parentage) was very much like what your Miss Bailey has done."[28]

Kelly raised the stature of her proverbial sisters, the legions of "Miss Bailies," widely under attack by progressive reformers and anti-Catholic xenophobes. Through her sweet stories she showed these teachers as accomplishing something of tremendous importance, the day-by-day integration of the children of immigrants into American life, offering them a springboard to the larger society. From those schools, the children of the Jewish immigrants, Miss Bailey's fictional students, went on to high school and so many to college and then the professions.

Few professional opportunities for the children of Jewish immigrants mattered more than schoolteaching itself, a powerful magnet for the daughters of Jewish immigrants. By the late 1910s handfuls began to graduate from normal schools, and then their numbers skyrocketed in the 1920s and beyond, as young Jewish women like Leah Boroff decided that they wanted to become teachers. They seized possibilities opening up to them, and by 1920 they made up over one-quarter of all the new teachers hired by the New York system. In the 1930s the percentage jumped to two-thirds, and in the interwar years, over three-quarters of the students in the city's teacher-training programs came from Jewish immigrant homes.

Their trajectory played as crucial a role in the movement of Jews into the middle class as it had for the Irish. Having acquitted themselves well in high school, they sought out work far beyond the garment factories and family-owned shops where their parents had labored. Schoolteaching provided Jewish women a practical and honored route into American cultural citizenship. Social work and librarianship attracted many as well, but schoolteaching outweighed them. Much white-collar office work lay beyond their reach, as Jewish women faced substantial discrimination when applying to work in corporate business settings, although untold numbers did go to work for city agencies.

Schoolteaching emerged as their most attractive professional goal. It offered steady incomes and carried with it, rightly, the mantle of professionalism and doing good work for the society, child by child.

Just as in the previous era, when Irish American women from poor, immigrant families became the teachers who conveyed the nuts and bolts of American life to newcomers, so too Jewish women, coming from similar homes, instructed subsequent generations of students. Jewish women swelled the ranks of the schoolteachers in New York, Chicago, Boston, and elsewhere; they served as the exemplars of northern, urban life to the African American children of the Great Migration, the Puerto Rican children whose families came to the mainland, and so many others.

The Jewish women who flocked to teaching in public schools starting in the 1920s benefited from the actions of the Irish women who preceded them. Irish American teachers had in their day struggled vigorously to improve their work conditions, and by the time the Jewish women entered the field, some victories had been won, and Jewish women reaped the rewards of those earlier efforts.

One example stands out. Most Irish women who taught school had not married. An unknowable number may have never intended to do so, preferring the single life. Most, however, did not marry because state law forbade married women from holding teaching positions, so those who married lost their jobs, independence, and status. But staying in the classroom, and thus staying single, meant giving up on domestic life, marital love, and children.

Yet by the time Jewish women entered the teaching force a quiet revolution had taken place, and restrictions on the employment of married women as teachers had been dropped in New York and elsewhere. Jewish women did not have to weigh such stark options.

That happened because Mary Murphy chose to launch a rebellion, challenging the system in 1904. A teacher in Brooklyn for a decade, she violated the law by marrying in 1901. She oddly remained in her job but received no pay. After protesting this outrage, the school board charged her with misconduct for teaching while married. She then sued on the grounds that she could not be dismissed because of marriage; the law, as specified in the city charter, stated that she could be fired only if she had engaged in behaviors like insubordination, neglect of duty, and the like. The case went up to the New York court of appeals, which found in her favor.

Murphy advanced the futures of Jewish women teachers. While it wasn't her original goal, she pushed the city to change its policy, and within a decade the Jewish women that entered the field had choices unavailable to the teachers before them. In the wake of the Murphy decision, schools liberalized further, no longer dismissing women who took off time for childbirth and to care for their young children, something of which Jewish women availed themselves.

Jewish women who taught school pointed out to researchers that as a profession it worked well with marriage and motherhood. Unlike social work or the other professions open to educated women, teachers enjoyed lengthy summers off, took advantage of regular school vacations, and could follow the same daily schedule as their children. Whether they knew it or not, they owed a debt to Mary Murphy for the opportunity to teach school, marry, and raise children.

So too Jewish women, single and married, found teaching attractive beyond the honor, service, and intellectual stimulation, because they enjoyed the steady paychecks with comparatively good wages. Never as high as they deserved or wanted, their earnings far exceeded what their parents had brought home, and the unions to which so many belonged pressed states and cities to raise teachers' salaries and, over time, to provide tenure, pensions, and a range of other job and income protections.

These benefits did not just arise out of the beneficence of state lawmakers, but rather states, pressed by increasingly robust unions, responded to the pressure of organized labor. Jewish women as teachers again reaped the advantages won for their profession by the Irish women who had led the fight.

Historically a difficult undertaking, the unionization of teachers revealed the divisions between male and female teachers, between elementary and secondary teachers, and between various ethnic and religious groups. Public officials and business interests claimed that teachers as public employees should have no right to unionize, and many teachers saw joining unions as affronting their professional status. Many in the public considered it unladylike for a teacher to belong to a union or to threaten to strike, never mind being on the streets brandishing a picket sign.

Those hurdles did not stop Irish women in the late nineteenth and early twentieth centuries. Margaret Haley and Catherine Goggin in Chicago battled the city's elites to get schoolteachers the right to unionize. Kate Kennedy had organized the first teachers' union in the 1860s in San Francisco, demanding equal pay for equal work for women teachers, a radical idea. These women paved the way for Lillian Herstein in Chicago and then, in 1930s New York, such labor activists as Dorothy Rose, Alice Citron, and Mildred Flacks.

These Jewish women's later activism as organized schoolteachers built upon the foundation laid for them earlier. The Irish women who pioneered in teachers' unions assumed a difficult challenge but, undeterred, linked their demands for economic security with the larger labor movement, encouraging teachers to recognize that acting collectively, like other workers, did not detract from their professional stature. Leonora O'Reilly in 1916, at an early organizing rally in New York, urged school-teachers to "stop thinking that they were better than ordinary workers," because just like those "ordinary workers," they needed unions.[29] Margaret Haley joined her on the dais, speaking to a predominantly Irish crowd. Starting out that year with one thousand members, the teachers' union, affiliated with the American Federation of Labor, grew to seven thousand in short order. A few months later the New York union joined with seven others representing teachers in various cities, forging the American Federation of Teachers. While it never represented the majority of the teachers, it amassed enough visibility and clout that within a few years it pressured the state and city to change policies in terms of allowing for maternity leaves and equal pay, and won for all teachers constant, if never large enough, raises in wages for all.

In this, then, Irish women paved the way for the Jews who followed them, having laid the groundwork and providing models for activism. Not that they all worked happily together within the unions, once Jews became the majority. From the 1930s through the 1950s, Irish and Jewish teachers formed separate unions, sparring over politics, mostly over communism, which the Irish Catholics hated and which many Jews embraced. In the 1930s their bitter arguments reflected the rise of Father Charles Coughlin, an outspoken anti-Semite.

The oversized role of Irish women as the teachers of Jewish youngsters inspired no criticism or complaint among the children or their parents or most Jewish communal leaders. Some immigrant parents took issue, sporadically, with school matters, focusing not on the classroom teachers but on the upper-echelon administrators and the various school boards, New York's in particular. When they protested Christian content or ceremonies in the schools, they found allies among Catholics, including teachers, who rightly discerned the heavy hand of Protestantism, something they recoiled against no less viscerally than Jews did.

In the rare moments when some New York Jewish parents protested school policies, Irish Catholic teachers and the ever-present Irish Tammany Hall joined them, literally and symbolically. Most notably in 1917 the Department of Education, spurred by education reformers and members of the business community, decided to adopt for New York City the Gary Plan, a reorientation of high school education. Jewish parents and students reacted in opposition, and Tammany Hall used the Jews' discomfort with the decidedly anti-Tammany plan as a golden opportunity to advance its own interests. It whipped the Jews into action, helping organize the protests in Jewish neighborhoods. The Jews, parents, children, and a number of communal agencies feared that the Gary Plan would diminish the academic content of their children's schooling, stalling their paths to success. Riots broke out in the heavily Jewish Browns-ville, a neighborhood in Brooklyn where students went out on strike. They rallied on the streets of Harlem and the East Side.

This happened during the mayoral campaign, one that some predicted would see the Jews abandon Tammany for the Jewish socialist Morris Hillquit. Tammany responded, distracting the voters from Hillquit, who campaigned against America's poten-tial entry into the world war. They campaigned against the Gary Plan as a threat to Jewish interests.

Tammany's candidate, John Hylan, born of immigrant par-ents from County Cavan, went out into Jewish neighborhoods stumping on his anti–Gary Plan, a surefire winner, he rightly reckoned. Hylan promised the Jews that he would "banish the . . . Gary system, which aims to make our public schools an annex to the mill and factory." If elected, he pledged these voters, he would make sure that "our boys and girls shall have

an opportunity to become doctors, lawyers, clergymen, musi-
cians, artists, orators, poets or men of letters, notwithstanding
the views of the Rockefeller Board of Education."[30]

Hylan, a lackluster candidate and then undistinguished
mayor, presciently touched upon something very real, namely
the dreams of Jewish parents of professional futures for their
children. Some who dreamed, in New York or elsewhere, discovered that Catholic universities could make their dreams
come true. Schools of higher education, particularly their professional divisions, attracted Jews, and although founded, administered, and supported by Catholics, nearly all Irish, they
made room for Jews.

Jesuits, Vincentians, Congregation of the Holy Cross, and
other Catholic religious orders established colleges and universities across the country in the late nineteenth and early twentieth
centuries, planting most in the big cities where the Irish immigrants and their children lived. Irish men who dominated the
American clergy founded the schools. The Irish constituted the
largest percentage of Catholics, particularly of second and third
generation in the United States, and they sustained this hefty
educational enterprise. And Jews, aspirants to the professions,
turned to these schools in substantial numbers.

Harry Roskolenko, a poet and novelist, as a young man
adrift toyed with becoming a lawyer. He recalled, "I figured
all I had to do was read the right books to be bright, apply
to Fordham, and I would enroll." Although he never went any
further than daydreaming, the fact that only one school came to
his mind reflected a historical reality. Founded by the Irish-born
archbishop John Hughes, succeeded then by John McCloskey,
Fordham became a mecca for Jewish students, and Roskolenko's memories revealed the Jewish comfort level with Catholic
schooling.[31]

Jewish attendance at these universities soared beginning in

the 1920s, coincident with the practices of most private schools, firmly in the hands of Protestants, which either imposed explicit quotas on Jewish admissions or did so stealthily. In 1921, a year before Harvard's president A. Lawrence Lowell announced his quota on Jewish admissions, joining the institutions that already limited Jewish enrollment, Loyola University in Chicago advertised for undergraduate students in the city's local Yiddish newspaper.

Word had gone out in the large Jewish population of the city that the Jesuit school, as a matter of policy, prohibited religious limitations on admissions. Jewish students flocked to it in appreciable numbers.

Chicago's other Catholic university, the Vincentian-affiliated DePaul, also declared that it did not restrict Jewish students. Dean of the School of Commerce, Father Comerford O'Malley, who later became chancellor, encouraged a local Jewish student, Abel Berland, to apply after the more prestigious University of Chicago turned him down. Berland could not afford DePaul's tuition, but O'Malley allowed him to take the courses anyhow, learn the material, and earn credits, which he could apply toward a degree when he had the funds. A wise move on O'Malley's part: Berland became a lawyer, developed a passion for collecting rare books and precious folios, joined DePaul as a trustee, and became a generous donor, repaying in many ways O'Malley and the school.

Irish American community leaders boasted of their universities' liberalism toward Jews, using it to point out the differences between themselves and their longtime antagonists, the elite Protestant Americans who claimed to be the true America. A speaker at the American Irish Historical Society's annual meeting in 1930 lumped in those institutions of higher education that discriminated against Jews with the Ku Klux Klan. He asserted that "the Klan," along with "the College Presidents . . . the

University heads," violated American ideals, naming as culprits "Garfield of Williams, Cutten of Colgate, Hibben of Princeton, Butler of Columbia, Lowell of Harvard." They, "all, are against true Americanism," both "in substance if not in form."[32]

He offered these words as Jews, community leaders, and ordinary people fretted over increasing discrimination at many private universities. Louis I. Newman, a Reform rabbi, worried enough about quotas and outright rejections of Jewish applicants that in 1923 he solicited the opinions of other Jewish leaders, compiling their responses to his poll in a book aptly titled *A Jewish University in America?* He and his respondents all recognized the extent and seriousness of the problem. They feared that the decisions of university and college administrators and trustees would dash the dreams of young Jews who hoped to become professionals.

They had heard stories from disappointed young Jewish men and women who had received polite rejection letters stating that because the school's Jewish quota had already been filled, their application had been turned down. These young people recognized that as Jews they faced hurdles having nothing to do with their intellectual abilities or academic achievements.

Their fears mirrored reality. A member of Yale University's medical school admission committee quoted, in writing, the words of his dean, who decreed, "Never admit more than five Jews, take only two Italian Catholics and take no blacks at all."[33]

That year journalists Heywood Broun and George Britt published an exposé, *Christians Only,* an account of the anti-Semitic practices rampant in American society. Giving much attention to education, the authors provided statistics and shared anecdotes demonstrating how many institutions, just like Yale University's medical school, deliberately limited, or in some cases fully excluded, Jewish applicants.

Broun and Britt did find one bright spot in this difficult situation. They declared that "the Roman Catholic colleges as a class usually have escaped the charge of anti-Semitism, not only those such as Georgetown and Notre Dame where there are few Jews, but also Fordham where the Jewish enrollment is large."[34]

Jewish exclusion from America's private universities continued to draw attention. In 1934 Claris Edwin Silcox and Galen Fisher, working under the aegis of the Institute of Social and Religious Research at the behest of the "National Conference of Jews and Christians and Jews" (*sic*: it should have read, National Conference of Christians and Jews), investigated anti-Semitism in America and paid attention to anti-Jewish policies in higher education. They concluded what many Jewish applicants knew all too well, that the majority of American private colleges and universities shut Jews out. They, too, pointed out that Catholic universities stood apart from the rampant discrimination.

These schools admitted Jews despite, or possibly because, the schools had meager endowments and perforce depended heavily on tuition money, which non-Catholics could pay just as well. Still, the two researchers marveled at the robust numbers of Jewish students admitted, attributing this fact to the urban spaces shared by the Catholic colleges and potential Jewish applicants.

Few Catholic schools existed in remote settings. The religious orders and dioceses that had founded them were located where (Irish) Catholics lived, places where Jews also clustered. Even in smaller cities like South Bend, Indiana, and Omaha, Nebraska, local Jewish students found places for themselves at Notre Dame and Creighton University, both of which enrolled a sizable number of Jewish students. Creighton's medical school produced the majority of Omaha's Jewish doctors.

These urban locales may help explain why more Jews than Protestants attended. Comparing Jewish enrollment at some two dozen Catholic schools to that of Protestants, the authors of a 1934 study stated that nationally "with a total student body of 30,607 . . . 3,299 (10.8 per cent.) were Protestants and 4,722 (15.4 per cent.) were Jews." Across the nation, Protestants obviously constituted a vastly larger portion of the population, but the urban environment and the still-simmering Protestant disdain for Catholicism kept their numbers down. Moreover, white Protestants faced no discrimination because of race or religion and enjoyed ample options when deciding where to study.

Jews, on the other hand, had limited choices, making Catholic schools attractive. Silcox and Fisher marveled at the numbers, declaring that "56.7 per cent. of the entire student body of one of these Catholic institutions in an area increasingly Jewish, were Jews," a statistic they repeated several times in their book, emphasizing the wonder and significance of it.[35]

By all accounts, these schools provided safe spaces for Jewish students to learn and acquire the credentials needed for professional careers. Many, like Fordham as of 1912, exempted Jewish students from the mandatory chapel and instruction in Catholic theology that was required of all students, not just undergraduates. Loyola's Jewish students founded a Jewish student organization in 1932, the Akibean Club, named for the second-century scholar Rabbi Akiba. The club combined Jewish cultural activities with intramural sports, and its members collaborated with other groups as they planned campus events. Notices appeared in the *Loyola News* announcing Akibean Club programs in the 1930s, and in 1932 the club sent greetings to "all our fond readers," wishing them "a very Merry Christmas and a Happy New Year."[36]

At the time, and in decades to come, Catholic universities cited their openness to Jewish students as a hallmark of their service to America. Notre Dame's long-running magazine, *The Ave Maria,* published an article in the 1950s—which later appeared in *Catholic Digest*—recounting the experiences of Sheldon Kaplan, a self-described Orthodox Jew who had attended the Jesuit Holy Cross University as an undergraduate. Kaplan had attended during World War II and claimed that not only had he received a top-notch education there, but the priests and his fellow students, "a group of predominantly Irish Catholics," had "left me a better Jew than I ever was before." More than once he brought some of his college friends, like John Shanley, Bill Sweeny, and John Shay, to his home in a "solidly Jewish section of Brooklyn," where "my mother, who would as soon lose an arm as break one of our strict dietary laws . . . always managed to see that our Catholic visitors got generous helpings of . . . prohibited delicacies which our own family was denied." She also made sure that she never served meat on Fridays when his college pals joined the family for dinner. In the years to come these same Irish Catholic friends attended Kaplan's wedding at the East Midwood Jewish Center. Having studied at Holy Cross, he surmised that "besides making me a more sincere Jew," the university and its faculty "did a little something to make my classmates better and more intelligent Catholics."[37]

Most Jewish students who attended these Catholic institutions opted for the professional schools rather than the undergraduate colleges, although some did pursue bachelor's degrees, attending such predominantly Irish institutions as Notre Dame, home of the "Fighting Irish," DePaul and Loyola in Chicago, and Providence College (PC). In 1920 Samuel Lockett enrolled in St. Francis College in Brooklyn, founded by Brother John McMahon, a Franciscan, and the brothers who ran the school, impressed by his academic distinction, recommended him for a scholarship to study medicine at University College Dublin. Returning eventually to Brooklyn, he served for a quarter century as the physician for the college's football team. Notre Dame's student newspaper reported on Jewish students as early as 1878, before it had established any professional schools, noting that the Jews had been celebrating their "Pasch" holiday (obviously Pesach, or Passover). In the 1890s a Jewish student donned a Notre Dame jersey to play on the gridiron, and the team's famous coach, Knute Rockne, recruited a handful of Jewish players.

Most of Notre Dame's Jewish students had grown up in South Bend as children of local immigrant shopkeepers and, like Abraham Plotkin, who eventually became a rabbi, lived at home while attending college. Because Plotkin lived in a city with no public institution to turn to, Notre Dame worked for him. So too Milton Cohen and Milton Borenstein, in-town Jewish students who attended Boston College in the 1930s, may have escaped some potentially unpleasant encounters that dorm life might have sparked. At all these schools existing records point to little interpersonal friction at the time, and the Jewish alumni's continued loyalty in postgraduation years suggests that few or no unpleasantries flared.

The story of Jewish students at Providence College, founded in 1917 by the Dominican order and administered jointly with the Diocese of Providence, followed that arc. It was created consciously as a local institution, and as such it addressed the aspirations of the rising generation of sons of the Irish Catholic working class. Its Irish founders, including Bishop Matthew Harkins, the child of Irish immigrants, and its trustees and supporters did not specifically define the school as Irish in writing, but by listing "Italian" students as a separate category from "Catholic" in official records, the college manifested its Irish core mission.

The handful of Jewish students at Providence, a small institution, tended like most of its student body to live at home, and most Jews enrolled in the college's preprofessional programs. A growing number in the 1930s, a high point of Jewish enrollment, attended the four-year undergraduate college. Max Novogroski, from the nearby town of Westerly, came to PC in 1922, opted for the premedical track, and benefited from the fact that the school exempted him from the mandatory daily class in "Christian doctrine."

Over the course of the 1920s the number of Jewish students rose yearly, and school records show that they hailed from the city's working-class neighborhoods and a few surrounding towns. They attended in almost exact proportion to the city's Jewish population. The school was located in the North End, close to where most of the immigrant Jews lived, which was surely seen as an asset.

A few Jewish students participated in PC's extracurricular activities, and a small number showed up on the roster of players on the school's football team, called the "Friars" in a nod to its Dominican auspices.

Low tuition meant that going to college did not take too big a bite from the incomes of struggling immigrant families, and living at home meant incurring no extra costs for room and board. One alumnus, Jerome Tesler of the class of 1942, recalled that "Within a few days after my application to Providence, I received, 'yes you can be a student here.' I think my mother was dancing with joy, and my father, of course, was pleasantly surprised because the tuition was within his means at the time. . . . The monies were kind of tight, and I think my father was quite happy that Providence College accepted me."[38]

Tesler arrived at PC during the 1930s, the highest point of its Jewish enrollment, when Jews made up almost 11 percent of the student body. Their numbers grew steadily that decade, when its president, Rev. Lorenzo McCarthy, embarked on a modernization campaign, striving to align the school closer to other American colleges, a fact that may explain the jump in Jewish student enrollment. Some PC Jewish students of the 1920s and 1930s, the years of McCarthy's presidency, who became doctors and dentists, expressed their gratitude by contributing money to a special fund in his honor. Their names, Paul Cohen, 1934; Hymen D. Stein, 1935; and Theodore Gorfine, 1943, still appear on a plaque in Harkins Hall, on the exterior of a building adorned with statues of saints.

Jewish alumni of these years recalled little anti-Semitism. Oral histories claimed that Jewish students felt fine at PC. One informant who attended right after McCarthy's presidency emphatically responded years later when asked if any students or faculty commented negatively about the Jewish presence: "No. No one said 'Jew' to you or nothing. In the public school they would, but not in Providence College."[39] He noted that PC had no quotas, unlike the more prestigious neighboring institution, Brown University.

Providence College, like DePaul and Fordham, St. John's, Loyola, and others, provided opportunities for professional advancement, something meted out to Jewish graduates stingily at other schools. This overshadowed whatever negative feelings these children of eastern European Jewish immigrants may have harbored about Christianity in general or Catholicism in particular. As they probably saw it, the fact that these schools existed to serve Catholic students, educating them and keeping them close to the faith of their parents, did not hamper their chance to learn. Jewish students did not, at the time or looking back, say anything negative about being taught by Catholic clergy wearing their clerical collars, who made up half of all instructors. They expressed no sense of discomfort about studying in rooms with crucifixes prominently hung on the walls.

Despite the all-pervasive Catholicism, shaped by Irish American culture, Jewish students showed up in large numbers. These schools left their marks on the history of America's Jews, particularly as they provided venues for the pursuit of professional education. Their schools of law, pharmacy, and commerce fostered the trajectory of young Jews from immigrant homes into income-generating, respectable work.

They also benefited from the fact that in early twentieth-century decades, precisely as the children of Jewish immigrants embarked on their professional educations, most schools did not require a student to have an undergraduate college degree; the less "elite" the institution, the less likely it was to require one.

Rather, young people, beneficiaries of public education and striving for professional work, could go directly from secondary school to professional programs. They could also transfer credits from two-year prelaw, premedical, or predentistry programs, like so many who had attended Providence College did.

Many urban Catholic institutions offered degrees—aside from those in medicine—through night schools, enabling students to work by day. Jewish aspirants seized these opportunities. Henry Monsky, the son of Orthodox immigrant Jewish parents who had moved to Omaha, ultimately became the president of B'nai B'rith, founded Omaha's Community Chest, partnered in a local law firm with an Irish Catholic classmate, Donald J. Burke, and became a close confidant of Father Edward Flanagan, founder of Boys Town; he started out at Creighton's night law school in 1909. Monsky worked for his stepbrother's jewelry and silverware business and attended classes when the store closed. The next year he switched to day classes and immediately became active in student life. He graduated first in his class in 1912. His loyalty to Creighton persisted for a lifetime; he chaired some of its largest fundraising campaigns, and, in appreciation, the school invited him to give the commencement address in 1925.

Monsky's experiences at Creighton differed little from those of many other Jewish alumni of Catholic professional schools, both in terms of their professional training and their subsequent careers. Despite rising anti-Semitism and the Depression, Jews experienced a steady move out of immigrant occupations toward nonmanual work, and out of the older city neighborhoods to newer and nicer ones they could now afford. The young and the American-born led the way.

Soaring rates of education, particularly focused on training for the professions, made a huge difference in American Jewish life, and so many opted to study law, medicine, dentistry, and pharmacy as vehicles to take them up and out, aided by the Catholic institutions founded to serve the sons of the Irish American working class but that took Jews in. These institutions had an enormous impact on their lives and, by extension, on American Jewish history.

The largely unacknowledged history of two examples of Catholic schools, almost exclusively Irish in terms of origins, administration, and student body—Fordham University in the Bronx and St. John's in Brooklyn—stand out. In the largest Jewish city in the United States, within the classrooms, laboratories, lecture halls, and moot courtrooms (where law students got the chance to practice the skills of their future profession) of these two Catholic schools, thousands upon thousands of Jews from the working class made their way into the professions.

Let us look at Fordham first. As of 1939, 6.2 percent of all practicing Jewish lawyers in New York City held Fordham degrees, with the number graduating that year from the Jesuit school in the Bronx larger than that of any other law school in the city other than Brooklyn Law. The figure situates this one school squarely within the fabric of New York's Jewish life. That "Fordham" automatically popped up in Harry Roskolenko's consciousness when thinking about law school testified to its place in the lives of ordinary Jews as they looked to the future.

The career trajectories of the legions of Jewish students who attended Fordham University School of Law offer a window into its importance. A list of their names and descriptions of their subsequent professional careers and civic activities would take reams of pages and would illuminate many tens of thousands of life stories. A few from those years have to suffice. A. David Benjamin, a Brooklynite who commuted to Fordham, graduating in 1919, became active in Republican politics. After years in private practice, he became a judge. Max Bloom, a Bronx native, graduated in 1931 and, after a career as a labor activist, served as secretary to two different New York State Supreme Court justices and helped to create New York's Liberal Party. David Edelstein attended Fordham as an undergraduate, then received his Fordham law degree in 1931. By 1945, after serving as an attorney in the Claims Division of the US Department of Justice, he became the assistant US attorney for the Southern District of New York. Irving Kaufman came to the Bronx campus by way of Brooklyn, and while on campus he achieved some distinction for his outstanding performance in Christian doctrine class, earning him the moniker "Pope Kaufman." A classmate of Edelstein's, he ascended to the bench as a judge of the US District Court for the Southern District in 1949 and achieved notoriety as the judge in the case of Ethel and Julius Rosenberg. Countless other Jewish graduates from Fordham stepped into law firms; government offices; city, state, and federal courts; as well as local politics from the 1920s onward.

But few achieved the fame of Louis Lefkowitz, raised on the Lower East Side. Having attended Fordham Law's night division between 1921 and 1925, he pursued politics, serving terms in the state assembly. Lefkowitz became a judge and then held, for twenty-two years, the post of attorney general of the State of New York. New Yorkers in decades to come might recognize his name from the imposing edifice of the Louis Lefkowitz State Office Building in Lower Manhattan, while at Fordham his name remains connected to an award for the best article in *The Fordham Urban Law Journal,* a publication made possible by his gift to his alma mater. In his many public pronouncements, Lefkowitz thanked the school, praising it for giving "me my start in life. I always referred to Fordham wherever I went."[40]

So too 1926 graduate Lou Stein made a sizable gift to Fordham to create the Stein Center for Law and Ethics, and along with Lefkowitz he fulfilled several of the goals envisioned by the law school's Irish Catholic administrators as they rolled out a welcome mat for Jewish students. These students, like any others, paid tuition. They went out into the world, made names for themselves in the profession, locally and nationally, and spoke well of Fordham as an institution that, as they described it, put into practice American rhetoric about equality and inclusion. These alumni gave back to it, enhancing its reputation, serving it, and providing ample financial gifts.

How did Jewish students fare in this overwhelmingly Irish Catholic environment? Although top administrators, all Jesuits, may have worried about the increasing number of Jewish students, Jewish students interviewed at the time or reminiscing in years to come did not recall hostility or the existence of a chilly environment.[41] Most lauded the school for its openness. An anonymous informant quoted in *Christians Only* told the writers that Jewish students represented 25 percent of the total. "The relationship between Jewish and non-Jewish students is pleasant, amiable, I might even say cordial. The professors are absolutely fair and impartial without even the slightest trace of anti-semitic prejudice." The interviewee continued: "In the one course taught by a priest, the Jewish students on the whole received much higher ratings than the non-Jewish." Jewish sources, defense agencies, and the press, ever vigilant about prejudice, had nothing to say on the matter.[42]

They also would have had no reason to complain about Fordham's College of Pharmacy, which opened in 1912 during the presidency of Thomas J. McCluskey, then closed its doors in 1921. Offering a three-year program of study, it enrolled so many Jewish students that within a few years they made up the majority. It had the distinction of being administered from its inception by a Jewish dean, Jacob "Jack" Diner. When officials from the Jesuit central office in Rome complained about the inappropriateness of having a Jew run a college within a Catholic university, McCluskey stood his ground, refusing to replace Diner and defending him as an outstanding head of the school.

Legions of Jewish students earned their pharmacy degrees at Fordham under Diner's tenure and beyond, moving into a respected profession that served the public in very practical ways and brought with it the chance for economic success.

In subsequent decades Jewish graduates of the College of Pharmacy as well as of the law school served as trustees of their respective institutions, further cementing relationships between them, the schools, and their fellow alumni. Whether elevated to the boards so that they could raise funds among other Jews, to demonstrate the schools' openness to Jews as opposed to the quotas that shut them out elsewhere, or as genuine acknowledgments that particular individuals had much good counsel to offer, sitting on these governing bodies constituted small parts of an emerging picture of Jewish integration in the United States facilitated by an institution deeply Catholic in mission and Irish in constituency.

So too the experiences of Jews at St. John's University in Brooklyn, in its law and pharmacy schools as well as the School of Commerce, now the College of Business, bore witness to liberal admissions, high levels of comfort, and the participation of Jews in the institutional life of a predominantly Irish and utterly Catholic school. As with other Catholic universities, while St. John's did not declare itself Irish, individuals with Irish surnames predominated as students, top administrators, including presidents, and trustees in the decades through the 1930s. Starting out in 1870 up until 1929, thirteen out of seventeen presidents had typically Irish names, and in 1929, as just one example, the five most important university administrators, all Vincentians, bore the surnames Cloonan, Reilly, Walsh, Ryan, and O'Grady.

With the university so firmly in the hands of these men, Jewish students applied, received admission, and studied at St. John's in a variety of professional programs. By 1939, for example, 10.7 percent of all Jewish lawyers in New York had studied at St. John's, only a decade after the law school's founding. As with Fordham, its low tuition, urban location, and availability of night classes made it an ideal setting for young Jewish women and men that were eager to move up in the world.[43]

The Jewish presence at St. John's can be seen in the statistics, but it can also be demonstrated in the words of at least one Irish Catholic student who studied side by side with Jewish classmates. Paul O'Dwyer came to New York from County Mayo in 1925, arriving with no exposure to Jews or Judaism before setting foot at St. John's law school a year later. O'Dwyer, later a New York City politician and lawyer, recalled that the school made "a good business" by capturing "a few honest dollars from the raft of young Jewish students, the children of East Side immigrants who had crossed the East River into Brooklyn and were hungering for a legal education." O'Dwyer, who would go on to collaborate closely with Jewish associates in liberal politics and progressive legal causes, overestimated the number, claiming that "Eighty-five percent of my class was Jewish and hungering and so too were the several Irish Americans and Italian Americans."[44]

Jews showed up in robust numbers as students and also as faculty, and their presence, rather than being obscured because of not being Catholic, loomed large. Maurice Finkelstein served on the original faculty of the St. John's School of Law in 1925, cofounding and advising the *St. John's Law Review.* The son of an Orthodox rabbi, he shared with his brother, Louis Finkelstein, chancellor of the Jewish Theological Seminary, a commitment to interfaith work. Harold Kleinsinger taught chemistry and physics to the students in the pharmacy school in the 1920s and 1930s. In the 1930s various volumes of the College of Pharmacy *Cosdamian Yearbook* opened with words of greeting from Kleinsinger, accompanied on the facing page with a morally uplifting statement, "The Oath and Prayer of Maimonides," composed by the eponymous twelfth-century Torah scholar, philosopher, and physician.

Jewish students established a highly visible presence on campus. In school publications, they made the fact of their Jewishness bold and prominent. As early as 1912 Jewish students at St. John's law school formed a chapter of Omega Chi, "the oldest Jewish legal society in New York City." *Res Gestae,* the school's yearbook, announced that the organization "has proven itself to be a worthy influence in shaping the character of men." In the early 1930s the campus newspaper serving the students in the business school, the *St. John's Analyst,* reported that a chapter of the national Avukah Society had been created to "promote the ideas and work of Zionism among American Jewish academic youth on the basis of cultural and practical activity." Subsequent issues reported that the society held meetings to discuss "Jewish problems" and activities to foster "the Hebrew language and literature, Jewish culture and tradition, to the student who feels the necessity for thus strengthening his Jewish background." Female Jewish students at St. John's appeared in the 1934 yearbook with a brief history of Gamma Sigma Tau, "the first Jewish Sorority in the School of Commerce," founded in 1929. Two years later the Jewish women studying law at St. John's formed a chapter of Tau Epsilon Delta, "a secret order composed of women of the Jewish faith," which was limited to "pre-law students, law students, and graduates of law schools of recognized standing." The roster of women who belonged to what seemed to be not so very secret a society included individuals who served on the law review, the moot court, and its women's club, an organization under the leadership of Jewish female students but open for all women studying law. Several of the women who belonged to Gamma Sigma Tau also listed their campus activities as members and leaders of the Justice Brandeis Society.

The existence of these Jewish organizations at St. John's and the degree to which their members felt free to proclaim their Jewish presence on campus testified to those members' high comfort level. They learned in what appeared to have been a congenial environment for Jews.

If the St. John's administrators behind the scenes were worried about the campus becoming not Catholic enough—or even possibly "too Jewish"—Jewish students seemed unaware either at the time or retrospectively. If some of the Irish students evinced hostility to their Jewish classmates, it garnered no attention in Jewish sources, which instead pointed out an undisguised Jewish presence with a deep sense of gratitude for the educations the students received, which would set them on a course toward professional achievement and further integration into American society.

One Jewish alumnus, Harold Cobin of the Class of 1927, shared in March 1938 in the alumni magazine his recollection of being a Jewish student on a Catholic campus and his understanding of what that experience meant to him in the present, a piece entitled "Democracy at St. John's." Looking back he recalled that he been very self-conscious about being "different," causing him to be "guarded . . . careful not to say or do anything which might possibly be a reflection on my race." While never shedding his sense of differentness, since a Jew on a Catholic campus had to be an anomaly by definition, he described his St. John's years as when "I became one with the others, making lasting friendships which I shall treasure throughout life."[45] He lauded St. John's as "an institution predominantly, in fact almost solely, Catholic" but profoundly "catholic" in its teaching and in extracurricular life, distinguishing between the name of the religion and the broader meaning of "catholic" as universal.

Cobin shared with his readers that he had run into some serious personal difficulties in his senior year and risked not graduating. But Father Ryan stepped in, "to the extent of taking over personally the straightening out of my affairs and insuring my graduation." This, to Cobin, personified the institution's "democratic spirit."

It is worth highlighting that Cobin's words appeared in a moment of deep existential crisis for the Jewish people around the world. Horrific news came from across the Atlantic. Nazi Germany had just annexed Austria, unleashing in its wake widespread brutality against the Jews; Jews from Germany and Austria, stripped of their citizenship, desperately sought places of refuge. Those events inspired Cobin to look back to "those years at St. John's." He wrote that memories of his student years "often recur in my thoughts these days when I read of European affairs and the sufferings of my people on what should today be called 'the Dark Continent.'" He asserted that "I owe those Vincentian priests who showed me how men can live and progress peacefully together despite differences in belief . . . I utter a fervent prayer that their work go on apace . . . that the world become *truly* safe for Democracy, 'with Liberty and Justice for all.'"[46]

Cobin employed those words derived from the Pledge of Allegiance, an aspirational credo of American citizenship memorized by millions of Jewish children from immigrant homes and taught to them by countless Irish American teachers, to thank Father Ryan and the Vincentians at St. John's for giving him "a poise, a calm self-assurance . . . the distinguishing mark of a college man."

Cobin extolled the now historic Irish-Jewish synthesis he experienced on a Catholic college campus, but just a few months earlier words of a different sort surfaced at another such school. A Jewish student, "D.J." at Providence College, wrote a revealing letter to the editor in the campus paper, *The Cowl*. He protested the newspaper editor's call for the United States to field a team at the upcoming Berlin Olympics, which Adolf Hitler would be presiding over. D.J. wrote as a Jew, declaring to his fellow students, "I am a Hebrew and I feel strongly that Hitler and his government has demonstrated so vile an attitude towards my race . . . and so un-American a treatment of visitors, that he and all that he stands for should be rebuked." To his overwhelmingly Catholic readers he depicted Hitler as a foe of their religion, too. Hitler, the young man noted, believes that he "can legislate out of existence the Eternal God," and that he "wants to supplant the great Christ with pagan Siegfried, simply because Christ was a Semite and a Jew." He ended his letter with a call: "Keep our sportsmen home."[47]

Not swayed, the editor wrote in response, "Seriously, do the Jews of Germany want us to go over?" Neither the anti-Nazi letter nor the pro–Olympic participation response (at least) was printed in the paper. But the clash between them reflected a collision taking place in late 1930s America between Irish

Americans, the door openers, and the Jews, who had needed and long appreciated those actions that provided them with American education and access to the benefits of American cultural citizenship.

6

In the Face of Coughlin and Hitler,
Still Standing Up for the Jews

The student who urged readers of *The Cowl* to support a boycott of the Berlin Olympics wrote as a Jew, angered at the Nazi persecution of the Jews. The newspaper's (likely) Catholic editor at the predominantly Irish school, Providence College, argued with equal fervor that the United States had no business in the matter.

They could not have been further apart in the last years of the 1930s, with Hitler's Germany following a steady course of removing Jews from public life, excoriating them, stripping them of their citizenship, and putting their lives in danger. From 1935 on, after the passage of the Nuremberg Laws, they experienced one humiliation after another, losing rights, property, freedom, and the right to life.

As the Jewish letter writer saw it, Americans of goodwill had an obligation to stop Hitler. As the editor saw it, Hitler's actions did not concern Americans. The two irreconcilable views separated Jews and Irish Catholics.

Yet at the same time, St. John's University's alumni magazine published Cobin's article, written as a Jew's homage to his alma mater, attesting to this Catholic school's welcome to him and other Jews. By providing a safe place for his people, he testified, St. John's fostered American democracy.

These contradictory stories are both emblematic of the Irish-Jewish state of affairs in the 1930s, both articulating views about the nation, the larger world, and each other.

Yet despite this and the wide appeal of the virulent and incendiary anti-Semite Father Charles Coughlin, who helped spark a high volume of anti-Jewish rhetoric more broadly in Irish American communities, Irish Americans also continued to speak out and act as defenders of the Jews, both at home and in the very dangerous big world.

They did so in ways that they considered in their own interests. They did so, as always, to showcase their service to the nation and their tolerance toward others, and as a sincere rebuke of those in their own communities who participated in the frenzy of anti-Semitism in America, which parroted Nazi talk abroad.

Irish Catholics in the United States experiencing those Depression years felt themselves diminished, stung, like all working people, from the economic disaster. Their reduced proportion of the population in the big cities dislodged them from their once-prominent place as the premier white European ethnic group, which had dominated urban life for generations. The eastern and southern European immigrants and their children who had arrived at the beginning of the century now outnumbered them. Institutions and neighborhood strongholds, once theirs, shifted to others. New York City elected its first Italian American mayor, Fiorello La Guardia, in 1933, beating Tammany. It never regained its dominance, nor did the Irish machines in other cities. In city after city where the Irish machines had long dispensed immediate relief, the agencies of the New Deal federal government stepped in, upending the old bargain the Irish politicians had long made with ordinary people, regularly trading votes for services.

Other changes in the 1930s likewise heralded a decline in Irish power. Jewish women and men took over the classrooms of New York City's schools and seized the teachers' union, using it to reflect their values. The great momentum in the labor movement of the 1930s came from the founding of the Congress of Industrial Organizations, in which the Irish showed little leadership. The momentum for the CIO came from John Lewis of the United Mine Workers, of Welsh parentage; the German American Walter Reuther of the automobile workers; the Scottish-born Philip Murray of the steelworkers; and Sidney Hillman, David Dubinsky, and Max Zaritsky, all Jews from the needle trades. While present in the CIO, Irish American labor activists played only supporting rather than leading roles and had little visibility or voice in forging New Deal labor policy.

Dropped down a few pegs on the domestic scene, these deeply Catholic Irish Americans furthermore considered their church abroad under vicious attack in the late 1920s and 1930s. They mobilized to defend it from the left, its mortal enemy. The anticlericalism of the revolutionary government in Mexico and the ensuing civil war between it and Catholic activists ended in 1929 with an estimated ninety thousand Cristeros, advocates for Christ and the church, dead. Later that decade the armed struggle in Spain between the government of the elected Republicans, secular liberals, and the church-backed rebels led by fascist Francisco Franco escalated Irish American hatred of leftists. Franco derived much of his support from the devout, who were horrified by the systematic stripping of lands and political authority from the church by the newly elected Spanish government.

Catholic periodicals around the United States reported in detail on the murders of priests and nuns at the hands of the Republicans in what had long been considered a Catholic fortress. Catholics in Europe and America prayed for the church and expended their political resources for this sacred cause. As the majority of Irish Americans, fervent anti-communists, saw it, liberals in the United States applauded these developments. They stood by idly while devout Catholics suffered.

Liberal Americans, even those uninfected by anti-Catholic zealotry, increasingly criticized the Catholic Church as a bastion of illiberalism. They argued that it had too much power in America, impeding free expression and choice of non-Catholics.

In 1934, for example, Cincinnati's archbishop John T. McNicholas, born in Ireland's County Mayo, created the Catholic National Legion of Decency and positioned it to wield a heavy hand in what movies Americans could watch. Across the country people flocked in the millions to Hollywood films, finding the shows on the big screen particularly attractive during the Depression, when a few pennies provided relief from stress. What they saw in their theaters did not reflect their tastes alone but rather had to conform to the Legion's Catholic standards of what might be too sexual, too risqué, too immoral. The Legion's actions raised the hackles of many Americans who felt strongly that such a body had no right to censor and control Americans' access to entertainment and ideas. Additionally, Jews owned many of the big movie studios, produced a large number of the films, wrote screenplays, and operated movie houses, and the Legion's assault on the movies further opened a chasm between the two groups.

In the 1930s Irish Americans began as never before to focus their public rhetoric on the Jewish question. In publications and pronouncements, in church bulletins and magazines, sermons and books, many conflated the categories communist and Jewish, claiming the two synonymous, a rhetoric that slid easily into depicting Jews as enemies.

This was an exaggeration to be sure, but a small yet visible minority of American Jews did endorse communism, valorizing the Soviet Union. They did so because early on after coming to power the Soviets banned anti-Semitism, and during the civil war following the Bolshevik Revolution the Soviet army rescued countless Jews facing escalating violence at the hands of defenders of the old regime. After Mussolini came to power in Italy and Hitler in Germany, communists took up the fight against fascism on the streets, in their publications, and on college campuses, leading the struggle. That, too, won over Jews, fearful of the rising Nazi menace.

The attraction of some Jews to communism transcended gratitude to the Soviet Union. Jewish adherents to the communist cause concluded that capitalism had to be undone. Only communism could solve poverty and inequality. They scoffed at the standard political parties, found American socialism weak and pathetic, and considered the Jewish-led labor unions to be tools of the bosses rather than true advocates for the workers. They saw the Soviet Union as an exemplar of progress and a bulwark against fascism, deserving their admiration and solidarity.

Jewish communists in America, like their counterparts elsewhere, supported clubs, publications, theaters, youth groups, summer camps, and schools. Yiddish banners fluttered at communist rallies. The *Morgen Freiheit,* a self-declared communist newspaper founded in 1922, sold tens of thousands of copies daily in the 1920s and 1930s.

Though they made up the single largest grouping within the Communist Party of the United States, Jewish communists remained a small minority among American Jews and had little influence in communal organizations. Most Jewish institutions, particularly unions and other socialist-oriented groups like the popular Workmen's Circle, expelled communists from leadership positions.

But Irish Americans lumped together the minority of Jewish communists with the far larger number of socialists—bitter enemies of the communists—as well as the vast majority of Jews who embraced liberalism, counting themselves among the staunchest devotees of the New Deal and Franklin Roosevelt. But all of these untold numbers of Irish Americans saw only that the Jewish left had stepped back and let the communists in Mexico and Spain destroy their church.

While Irish voters remained true to the Democratic Party in the 1930s and, like Jews, contributed to the New Deal coalition, fissures between the two groups began to shake the foundations of a previously sturdy mutually useful political alliance. Jews broke ranks in the 1933 mayoral election in New York City and tipped the scales for the Republican candidate, La Guardia.

La Guardia had hoped that this might happen, and his campaign, to win over Jews, released an article published in 1915 in *The Catholic World* by Joseph McKee, one of the candidates running for mayor on the recently created Recovery Party ticket. Tammany had endorsed Democratic mayor John P. O'Brien, who had taken the post in a special election in 1932, which caused McKee, a Tammany stalwart in past years, to bolt and form a new ad hoc party so he could run.

A former teacher at the heavily Jewish DeWitt Clinton High School in the Bronx, McKee had in that long-forgotten article praised the intellect of his Jewish students. They, he wrote to his fellow New York Catholics, who do not "belong to us, will be the lawyers, the doctors, the educators, the professional men of the coming generation." He chided Catholics for not sending their sons in larger numbers to public high schools like De-Witt Clinton, opting instead for lesser quality sectarian schools. Of the five thousand boys at the school, McKee enumerated, "hardly 10 per cent are Christians, and it is a rare thing even to hear an Irish Catholic name!" No wonder, he predicted, the Jews will overtake us.

But McKee sealed his fate with Jewish voters when they read

the republished article. He lamented that his quick-minded, intellectually sharp Jewish students, bound for great things, sadly had gravitated toward socialism, having cast off "the obligations of the orthodox Judaism of their fathers and mothers." The boys replaced Judaism with a politics "whose ambition is the furtherance of Socialistic dogma."[1]

A barely noticed piece in 1915, in 1933 it offended many New York Jewish voters who read it as anti-Semitic, not so unlike the rhetoric running rampant in Europe. The election in New York took place just after Germans voted Hitler into office. He had come to power using similar tactics, warning that Jews would supersede real Germans (and that these Jews supported the left).

By connecting Jews to communism, and from there identifying them as a foe to be defeated, such rhetoric ushered in a new era in Irish-Jewish interactions, one seemingly far different than the mutually useful cooperation of earlier decades.

During the 1930s, the unmistakable chords of anti-Semitism rumbled through the land, and Irish American voices joined in. Father Charles Coughlin became the chief apostle of the creed of Jews as communists and Jews as enemies of good, hardworking Americans. He became the darling of the Irish American masses. His weekly radio broadcasts and publications had begun earlier in the decade, but by the mid-1930s they became monomaniacally anti-Jewish, anti-communist, and additionally, anti–New Deal.

Certainly many others—non-Irish and non-Catholics—spewed forth the same ugly defamations of the Jewish people as well. Demagogues like William Dudley Pelley and his Silver Shirts, and Gerald Winrod, dubbed the "Jayhawk Nazi" because he hailed from Kansas, dipped into the identical rhetorical trove. Winrod's newspaper, *The Defender,* reached hundreds of thousands, and in it and on the lecture circuit, he fed his believers a steady poisonous diet about Jews as agents of Satan, apostles of Stalinist communism.

American Jews fretted about them all, but Coughlin mattered most. He had a bigger public persona, appearing on the cover of *Time* in 1934. He hobnobbed with many Irish American notables, including Joseph P. Kennedy, whom Roosevelt nominated to the Securities and Exchange Commission and then the US ambassadorship to Great Britain in 1938.

Much of Coughlin's early support, including from prominent Irish Americans like Kennedy and Boston's mayor James Michael Curley, predated the priest's turn against Roosevelt and against the Jews, but those relationships had already been forged, giving Coughlin a stature and respectability Pelley and Winrod never commanded.

Before 1936, for the most part Jews had nothing to say about Coughlin and his broadcasts, paying him little attention. At that time, his attacks were focused on the businesses that had brought about the Depression and caused so much suffering. But his break with the New Deal, simultaneous with his slide into blatant and constant anti-Semitism, via his radio broadcasts, beamed from Royal Oak, Michigan, and his rotogravure magazine, *Social Justice,* launched that year, elevated him to their greatest American enemy. His reproduction of *The Protocols of the Elders of Zion* in *Social Justice* connected Coughlin to Hitler and his increasingly powerful campaign against the Jews.

Coughlin's talk against Jews transcended ugly words, themselves frightening enough for a people on edge. Several thousand of his followers, mostly Irish and German Americans, joined the Christian Front, an organization founded in 1938. They harassed Jews, beating them up in the streets, and attacked attendees at communist and socialist meetings. They hawked their publications in front of Catholic parishes on Sundays in

Irish neighborhoods in Boston, New York, Chicago, and elsewhere. Their presence seemed to disturb none of the faithful
who went to and from Mass.

As Germany moved against its neighboring countries and
escalated its campaign of terror against the Jews, Coughlin
and the heavily Irish Catholic Christian Front told an American public wary of joining any military action against Germany
that only Jews wanted to drag America into a European war.
They wanted to put American lives at risk for the sole purpose
of helping Jews.

Hardly alone among Americans to oppose United States involvement on the grounds that it would serve Jewish interests
only, Coughlin's voice contributed much to that descant. Echoed
by the student editor of *The Cowl,* antiwar sentiment rumbled
through Irish American communities, too. Not an expression of
pacifism, this talk rather reflected the torrents of anti-Semitism
that Coughlin helped stir up.

Even after the United States finally entered the war in 1941,
Coughlinites persisted in blaming the war on the Jews, and although the vast majority of Irish American men—perhaps even
that student from Providence College who edited *The Cowl*—
donned uniforms, manifesting unalloyed patriotism to the United
States, the antiwar discourse around Irish neighborhoods and institutions did not die, still insisting that Jews alone wanted the
war.

After the United States declared war, Coughlin persisted in
lauding Hitler as the best bulwark against communism. Even
Irish Americans who did not listen to Coughlin—those who
never harmed any Jews or even uttered anti-Semitic words—
often considered communism the greatest threat that stalked
the world. The strategic alliance between the United States
and the Soviet Union complicated their feelings about the war.
While Coughlin was forced to retreat from the public eye in

1942, his opposition to the war, to communism, and to Jews did not fully evaporate.

That Ireland remained neutral while other nations fought may have likewise contributed something to keeping alive pockets of Irish American support of Coughlinism, even after he left public life, not of his own volition. Eamon de Valera, Ireland's president, infamously paid a condolence call at the German Legation upon news of Hitler's death in 1945. His decision to sign the memorial book for Hitler inspired little outrage among Irish Americans, although Kerry-born labor leader Mike Quill, head of the New York Transport Workers Union, minced no words in damning de Valera, saying that by expressing sympathy for Hitler, the taoiseach had stooped so low, doing something that even "no English enemy" would have done.[2]

American Jews, however, even the most ardent critics of the Soviet Union among them, saw and lived the era differently. The horrific turn of events in Europe, starting in 1933 with Hitler's ascent to power, could not have been more ominous. Anti-Semitism, never completely absent from political life in Europe, spread quickly as the dominant force across the continent. Back there, the places where they had come from and where so many still had family and friends, Jews moved along a path from citizenship to demonization, dehumanization, and mass extermination. In those back-home places, whole Jewish communities were disappearing.

Hatred of Nazism and anxiety over the fate of the Jews pervaded American Jewry. Even with the Christian Front nearby, they were themselves quite safe, but they read daily in Jewish and general newspapers about the ghettos, and how Jews had lost their livelihoods, properties, citizenship, and rights. They could see pictures in the press of Jews wearing the mandatory Star of David, which they had been forced to sew on to their clothing. They heard in synagogues, community meetings, and during Yiddish radio programs about forced relocations. As the war raged on, they slowly learned details about the staggering death tolls of Jews just like themselves—women, men, and children in the millions who had succumbed to starvation, disease, gas chambers, and mass shootings in forests and ravines.

This motivated them to act, and despite their lack of power, internal divisions, and small numbers, they attempted to do what they could to help from the safety of their American space. They put a high priority on enlisting assistance, real and symbolic, from their non-Jewish neighbors willing to join them in awakening the public and the government to the dangers posed by pro-Nazi groups at home, to the emerging cataclysm on the world stage, and to the imperative of rescuing imperiled Jews.

They realized, much to their chagrin, that they had little power to do anything meaningful about what went on in Germany and then the rest of Europe. They understood with frustration that they had essentially no clout to affect immigration policy as a means of rescue for Jews.

But as for pro-Nazi, anti-Semitic groups in their own communities, they saw an opportunity to make a difference. As Jews saw it, the Christian Front and others like it at work in Irish neighborhoods, such as the Christian Mobilizers, differed little from the Nazis. If given a chance, these domestic terrorists would move America closer and closer to the German model. At a monster rally held by the Christian Front at New York's Madison Square Garden after Kristallnacht, banners fluttered in the air proclaiming, WAIT UNTIL HITLER GETS TO AMERICA.[3]

These groups had to be stopped, and for this, Jews turned to non-Jews, Irish Americans among them, whom they considered perfect allies. They reached out to and welcomed all who would help, but Irish Catholics had a particular role to play as Jewish activists crafted their strategy.

With their political visibility and demonstrative Catholicism, they could not be accused of acting in self-interest when speaking out against Nazism and for the Jews. That they shared ethnic and religious ties with Coughlin made them especially attractive partners in this project that was so important to American Jews. Given the anti-Semitism percolating among Irish Americans, American Jews involved in shaping a response to the domestic and global crises of the 1930s believed that Irish American participation could do particular good. Having notable Irish Americans and their publications advocate for Jews offered a potential route to disarming the Coughlinites who held such sway in many Irish parishes. And not incidentally, Irish Americans had been speaking out for Jewish causes since the latter part of the nineteenth century.

Irish Americans might, Jews hoped, be moved when Al Smith—the "Happy Warrior," their hero so viciously pilloried by Protestant America in 1928—took up their cause. He did so numerous times during the 1930s and then during the war. Jewish community leaders turned to him to advocate for refugees or to serve as a channel of communication with the pope. Smith appeared repeatedly at public gatherings protesting Nazi persecution of Jews, and his name was regularly seen on documents expressing outrages being perpetrated in Germany and elsewhere at the hands of the Third Reich.

They asked for more from Irish Americans, and they got it. When Samuel Dickstein, a Jewish Tammany Hall politician and congressman from Brooklyn, sought to form a special congressional committee to investigate un-American—that is, pro-Nazi—activity, he hesitated to serve as chair. For him to do so, he feared, would tarnish the committee, which would be seen as simply the efforts of a Jew working for the Jews. So he enlisted his colleague, Massachusetts congressman John McCormack, a close ally of Jewish causes, a darling of his Jewish constituents, and an Irish Catholic who represented a large Irish constituency, to front for him. McCormack, by working with Dickstein to expose Nazis, sent a message to the largely Irish women and men who sent him to Congress.

McCormack, whom Boston Jews sometimes called "Rabbi John," had been speaking out against Hitler and anti-Semitism even before Dickstein approached him. As soon as Hitler came to power, McCormack addressed the House, declaring, "Mr. Speaker, I may no longer refrain from expressing my condemnation of the policy being pursued by the present German Government, particularly as it applies to a ruthless agonizing of the Jews." Speaking as someone from a district with a robust minority of Jewish residents, he proclaimed to the Christian majority in Congress and the Catholic majority in his home district that "Christianity cannot ignore the debt she owes to Judaism." He continued that "I always have and always will" condemn "the attempt of the Hitler regime to destroy" the Jews.[4]

Irish support of the Jewish campaign against Nazism and its supporters in the United States at times played out in a number of states. In 1934 John J. Rafferty, with his Jewish colleague Sam Pesin, sponsored the Anti-Nazi Act in the New Jersey General Assembly, legislation designed to prohibit the dissemination of propaganda targeting any religious or ethnic group. Despite its dubious constitutionality, Pesin and Rafferty hoped that they could put the brakes on the spread of Nazi-printed materials in the Garden State. Irish-born representative Thomas Dorgan of Boston pushed the Massachusetts General Court to adopt a resolution in 1936 that stated that the body "views with alarm that certain inhabitants of Germany are being persecuted on account of their religious faith and nationality." When Baron Kurt von Tippelskirch, the German consul general in Boston, protested the state action, Governor James Michael Curley retorted that "right-thinking men and women the world over" found Nazism and Tippelskirch's government abhorrent. The

American Jewish Year Book hailed this as significant despite its purely symbolic import.[5]

Speaking out against Nazism and its Irish American henchmen occasionally put Irish politicians in potential conflict with others in their communities. William O'Dwyer, at the behest of Maximilian Moss, a Brooklyn Jewish community leader and political figure, lambasted anti-Jewish, pro-Nazi activities in 1939 when running for district attorney. He challenged his Irish constituents to disassociate themselves from the Christian Front. O'Dwyer recalled in his memoir that Moss, along with Nathaniel Kaplan and Eddie Silver, had come to him, seeking his help and impressing upon him that "the Jewish community, and particularly the younger ones, would no longer tolerate" the marauding violence of the Coughlin-inspired Front. O'Dwyer stumped through Irish Catholic neighborhoods and warned the crowds that, if elected, "hooliganism on the streets of Brooklyn would not be tolerated." Looking back at that campaign, O'Dwyer said that he "was pleasantly surprised when the vast majority applauded." He noted that while "I had not heard the last of the Christian Front . . . I succeeded in separating them from the Irish American community."[6]

Outside of the political sphere, Jewish organizers of anti-Nazi events made sure to include visibly Irish figures and give them prominent billing. When actor and singer Eddie Cantor organized a mass rally in Los Angeles's Shrine Auditorium in 1938, he asked Congressman Jerry J. O'Connell to share the stage with him.

Irish groups and notables did not necessarily have to wait for Jews to ask them to speak out against Nazism at home and abroad. New Jersey's Knights of Columbus condemned the activities taking place at the Nazi's Camp Nordland in Iliff, New Jersey, as "a harvest of religious intolerance in America." The Knights organized a mass meeting in November 1938 to protest

Kristallnacht, featuring the president of Seton Hall University, James F. Kelley, who condemned Nazism as a "leap backward over thousands of years" as he pleaded with his fellow Catholics to ignore the "anti-Semitic vilifications" flooding their mailboxes from "unknown" sources.[7]

One event particularly stands out as Irish Catholics joined in the chorus of outrage after Kristallnacht. It gave the organizers a chance to condemn Coughlin and his followers while expressing disgust at the events in Germany. On November 16, 1938, just a few weeks after the pogroms in Germany, Catholic bishops from across the country, along with Al Smith, broadcast over the competing NBC and CBS radio networks a program called "Catholic Protest Against Nazis." Covered on the front page of The New York Times the next day, the broadcast had been organized by the National Catholic Welfare Conference. NCWC leaders like Fathers John A. Ryan, Maurice Sheehy, and Edward Mooney had issued individual statements of protest as well, and all three attended rallies well before Kristallnacht, making the conference an obvious sponsor of the unprecedented radio program that brought the two networks together to speak out for the Jews and against the Nazis.

Whether too late or not, by May 1939 the formation of the Committee of Catholics to Fight Anti-Semitism (later Committee of Catholics for Human Rights) entered into the organizational life of Catholic communities to expose the yoked evils of Nazism and Coughlinism. It enlisted such Irish Catholic notables as the archbishop of Newark, New Jersey, Thomas J. Walsh, also founder of the Catholic War Veterans; Father John M. J. Quinn of the Bronx, New York; and Msgr. Edward J. Higgins of Queens, who joined John A. Ryan to "reach those who, contrary to the teachings of Christianity and the principles of democracy, are taking part, unfortunately, in spreading race and minority hatreds in the United States." With chapters in half a dozen cities, it not surprisingly got Al Smith to join and is-sue a statement that declared that "no Catholic can be an anti-Semite, because the Catholic Church teaches charity and love of your neighbor." To galvanize the Catholic public, it launched its newspaper, *The Voice*, on the opening day of the 1939 New York World's Fair, and by July of that year, over one hundred thousand copies went into circulation.[8]

The list of public statements articulated and political acts undertaken by Irish Americans condemning the Coughlinites at home and the war against the Jews abroad could fill pages. They did not emanate from a single source, but rather one by one they resounded in the public sphere, to be heard by other Catholics and other Americans, Jews included.

No monolithic Catholic Church could command its flock as to what to think and do, and Irish Catholic clergymen di-vided among themselves, as did Catholic publications and lay-people, speaking on their own as Catholics about Coughlin, the Jews, or developments in Europe. A not-insignificant number of Catholic priests and Catholic publications applauded him. The laypeople in Irish Catholic communities who approved of Coughlin's words against the Jews cannot be counted, and say-ing that they numbered in the millions would be no exaggera-tion.

Yet they alone did not represent all of the Irish Catholics in America. Those who joined the chorus against anti-Semitism did so in the name of Catholicism, as proud Irish Americans who considered their actions in defense of the Jews as a way to demonstrate their American values while defending their faith tradition and ethnic community.

Patrick Henry Callahan, for example, an industrialist and progressive Catholic layman, published a newsletter out of his hometown of Louisville, Kentucky, the *Callahan Correspondence*. Devoted to a range of causes, including support of Prohibition, by the late 1930s it mainly focused on exposing anti-Semitism. Highlighting the horrors of Nazi Germany to his readers, he took to the airwaves on Louisville's NBC station, challenging Coughlin and proclaiming that the priest did not speak for all Irish Catholics. As to why he focused so much on Coughlin and Nazism, Callahan explained to Rabbi Stephen Wise, "How long do you think it will be before the Catholics are in the frying pan again?"[9]

In a similar vein, the Catholic Press Association in the wake of Kristallnacht joined the outcry excoriating Hitlerism and its persecution of the Jews. While not explicitly Irish, the association primarily represented young men and women who came from Irish American families, who made up the majority of Catholic college attendees. The editors minced no words, resolving that "In this tragic hour for the Jews in Germany, Catholic students are impelled to express their deep anxiety over the rising tide of anti-Jewish feeling in the world." Such persecution, the organization declared, ran counter to Catholic teachings, which "oblige us to take a front position in the battle against racial hatred and intolerance always, but particularly at this time and in the United States," so inundated by Coughlin's ugly bombast.[10]

As with Callahan and so many more, to these Catholic college journalists, taking on the cause of the Jews provided a way to show that not all Catholics indulged in bigotry and that their faith put them on the side of the angels.

Like the young journalists, the more seasoned editors of the Jesuit magazine *America*, despite the hefty attention it paid to the evils of communism, still noted that "If Father Coughlin is a thorn in the side of the Jews, he is also a thorn in the side of the Catholics." Consistent with many other Catholic critics of the radio priest of Detroit, the editorial in *America* opined that "if he is arousing anti-Semitism, he is also arousing anti-Catholicism."[11]

The other major Catholic publication of the time, *The Commonweal*, upon Hitler's stepping into office in 1933 declared itself "firmly associated" with Jewish protests. It, like *America*, defined communists as an existential threat to the church, but that position did not prevent the magazine from editorializing against Nazism as it declared that Hitler's attacks on Jews stemmed from anti-Semitism and not anti-communism. Both publications persisted in pointing out the threat of communism, but not at the expense of "Mrs. Cohen, the delicatessen lady around the corner, and Meyer, the insurance collector." John Cogley, writing in *The Commonweal*, depicted Coughlin's followers as having "confused . . . anti-Communism . . . with anti-Semitism," ignoring the reality that they inflected "pain and insult" upon "innocent, godly Jews." And as to Germany, "nothing more than the overthrow of Hitlerism by the German people itself will bring justice to the Jews and other oppressed minorities, including Catholics," its editors wrote.[12]

The grim 1930s provided an opportunity for some Irish Catholics to use advocacy for Jews as a way to reorient the church. They sought to bring it into line with liberalism, a broad idea that America as a progressive, modern nation could not and did not share in the hatreds inherited from the European past. Even as discriminatory practices against Jews remained firmly in place, individuals associated with liberalism, mostly Protestants and the well-connected, stood up against anti-Semitism. Organizations like the National Conference of Christians and Jews, which created Brotherhood Week in the 1930s, the YMCA, the YWCA, the Boy Scouts, the Girl Scouts, and many more, particularly after the 1920s with the flourishing of the Klan, sought ways to reach out to Jews and disassociate themselves from anti-Semitism, hoping to forge an America devoid of religious and racial hatred.

Annually the *American Jewish Year Book* listed the speeches, programs, books, pamphlets, and discussion groups organized by non-Jews, often with the encouragement of Jews, to expose anti-Semitism and call for a tolerant America. As to religious bodies and clergy, Protestants had predominated these lists.

Those Catholics who spoke up for the Jews in the 1930s wanted the same for themselves and their faith community, never knowing when anti-Catholicism would rear its head again. They wanted to soften the liberal's critique of American Catholicism as uninterested in interfaith work to promote goodwill.

Catholics had previously been infrequent and desultory participants in interfaith work. Many clergy held to the position that their theology prevented them from fully articulating statements about the importance of respect for other religions, a principle that lay at the heart of liberalism. Their history of building and sustaining parochial education, even though the majority of their children in fact attended public schools, bothered liberals who suspected that such behavior meant that Catholics did not want to engage with those who adhered to other religious traditions.

Additionally, Americans had long associated Irish immigrants and their sons with rowdyism, as thugs who beat up people on the street, usually under the influence of alcohol. References to their proclivities toward uncontrollable violence coursed through American popular culture, and the image of the tough Irish hooligan who thought with his fists enjoyed great currency.

Coughlin's dramatic appearance on the American scene as the most visible, loudest, most notable anti-Semite, who sounded like a Nazi, shook those Catholics who had been laboring to reverse the image of their church as a bastion of reaction. Marauding bands of Irish members of the Front, pummeling unsuspecting Jews, fit the deeply embedded Irish stereotype while tying them—with their distinctive Irish names as reported in the press—with the murderous Nazi thugs who made Germany's streets hell for Jews.

The events of the 1930s and the chance to stand up for the Jews served this swath of Irish Catholic America, which feared that Coughlin and his ilk harmed their people, that the larger American public would consider that he and his pro-Nazi bands validated the belief that Catholicism had no place in America. Young Irish American men, armed with razor blades and baseball bats, they worried, confirmed Americans' views of Irish uncivility. As they addressed their own people while reaching out to Jews and the larger American public, they sought to repair their own image, showcasing a modern, liberal, and religiously tolerant face of Irish America.

Living as they did with anti-Catholicism, the memories of, for example, the rhetoric surrounding Al Smith's campaign, with its blatant assertions that Catholics could never be good and real Americans, still ringing in their ears, they shuddered at what they saw going on in their own communities.

The efforts of Irish Americans to offer a countermessage to Coughlin's ran through their public culture of the late 1930s. Within the span of three months, Michigan's governor Frank Murphy, the son of two Irish immigrants, spoke at both the golden anniversary of Yeshiva College, the nation's only Jewish institution of higher education, and at the Irish American Association of Lackawanna County. To the Jews gathered to celebrate Yeshiva College he decried the anti-Semites among his own group who claimed that "Jews are communists. We must condemn" them, he told the Orthodox Jews. The governor proclaimed that Irish Catholics needed to remember the common heritage of Jews and Christians. He cited "the many contributions the Jews have made to civilization" and excoriated the one "who . . . tars the entire Hebrew race with the same brush." He followed his January 1937 remarks to the Orthodox Jews with a talk to Irish Americans in Scranton, Pennsylvania, a community of steelworkers and coal miners, immigrants and their progeny. "Children of the Rosaleen," a metonym for the Irish people popularized by nationalists, "with all their sorrows can bring a rich moral and spiritual contribution" to "the New Fight for Freedom." Gently nudging them to embrace "the same . . . spirit they have demonstrated through the generations that are now history," he called on them to participate in "the undoing of social and economic wrongs, and . . . the elimination of every injustice." While not calling out Coughlin by name or identifying his followers, some of whom might have been sitting in front of him, Murphy offered his fellow Irish Americans a message different from that of the other Irish Catholic Michigander.

Other notable Irish Americans did not ask their readers and listeners to read between the lines with such oblique words. Msgr. John A. Ryan took to the air to deliver an anti-Coughlin radio broadcast, directed at his fellow priest's anti-Semitism and his attacks on the New Deal. Ryan directly called Coughlin's words "ugly, cowardly, and flagrant calumnies." Ryan held up as good and honorable Americans labor leader David Dubinsky and Felix Frankfurter, a newly appointed Jewish justice of the US Supreme Court, rather than as communist stooges, as Coughlin called them.[13] So too Coughlin's own bishop, Edward Mooney, immediately upon the first openly anti-Semitic broadcast in November 1938, a few days after Kristallnacht, wrote in *The Michigan Catholic* that the words the faithful may have heard on the radio should be understood as "totally out of harmony with the Holy Father's leadership," and that he, like the pope, condemned "Catholics who indulge in speeches or writings which in fact tend to arouse feelings against Jews as a race."[14]

The anti-Coughlin Catholic clergy who came to the defense of the Jews included Rev. R. A. McGowan, assistant director of the Department of Social Action of the National Catholic Welfare Conference, who pointed out to members of that organization that "Father Coughlin forgets the remarkable work for economic justice done by the Central Conference of American Rabbis." Father Maurice Sheehy, also of the National Catholic Welfare Conference, offered a twinned condemnation of the Nazi brutality of Kristallnacht and Coughlin, who claimed that the Jews had brought it all on themselves. Rev. Fulton J. Sheen, based then at the Catholic University of America, also linked Coughlin and Hitler together and asserted that Coughlin provoked anti-Catholicism. *The Commonweal* warned its readers that they should imagine anti-Semitism as a coin that on the obverse side read NO POPERY, appealing to their self-interest and asserting that Jews and Catholics shared common enemies. The roster could go on.[15]

Irish Catholics talked among themselves about Coughlin, his affinity to Nazism, and the threat he posed for Catholics in America. Daniel J. Tobin, an Irish immigrant and president of the International Brotherhood of Teamsters, warned James Farley, postmaster general of the United States and the son of Irish immigrants, of the dangers posed by Coughlin, advising that the priest's influence ought not "be sneered at."[16]

Frances Sweeney did not need anyone to tell her not to sneer at Coughlin. She took him on directly and unafraid. She took on her own bishop, William O'Connell, whom she excoriated for being too soft on Coughlin and his followers, too mealy-mouthed in his choice of words as he sort of condemned the priest. Sweeney, in her self-published newspaper, the *Boston City Reporter,* took on Coughlin's minions in Boston, a city that James Michael Curley described as the "strongest Coughlin city in the world," with the largest number of members on the rolls of the Christian Front.[17]

The daughter of an Irish-born Boston saloonkeeper, Sweeney

grew up in the working-class neighborhood of Brighton and was educated at Mount Saint Joseph Academy. She filled her paper with no-punches-spared articles and editorials against Coughlin, the Nazis in Germany, their clones in Boston strutting around as members of the Christian Front, and the city's Irish Catholics who cheered for Coughlin. She took aim at those Irish Catholics who just stood by silently and did nothing to quell anti-Semitism. Irish Catholics, she argued in her columns, had an obligation to behave better given their own bitter history of persecution in America.

Sweeney originally intended the paper, which provided teenaged Nat Hentoff with his first job as a reporter, to concentrate on local political corruption, but the chance instead to expose fascists in the form of Coughlinites made the ordinariness of graft in municipal government less important. Sweeney informed federal agents about the connections between local Bostonian Francis P. Moran, son of immigrants from County Mayo, and George Sylvester Viereck, a poet and high-profile member of the Friends of the New Germany, an unabashed pro-Nazi, pro-Hitler organization. She lambasted Bishop O'Connell so often that he summoned her to his office and threatened her with excommunication.

Notwithstanding her devotion to Catholicism, Sweeney paid no attention to O'Connell's threats and took upon herself the duty of keeping tabs on Moran and then reporting his activities to the FBI. Sweeney stood up at a rally in South Boston and verbally challenged Father Edward Lodge Curran, a Coughlin henchman sometimes called the "Father Coughlin of the East," while the priest spoke to the crowd of two thousand. Offended by her actions, some burley attendees dragged her out of the hall amid a chorus of jeers and obscenities. That did not stop her, though.

In his 1943 expose, *Under Cover: My Four Years in the*

Nazi Underworld in America, John Roy Carlson paid homage to Frances Sweeney, saying that what she undertook in Boston resembled "digging a mountain with a hand spade," pointing to what she published in the *Boston City Reporter,* and also her work with the *Boston Herald,* in organizing the Rumor Clinic in 1942.[18] She convinced the mainstream, widely circulating city paper to choose one rumor about the "Jews" heard that week in the city, and she, along with other volunteers who had established themselves as "morale wardens," exposed those who had started the rumors and then proved their falsity.

Sweeney ran a local operation, but the national media picked up on her work. Articles in *Life* and *Reader's Digest* gave it wider exposure. That in turn led to the founding around the country of clinics like hers in Boston.

Sweeney, who died before the war's end, did even more, using her voice as an Irish Catholic to come to the aid of Jews. She got the city council to ban the sale of the pro-Nazi magazine *Catholic International* from the city's largest newsstands, and helped bring about the dismissal of the city's police commissioner after exposing how the overwhelmingly Irish and Catholic police ignored the violence perpetrated on Jews by the Christian Front and instead harassed the Jewish victims of their assaults.

In 1942 Sweeney became the secretary of the newly formed American Irish Defense Association, which included among its members Edward Flynn, chair of the Democratic National Committee; General John F. O'Ryan; and a number of clerics. Among its accomplishments, it convinced the Brooklyn Character and Fitness Committee of the Brooklyn Bar Association to refuse membership to John F. Cassidy, a leader of the Front.

No wonder then that upon her death Bishop Bernard Sheil of Chicago, a champion of Sweeney in her confrontation with O'Connell, posthumously awarded her the Pope Leo XIII Medal for combating prejudice. No wonder also that Hentoff, the

Jewish boy reporter in the 1930s, remembered her decades later, dedicating his autobiography, *Boston Boy,* to "Frances Sweeney, editor of the *Boston City Reporter,* for whom I reported on anti-Semitism, and in all of Boston, the woman I most admired, sometimes feared, and ridiculously loved."[19]

Frank Hogan, like Sweeney, also did not dismiss the threat posed by Coughlin to Jews and Catholics alike, although he delivered his condemnation in a very different way than Sweeney, one that undoubtedly reflected his place in American life and politics. A lawyer who became president of the American Bar Association in 1938, Hogan, unlike Sweeney, moved in high circles, having served as personal attorney to President Warren Harding and banker Andrew Mellon. An embodiment of the Irish American success story, he made it from very humble beginnings, raised by a widowed mother, Mary McSweeney Hogan, on her wages as a seamstress to become the founder of one of Washington, DC's most prestigious law firms, Hogan & Hartson.

Perhaps the prestige he had come to enjoy by the mid-1930s allowed him to raise the most powerful Catholic voice to attack Coughlin. On December 11, 1938, just after the priest had signed off the air, Hogan came on and made the case against Coughlin, speaking in the name of Catholics. He gave his half-hour speech, carried by the same thirty-four stations around the country that gave Coughlin his airtime, at the behest of the General Jewish Council, as well as the American Jewish Committee, the American Jewish Congress, B'nai B'rith, and the Jewish Labor Committee, addressing primarily his coreligionists. "An American Catholic Speaks on Intolerance" may not have named Coughlin, but it unmistakably spoke for the Jews. "Whenever Jews are persecuted," Hogan began, "there too other creeds and races will soon or later be persecuted." Drawing on recent history, he invoked the Ku Klux Klan, which had been at the height of its membership and influence less than two decades earlier, and continued: "One thing is becoming even more clear to serious students of history. That the Jews have become the barometer of democracy throughout the world. Where they are oppressed, as in Germany, democracy and freedom have been utterly destroyed, and Christians have also suffered. Where they are the equals of all citizens, as in America, democracy lives and flourishes, and all men are free, whatever their faith." Hogan refuted Coughlin's charges about Jews as communists and stated unequivocally that "We Catholics cannot permit men of ill will to preach in America bigotry and anti-Semitism without raising our voices in protest." On the contrary, he demanded that they had to "stand shoulder to shoulder with all Americans in viewing with horror the atrocities committed against Jews in Nazi Germany."[20]

Not one to remain silent, Coughlin, knowing in advance that Hogan would be speaking right after and against him, blustered, "Oh, how can the General Jewish Council and the Jewish Community Councils" purposely engage another Catholic to do their dirty work as they tried to silence him? How low of the Jewish groups to launch their attack "through the lips of a fellow religionist, and with the voice of a fellow descendent of the same Irish race which suffered death and persecution—how can they be so unkind?"[21]

Despite the bonds of Catholicism and Irish ancestry, Hogan felt duty bound to be the voice of Catholicism in the face of Coughlin. Hogan's speech, like those offered by other Irish Catholics at the time, as they sought to quell Coughlinism within the Irish communities and as they sought to prove themselves as defenders of democracy to American non-Catholics, made three points. First, he (and they) simply demolished and disparaged Coughlin's arguments as lies, as baseless slander. Second, Hogan pointed out that the Coughlin phenomenon had the potential to revive virulent anti-Catholicism in America based on a belief that the church and American democracy could never be reconciled. Additionally, Hogan feared that Coughlin threatened to split the church apart. Too many Catholics supported him, and yet so many hated him.

With this final point Hogan, like so many other Irish Catholics, had no choice but to admit Coughlin's appeal among the faithful. But these words and those in much of the Catholic press, in radio broadcasts and in statements from clergy, showed that enough Catholics found the anti-Semitism so abhorrent that they would abandon the church that harbored Coughlin and his followers.

Jeremiah Mahoney, like Frances Sweeney and Frank Hogan, did not downplay the situation or dismiss anti-Semitism and the threat from Nazi Germany, either. Whether facing the Nazis in New York or in Europe, Mahoney took upon himself the role of advocating for Jews.

The son of immigrants from Ireland, Mahoney's father, like so many of his generation, made a life for himself as a New York City police officer. That in turn allowed Jeremiah to attend college and law school. A talented athlete, he qualified for the 1908 Olympics in track, but his job in the office of the city comptroller prevented him from going to London to compete in the games.

Nothing in Mahoney's life up to 1935 pointed to any particular Jewish connections or interests, other than the simple fact that he had grown up on the Lower East Side, attended public schools there, and earned his bachelor's degree at the predominantly Jewish City College of New York, all putting him in proximity to Jews.

But a fortuitous combination of sports and political ambitions propelled Mahoney into the world of Jewish concerns. A lawyer in private practice, like many Irish men he turned his attention to politics to advance his career, aligning himself with Tammany Hall. Al Smith in 1923, as governor, rewarded him with a judgeship.

Athletics continued to matter to him. He joined and then served as an officer of the New York Athletic Club. From there he rose in the world of amateur athletics, and by 1934 the Amateur Athletic Union of the United States (AAU) elected him its president, which automatically gave him a seat on the board of the American Olympic Association, perhaps for Mahoney a poignant moment given that he had two decades earlier qualified to participate but could not.

What began as an avocation and personal passion, however, changed dramatically and transformed his life. Within a year of Mahoney's election to the AAU presidency, the issue of Nazism, Hitler, and the Jews cast him into the politics of the athletic world.

In 1933 the world Olympic body had named Berlin as the site for the 1936 games. Over the course of the intervening three years Berlin became a very different place, serving now as the capital of the Third Reich, which had commenced its campaign of terror against the Jews.

The American Jewish Congress contacted Mahoney because he sat on the official body that had oversight of the United States participation in the world games. The Jewish defense organization asked him to get involved in its efforts to draw attention to the matter. What, they asked him to find out, would it mean to American Jewish athletes? How would US participation in the Hitler Olympics signal a legitimization of the regime, which had already stripped Jews of their citizenship? How would it look to the world if American athletes saluted Hitler, who no doubt would be in the reviewing stand?

Mahoney took on the matter zealously, poring over research undertaken as to the status of Jewish athletes in Germany, and within a year he rose to leadership of a movement advocating that the United States not go to Berlin, that its athletes stay home in protest.

He found and then disseminated the evidence supplied to him by German sources that attested to the fact that Jews had been expelled from sports clubs and other public facilities where they in the past would have trained, that Jews could not compete in Germany against other Germans, and that the high jumper Gretel Bergmann had been booted from the German team. Enough proof for him, he declared that "there is no room for discrimination on grounds of race, color or creed in the Olympics." The AAU, the organization he represented, had previously accepted the invitation to participate in the games so long as Germany would honor a "pledge that there would be no discrimination against Jewish athletes," these words drawn from his 1935 pamphlet, "Germany Has Violated the Olympic Code."[22]

Mahoney declared that Germany had violated this pledge, and he called for a boycott.

Mahoney led the public charge, going head-to-head with the president of the US Olympic Executive Committee, Avery Brundage, known widely for his openly anti-Jewish remarks. Mahoney stood up to Brundage and enlisted his Irish and Catholic network to join him, in hope of pressuring the executive committee. He convinced Governor Curley and Al Smith to join the protests and rallied newspapers to join his call. The Catholic War Veterans joined him, and he asked Senator David I. Walsh of Massachusetts to introduce legislation in Congress calling for a boycott. Mahoney's words must have moved *The Commonweal* to declare that United States support of the games would by extension approve the "anti-Christian" doctrines of Nazism.

The *American Jewish Year Book* of 1936–1937 hailed

Mahoney as "the recognized leader of the anti-Olympic movement," reporting on his nationwide radio broadcast on the subject, in which he shared with the American public his outrage at the "formidable list of Nazi violations of the Olympic pledge."[23]

Foreshadowing the spat that played itself out in the pages of the Providence College newspaper between the Jewish student D.J. and its editor, Coughlin not surprisingly opposed any boycott as an action only serving Jewish interests.

In the end, Brundage prevailed; Mahoney lost, vacating his seat on the US Olympic organizing committee. Brundage's argument that the host country had the right to set the terms of the games held sway, and a majority of the members of the commission felt satisfied or did not care much about the fate of the Jewish athletes.

Brundage, however, believed that he had public opinion on his side and asserted in the course of the debate that Jews, communists, and Mahoney advocated boycott. Brundage further disparaged Mahoney with the charge that he actually did not care about the Jews or Jewish athletes but only thought about crass politics, hoping to capitalize on his advocacy to get the Jewish vote in the upcoming mayoral election in New York City. Brundage relied in this on the pervasive anti-Irish stereotype of the dirty machine politician with no agenda beyond wanting to win at the ballot box at any cost.

Mahoney did indeed have politics on his mind and his eye on the New York City mayoral race for 1937. He may very likely have thought that Jewish voters would look favorably upon him for his boycott work. Whether he took the lead on the boycott to curry favor with Jewish voters or not, he did set himself up to challenge La Guardia, who was then finishing up his first term in office. Both La Guardia and Mahoney supported the New Deal. Their agendas differed little. So when La Guardia allowed the unabashedly Nazi-affiliated German

American Bund to march through the streets of Yorkville, a predominantly German neighborhood with a good sprinkling of Irish residents, Mahoney found a splendid opportunity to distinguish himself. No friend of the Bund, La Guardia realized that he had no legal right to ban the march, but Jewish community leaders, the Jewish press, and the Jewish public clamored for him to quash it, considering it an affront to see Nazis strut through the streets of the most Jewish city in the United States. While the mayor banned Bund marchers from wearing their uniforms and singing their songs as they marched, Mahoney took up the matter, seeing it as a possible wedge issue with which he hoped to pry the Jewish vote away from the popular La Guardia. In the public debates, Mahoney posited himself as the stronger anti-Nazi, the more pro-Jewish advocate of the two.

Mahoney lost the election, but even after giving up on electoral politics, he seized more opportunities to advocate for Jews and oppose Hitler, demolishing, as such, Brundage's claim that he had led the boycott movement for purely political reasons.

With no more interest in running for elected office, Mahoney joined the executive committee of the American Irish Defense Association (AIDA), on which Frances Sweeney served as the secretary, participating in its campaigns against the Christian Front and Coughlin. And in December 1941, while Coughlin still thundered on and voices still rattled in Irish American communities against the newly declared war as a Jewish project, Mahoney, through the AIDA, held rallies to drum up support for the war among Irish New Yorkers.

Speaking at rallies around the city, along with Father Vincent Brown, also a member of the American Irish Defense Association, Mahoney called on the Irish public to "Defend America! Stop Hitler Now!" One of the rallies took place in the meeting hall of the Shamrock Society, and the organizers declared in their publicity flyers THE WEST SIDE IRISH ARE WITH YOU—MR. PRESIDENT. The flyer depicted FDR in one corner with drawings of the heads of Irish Americans labeled underneath, COP, TEAMSTER, LONGSHOREMAN, FIREMAN, HOUSEWIFE, and a female, marked as employed in an OFFICE.[24]

These were the faces of New York, and by extension, of America's Irish working class, the hard core of Coughlin's supporters. Mahoney and Brown and the AIDA sought to wean them from Coughlin, his unpatriotic flirtation with Nazism, the nation's enemy, and foster their support of their Jewish fellow citizens.

As Coughlin still raged on the airwaves against the Jews, the communists, the war, and Roosevelt, whom he had for years claimed was really a Jew, Mahoney, like Sweeney and Hogan and other Irish Americans, continued to stand up for the Jews. They projected a different Irish America from that which Coughlin described, and they labored to hold back the torrents of anti-Semitism awash in their communities. They did not hesitate to affirmatively identify themselves with the Jews in their truly most devastating hours.

Their words and actions demonstrated a strategic alliance that far transcended simple gain. Rather, as they saw it, by succumbing to anti-Semitism, the Irish had harmed themselves, aligned themselves with the world's most reactionary, nefarious force, the one that Americans would shortly meet on so many European battlefields. To protect their own people, to defend the good name of the Catholic Church and the Irish in America, they offered a counterimage, one that stood up in solidarity with their neighbors in distress.

As these three individuals, along with Paul O'Dwyer, Msgr. Ryan, Al Smith, James Michael Curley, the editors of *The Commonweal,* and even the staff of the St. John's University alumni magazine saw it, no good could come of America's Irish Catholic population embracing reaction and illiberalism, and most of all, from being the loudest voice for anti-Semitism at that fraught moment in time.

Conclusion

In this the Irish American defenders of the Jews echoed the words and actions of those who came before them, who also championed Jews to champion themselves, including but hardly limited to Charles P. Daly, John Boyle O'Reilly, his daughter Mary, Leonora O'Reilly, Myra Kelly, John Fitzpatrick, the Knights of Columbus, who launched the Racial Contributions to America book series, and so many more who had declared that by standing up for the Jews, they shored up their own standing in America. By championing the Jews, by opening doors for them, they demolished the widely heard charge of their unfitness for American citizenship, as Irish women and men and as Catholics. In standing with the Jews, they could claim their rightful place in America as they acted in a way exactly opposite to what their defamers claimed. By paving the way for Jewish integration, Irish Americans sought to secure their own comfort in America. By defending the Jews against their old enemy, Protestant anti-Catholicism, they asserted that they deserved the respect that was widely denied to them. They were entitled to full American cultural citizenship, something their antagonists, who declared the nation a bastion of Protestantism, considered these Irish Catholics never capable of achieving.

Jews benefited mightily from others making their case for them in the public arena. They obviously gained much in practical terms, whether in the labor movement, the public schools, the Catholic universities, or the smoke-filled rooms of sundry political machines, places from which the Irish who had come earlier launched them into American life. Each of these served as stepping stones on the Jews' American journeys, providing them with jobs, political offices, education, and the tools they needed to advocate for themselves in their workplaces.

Beyond door opening, for Jews to have others speak for them, to make their case when they found themselves the victims of discrimination and violence, mattered. More than deriving the satisfaction of not feeling alone in a hostile world, having someone else take up their cause allowed them to lay low. When Jeremiah Mahoney, or decades earlier Michael Davitt, could attest to Jewish suffering, no one could accuse them of exaggerating. When Congressman Dickstein gave the chair of his committee dedicated to exposing Nazis in America to John McCormack, he admitted that an Irish Catholic would be a more believable voice because he could not be dismissed as self-serving. When at the beginning of the century Mary Boyle O'Reilly declared that blood libel was a Christian crime against the Jews, she could hardly be seen as overstating the case to advance her own interests. When Charles P. Daly held up the Jews as exemplars of good Americans, who could quibble with him?

Having these Irish Catholics in their corner defending them meant that Jews did not have to always engage in self-defense. Letting the words come out of the mouths of others prevented them from being viewed as complaining too much, whining too loudly, or drawing too much attention to themselves.

This strategy worked immensely well for both the Irish and

the Jews. They both gained, and their twinned story helps us see that no one succeeds on their own, and that the people in a complex democratic society always have reasons to stand up for each other. Not a matter of altruism, this relationship made sense, and by making sense, both groups benefited.

This strategy worked no less well for the nation as a whole. While the Irish and the Jews did what they did, each group for themselves, their work together also left its mark on America writ large. Jews and Irish in concert with each other played a role in loosening the Protestants' iron grip on the nation, demolishing their claim that by virtue of being first, Protestantism, the dominant religious tradition of the founders, had the right to keep on charting the nation's course. The Irish and the Jews, as allies, pointed out that the United States owed its existence to women and men of many faith traditions, and that the Constitution guaranteed religious freedom, both its free exercise and freedom from any establishment, to all.

White Americans with long and deep roots in American soil, with family origins also somehow traceable to England, had no express right to govern and define the nation, according to the Irish and the Jews. The ancestral legacies of the old elites did not guarantee them a lion's share of authority or privilege. Those whose families had come from Ireland and, like the Jews, from central and eastern Europe shared in the same full bundle of rights. While the nation's torturous confrontation with race has dragged on into the twenty-first century, these two groups, with the Irish in the lead, challenged a firmly established belief that possessing the right origins and the most prestigious identities guaranteed some individuals privileges over others.

These two peoples, as embodied in the Irish political machine and the Jews whom they incorporated into it, helped open up the democratic process, declaring in their actions, which sprouted from the streets to the political clubs and the ballot box, that politics belonged to the people. Power should rest with those who showed up on Election Day and voted. The more people who voted, the better. Those who encouraged ordinary citizens to claim the franchise deserved credit, rather than the elites who thought that they knew better and sought to restrict it. Just as the Irish had recognized that they could never hold on to power without casting their nets wide and including the Jews, so too Jews, when and where they moved to political center stage, made a point of reaching out and encouraging new groups of outsider voters.

The Irish and the Jews, through their activism in the labor movement, did nothing less than help push forward innovations once considered radical, like the right of workers to organize, minimum wage, maximum hours, and on-the-job safety and health protections. In their collaborations they drove home the point that bosses ought not have the right to exercise a free hand over those whom they employed. They called upon the state to intercede on behalf of workers, to create a more level playing field between employers and employees. They together, through union campaigns, gave us the five-day workweek, state-mandated collective bargaining, and more. In this the Irish, who had come on the labor scene first, impressed upon the Jews that only the unions would make them strong. Over time, the Jewish-led unions had to extend that same message to new workers who also sought economic security for themselves and their families.

Likewise, just as Irish Catholic women had educated Jewish immigrant children, guiding them to English literacy and exposing them to American skills, broadly defined, so Jewish teachers, mostly women as well, and particularly in New York, served on the front line for the African American children of the Great Migration and the youngsters whose parents arrived from Puerto Rico and the islands of the Caribbean in the decades surrounding World War II.

Both cohorts of teachers saw what they did as more than a job, although it was that, too. They understood it as a civic calling, considering their years in so many classrooms as tools in the effort to make the nation great. Rather than defining education as something to be doled out at the lowest cost to taxpayers and to keep the poor bereft of robust futures, Irish and Jewish schoolteachers defined their classrooms as engines of mobility for the children of so many newcomers, whose parents, like their own, had entered America at the bottom of the economic ladder. They saw the lessons that they had received, and that they then in turn imparted, as crucial to shaping a common culture that incorporated diversity yet celebrated unity.

Together, Irish and Jews created an exuberant, decidedly urban, American vernacular culture, which in turn opened doors for others. They had done so for themselves, but they set in motion, whether intentionally or not, a dynamic that engulfed others and as such opened doors for them. They nudged their fellow Americans to see the category "American" as a capacious one that had no boundaries as to who could be included.

Perhaps the final word might go to the Irish and Jewish songwriters of the early twentieth century William Jerome and Jean Schwartz, who not only wrote the song "If It Wasn't for the Irish and Jews" but also entertained the American public with the 1911 composition "They're All Good American Names," which jingled:

The men who lead the world today in all athletic games
Are brawny sons of Uncle Sam, with good old Yankee
*   names.*
Brady and O'Toole, Dooin and McColl,
McInerny and McBarney, Harrigan, McVey and
*   Kearney . . .*
Connie Mack and John McGraw, all together shout Hurrah!

The song did not end there:

There's Rosenheimer, Jacobs, Weiner,
Gimble, Sax and Straus. . . .
They're all good American names![1]

Schwartz and Jerome, born Flannery, could have thrown into the stew Italian, Greek, Polish, Lithuanian, Portuguese, German, and so many other names. So too today's songwriters can add new ones, derived from a multiplicity of places from around the world, names in Spanish, Chinese, Vietnamese, Swahili, Persian, Korean, Urdu, Tamil, Arabic, Creole, Hindi, Tagalog, and on and on, "all," like those of the early twentieth-century song, "good American names."

ACKNOWLEDGMENTS

I have been waiting for a long time to write this part of the book, the one in which I get a chance to thank those who made it possible. Colleagues, librarians, and archivists, grant givers, friends and family all have a hand indeed in every piece of historical writing.

Every book has an origin story, and the genesis of this one begins with the names of some key individuals and one gem of an institution that launched my interest in this subject.

This book began in the summer of 2017, when a dean at New York University, my then institutional home, asked me to step into a leadership vacuum and serve for a year as the interim director of Glucksman Ireland House.

The façade of the beautiful townhouse on Fifth Avenue just north of Washington Square bears the names of its donors and founders, Lou Glucksman and Loretta Brennan Glucksman. Their vision of scholarship, academic study for NYU students, and community programming infuses the house, and being its director, even for just the one year, obliged me to consider both aspects as I took over.

It happened that my stewardship of the house coincided with

its twenty-fifth anniversary. The staff, in particular the dynamic Miriam Nyhan Grey, who gets my first and maybe loudest acknowledgment here, decided that, in honor of that moment, the year's public lectures would focus on the Irish-Jewish encounter in America, providing a context for thinking about the dynamic pair of Lou and Loretta.

I had no choice but to give the first talk in the series, and I worried that I would mostly catalog troubling moments in that encounter, including the shadow of Father Charles Coughlin, the unabashed anti-Semite, who in the 1930s spewed forth to his radio listeners a pro-Hitler message. But preparing the talk took me down a very different path, and what appears in these pages represents a fresh look at that history.

So, my thanks must begin with Miriam, as well as Loretta Brennan Glucksman, who embraced me and encouraged me, making me feel like an insider. Likewise, Ted Smyth, Judith McGuire from the GIH board, as well as Professor Marion Casey all cheered me on and provided me with great support. I handed over my temporary directorship to Kevin Kenny, who has been with me all the way on this project, listening to me and reading with laser-sharp precision the manuscript in its earliest form.

I cannot say too much about Ireland House as a setting for intellectual work and as a place that understands that the history of one group in a complex society can never be disconnected from that of others, the theme here in this book.

Along the way, I benefited much from the librarians at NYU's Bobst Library: Guy Burak never hesitated when I bombarded him with questions, and since much of my research took place during COVID times, my questions were many. Guy was there with me during the pandemic and after, as I scrambled for a way to work around closures and lack of access to archives and libraries. Shannon O'Neil at the Tamiment Institute likewise provided much help in accessing the holdings of this jewel of a collection.

Additionally, a good deal of the research took place "at" the New York Historical Society, and librarians there and at the New York Public Library accommodated the searches I undertook from home, due to the limitations of COVID closures. Librarians at St. John's University in New York brought me amazing material that truly impacted this book.

Professor Arthur Urbano at Providence College shared much with me about the history of Jewish students at this school, founded and led by Dominican friars, and Professor Susie Pak at St. John's University provided me with an overwhelming amount of material about the Jewish students who studied there under the guidance of the Vincentian Fathers. Professor Pak truly served as a sounding board for my ideas and as a font of empirical information that I would never have had access to.

Two of my doctoral students had a hand in this as well. Hadas Binyamini culled the American Jewish press, uncovering a rich trove of material, while Gavin Beinart-Smollan read the manuscript and gave me great feedback, heeding my advice that he should not worry about offending me with sharp and probing criticisms.

As to the always important matter of financial support, I received a Hibernian Research Award from the Cushwa Center at Notre Dame University, funded by the Ancient Order of Hibernians and the Ladies Ancient Order of Hibernians. Having been chosen to be the D'Angelo Distinguished Visiting Professor in the Department of History at St. John's University, an honor provided by Peg and Peter D'Angelo—who wondered if I might not next turn to Italians and Jews—not only helped me defray research costs but also provided me with an introduction to the world of Jewish students at Catholic universities. It also gave me the chance to publicly articulate in a formal talk, for the first time, the framework for this study.

I spent an entire year at the Herbert D. Katz Center for Advanced Judaic Studies as the Louis Apfelbaum and Hortense Braunstein Apfelbaum Fellow, which made a major difference in moving the project forward. Its director, Professor Steven Weitzman, and the organizers of that year's program, "America's Jewish Questions," led by Professors Lila Corwin Berman, Deborah Dash Moore, and Beth Wenger, enabled me to think and to research as I pondered the contours of this particular American Jewish question. I learned so much from them, from their probing questions and cheerful support. The other fellows at the Katz Center all shaped my thinking.

Special thanks to Professors Jeffrey Gurock of Yeshiva University—himself a scholar of Jewish athletes at schools like St. John's—Laura Vapnek, a St. John's University scholar of women and labor history, and James Barrett, University of Illinois, one of the foremost historians of Irish America, who all wrote letters of support for me and, importantly, asked me great questions in the process, which gave me pause. I thank them.

This is the second time that I get to thank my agent, Don Fehr of Trident Media, for again taking me on and shepherding my path, which led me to St. Martin's where I have had the pleasure of working with fine, solid, and helpful editor Kevin Reilly, who has been an enthusiastic supporter of the book and patient with me.

Finally, and never finally, my family has always been there for me during this and previous undertakings. Steve read the manuscript, as he did my MA thesis a half century ago, in its messiest form. He also, somewhat to my chagrin, constantly described to others in social gatherings what I was writing, while I wanted to keep my work under wraps. But many of those to whom he mentioned that I was writing a book on Irish and

Jews in America had useful insights and often offered me some fruitful leads to follow. His desire to share my work with the world always made me feel good.

Shira, Eli, and Matan, Eugene, Anh, and now Gabriella in countless ways are always there with me. They are my greatest treasure.

NOTES

1. American Meeting Places

1. Robert Woods, *Americans in Process* (Boston: Houghton, Mifflin, 1902), 282–83.
2. Theodore H. White, *In Search of History: A Personal Adventure* (New York: Harper & Row, 1978), 28.
3. Harry Roskolenko, *When I Was Last on Cherry Street* (New York: Stein and Day, 1965), 2–3.
4. Sophie Ruskay, *Horsecars and Cobblestones* (New York: Beechhurst Press, 1948), 60.
5. Abraham Bisno, *Union Pioneer: An Autobiographical Account of Bisno's Early Life and the Beginnings of Unionism in the Women's Garment Industry* (Madison: University of Wisconsin Press, 1967), 56.
6. David Julius Seligson, *Rabbi, Chaplain and Burra Sahib* (n.p., 1994), 7.
7. Harry Golden, *The Right Time: An Autobiography* (New York: Putnam, 1969), 51, 73, 104.
8. Nat Hentoff, *Boston Boy: Growing Up with Jazz and Other Rebellious Passions* (Philadelphia: Paul Dry Books, 2001), 24–25.
9. Woods, *Americans in Process,* 282–83.
10. Marcus A. Jastrow, "The Causes of the Revived Disaffection Against the Jews," *American Hebrew,* June 20, 1890, 122.
11. Michael Gold, *Jews Without Money* (New York: H. Liveright, 1930), 163, 165.
12. Quoted in Gil Ribak, *Gentile New York: The Image of Non-Jews Among Jewish Immigrants* (New Brunswick, NJ: Rutgers University Press, 2012), 67.

13. Bella Spewack, *Streets: A Memoir of the Lower East Side* (New York: Feminist Press, 1995), 118, 119.

14. Thomas Jesse Jones, *The Sociology of a New York City Block* (New York: Columbia University Studies in the Social Sciences, 1904), 12, 64.

15. "Floating Facts," *Jewish Messenger,* Oct. 8, 1875, 3.

16. "Floating Facts," *Jewish Messenger,* June 2, 1876, 6.

17. "New Renderings of an Old Legend," *American Hebrew,* Dec. 3, 1897, 132.

18. Edward J. Flynn, *You're the Boss* (New York: Viking Press, 1947), 46.

19. Rose Schneiderman, *All for One* (New York: P. S. Eriksson, 1967), 52.

20. Charles Ffrench, *Biographical History of the American Irish in Chicago* (Chicago: American Biographical Publishing, 1897), 130.

21. Conan Shaffer, "Patrick and Levy," *Sentinel,* Sept. 13, 1912, 19.

22. Hentoff, *Boston Boy,* 45.

23. Jones, *Sociology of a New York City Block,* 110.

24. Philip Cowen, *Memories of an American Jew* (New York: The International Press, 1932), 28.

25. Rabbi L. Wintner, "Father Malone," *Jewish Messenger,* Jan. 19, 1900, 5.

26. Francis P. Duffy, *Father Duffy's Story: A Tale of Humor and Heroism, of Life and Death with the Fighting Sixty-Ninth* (New York: George H. Doran, 1919), 106.

27. S. N. Behrman, *The Worcester Account* (New York: Random House, 1954), 33.

28. Quoted in Patrick R. Redmond, *The Irish-American Athletic Club of New York: The Rise and Fall of the Winged Fists, 1898–1917* (Jefferson, NC: McFarland, 2018), 39.

29. Quoted in Robert Snyder, *The Voice of the City: Vaudeville and Popular Culture in New York* (New York: Oxford University Press, 1989), 119.

30. "Local News," *Jewish Messenger,* Mar. 19, 1880, 2.

31. "Richard O'Gorman Lecture," *Jewish Messenger,* Apr. 13, 1877, 5.

32. Quoted in Leonard Dinnerstein, *Anti-Semitism in America* (New York: Oxford University Press, 1994), 40.

33. "The Irish Relief Fund," *Jewish Messenger,* Feb. 20, 1880, 2; Alpha, "The Irish Collection," *Jewish Messenger,* Feb. 20, 1880, 4.

34. "Jewish Charity and Irish Distress," *American Hebrew,* Feb. 12, 1880, 146.

35. Hanna Sheehy-Skeffington, *Call,* Feb. 19, 1918, 1.

36. Quoted in Brian Hanley, "'The Irish and the Jews Have a Good Deal in Common': Irish Republicanism, Anti-Semitism and the Post-war World," *Irish Historical Studies* 44, no. 165 (2020): 57–74, https://doi .org/10.1017/ihs.2020.5.

37. Quoted in Meaghan Dwyer-Ryan, "Ethnic Patriotism: Boston's Irish

and Jewish Communities, 1880–1929" (PhD diss., Boston College, 2010), 145.

38. "'Tay Pay' on Britain's Promise of 'The Promised Land,'" *Sentinel,* Nov. 30, 1917, 17.

39. "Lawndale Civic Center," *Sentinel,* Jan. 24, 1919, 23.

40. Hyman L. Meites, "Home Rule and the Jews," *Sentinel,* June 19, 1914, 17–18.

41. Louis D. Brandeis, "Why I Am a Zionist," *Sentinel,* Nov. 27, 1914, 21.

42. "Nineteenth Annual Report of the American Jewish Committee," *American Jewish Year Book,* vol. 28 (1926–1927), 471.

43. "True Charity," *Jewish Messenger,* Aug. 15, 1902, 6.

2. Defending the Jews

1. Mary Boyle O'Reilly, "Mary Boyle O'Reilly, in Russia, Investigates 'Ritual' Murder," *Day Book* 3, no. 7 (1913): 1–4.

2. "Beilis and Frank," *Yidishes Tageblatt,* Apr. 29, 1915, 4; "Beilis Family Comes to America," *Yidishes Tageblatt,* Oct. 14, 1913, 4.

3. Quoted in Edmund Levin, *A Child of Christian Blood: Murder and Conspiracy in Tsarist Russia; The Beilis Blood Libel* (New York: Schocken Books, 1914), 243.

4. Reproduced in Philip Cowen, *Prejudice Against the Jew: Its Nature, Its Causes and Remedies; A Symposium by Foremost Christians Published in "The American Hebrew," April 4, 1890* (New York: Philip Cowen, 1928), 123–24.

5. James Michael Curley, "Exercises in Memory of John Boyle O'Reilly," *Journal of the American-Irish Historical Society* 16 (1917): 257.

6. Charles Patrick Daly, *The Settlement of the Jews in North America* (New York: P. Cowen, 1893).

7. *American Jewish Year Book,* vol. 28 (1926–1927), 112.

8. Daly, *Settlement of the Jews in North America,* 2.

9. Quoted in Albert M. Friedenberg, *Publications of the American Jewish Historical Society,* vol. 1 (1903), 101–15.

10. Quoted in Harold Earl Hammond, *A Commoner's Judge: The Life and Times of Charles Patrick Daly* (Boston: Christopher Publishing House, 1954), 271.

11. Daly, *Settlement of the Jews in North America,* vi; Charles P. Daly, *The Jews of New York* (New York: American Hebrew, 1883); Max J. Kohler, *Charles P. Daly: A Tribute to His Memory* (New York: American Hebrew, 1899).

12. Max Kohler, "Charles P. Daly," *American Hebrew* 9, no. 29 (1899): 1.

13. Michael Davitt, *Within the Pale: The True Story of Anti-Semitic Persecution in Russia* (Philadelphia: Jewish Publication Society of America,

1903); Edward H. Judge, *Easter in Kishinev* (New York: New York University Press, 1992); Steven Zipperstein, *Pogrom and the Tilt of History* (New York: W. W. Norton, 2018).

14. Davitt, *Within the Pale,* 107.

15. Maxmillian Heller, "The Year 5663," *American Jewish Year Book,* vol. 5 (1903–1904), 21.

16. David Philipson, "Jewish Authorship," *American Jewish Year Book,* vol. 15 (1913–1914), 37.

17. "A List of Leading Events in 5667," *American Jewish Year Book,* vol. 9 (1907–1908), 509.

18. Heller, "The Year 5663," 21.

19. Quoted in Till van Rahden, "Beyond Ambivalence: Variations of Catholic Anti-Semitism in Turn-of-the-Century Baltimore," *American Jewish History* 82, no. 1/2 (1994): 7–42.

20. Finley Peter Dunne, *Mr. Dooley in War and Peace* (Boston: Small, Maynard, 1899), 234–38.

21. "Dooley on the Jews," *Lake County Press,* Feb. 12, 1903, 3.

22. Ibid.

23. Quoted in Thomas Gossett, *Race: The History of an Idea* (Dallas: Southern Methodist University Press, 1963), 207.

24. "Some Ways in Which History Is Falsified," *Journal of the American-Irish Historical Society* 1 (1898): 82, 87.

25. Quoted in A. L. Todd, *Justice on Trial: The Case of Louis D. Brandeis* (New York: McGraw-Hill, 1964), 74.

26. Ibid., 189, 249.

27. Quoted in James McGurrin, *Bourke Cockran: A Free Lance in American Politics* (New York: Charles Scribner's Sons, 1948), 298, 320, 333.

28. Peter Wiernik, *History of the Jews of America: From the Period of the Discovery of the New World to Present Times* (New York: Jewish Press Publishing, 1912), 315.

29. David I. Walsh, "Our Debt and Duty to the Immigrant," *Jewish Advocate,* Mar. 13, 1919, 7.

30. "Annual Meeting of the Society," *Journal of the American-Irish Historical Society* 26 (1927): 271, 278.

31. "Thirty-First Annual Dinner of the American-Irish Historical Society," *Journal of the American-Irish Historical Society* 28 (1929–1930), 272.

32. "Addresses Delivered at the Twenty-Ninth Annual Dinner," *Journal of the American-Irish Historical Society* 26 (1927), 303.

33. Harry S. Linfield, "A Survey of the Year 5682," *American Jewish Year Book,* vol. 24 (1922–1923), 94.

34. Quoted in Mark Paul Richards, *Not a Catholic Nation: The Ku Klux*

Klan Confronts New England in the 1920s (Amherst: University of Massachusetts Press, 2015), 180–81, 197.

35. Quoted in Christopher J. Kauffman, *Patriotism and Fraternalism in the Knights of Columbus: A History of the Fourth Degree* (New York: Crossroads Publishing, 2001), 284–85.

36. George Cohen, *The Jews in the Making of America* (Boston: Stratford, 1924), 27–28.

37. Hugh Hastings, "Irish Stars in the Archives of New York Province," *Journal of the American-Irish Historical Society* 9 (1910): 158, 356.

38. "Minutes of Annual Meeting," *Journal of the American-Irish Historical Society* 19 (1920): 27–52.

3. The Gatekeepers of American Urban Politics and the Jews Who Entered

1. D. M. Hermalin, "The Roumanian Jews in America," *American Jewish Year Book,* vol. 3 (1901–1902), 96.

2. Theodore H. White, *In Search of History: A Personal Adventure* (New York: Harper & Row, 1978), 20.

3. Quoted in Meaghan Dwyer-Ryan, "Ethnic Patriotism: Boston's Irish and Jewish Communities, 1880–1929" (PhD diss., Boston College, 2010), 94.

4. Nat Hentoff, *Boston Boy: Growing Up with Jazz and Other Rebellious Passions* (Philadelphia: Paul Dry Books, 2001), 104.

5. Quoted in Lawrence J. McCaffrey, "Irish American Politics: Power with or Without Purpose?" in P. J. Drudy, *The Irish in America: Emigration, Assimilation and Impact* (Cambridge: Cambridge University Press, 1985), 171, 175.

6. Robert A. Woods, *The City Wilderness: A Settlement Study* (Boston: Houghton, Mifflin, 1898), 135.

7. Eddie Cantor as told to David Freeman, *My Life Is in Your Hands* (New York: Harper and Brothers, 1928), 44–45.

8. Harry Golden, *The Right Time: An Autobiography* (New York: Putnam, 1969), 104.

9. Quoted in "Memorial Addresses Delivered in the House of Representatives of the United States in Memory of Daniel J. Riordan, Late a Representative from New York, Sixty-Eighth Congress," May 4, 1924 (Washington: Government Printing Office, 1925), 27, https://babel.hathitrust.org/cgi/pt?id=mdp.39015070224400&seq=11.

10. Quoted in Terry Golway, *Machine Made: Tammany Hall and the Creation of Modern America* (New York: Liveright Publishing, 2014), 155.

11. John Daniels, *America via the Neighborhood* (New York: Harper and Brothers, 1920), 297.

12. Quoted in Batya Miller, "Enforcement of Sunday Closing Laws on the Lower East Side, 1882–1903," *American Jewish History* 91, no. 2 (June 2003): 279.

13. *Jewish South,* August 27, 1897; "Chicago, Ill.," *American Hebrew,* Aug. 20, 1897, 455.

14. John F. Ahearn Papers, 1904–1909, Scrapbooks, MS 3074, New York Historical Society.

15. Michael Gold, *Jews Without Money* (New York: H. Liveright, 1930), 207–8.

16. *American Jewish Year Book,* vol. 9 (1907–1908), 509.

17. Quoted in John T. Galvin, "Patrick J McGuire: Boston's Last Democratic Boss," *New England Quarterly* 55, no. 3 (September 1982): 392–415.

18. Quoted in Steven P. Erie, *Rainbow's End: Irish-Americans and the Dilemmas of Urban Machine Politics, 1840–1985* (Berkeley: University of California Press, 1988), 103.

19. Ibid., 86.

20. Rocco Corresca, "Biography of a Bootblack," *Independent* 54 (1902), 67.

21. Golden, *The Right Time,* 84.

22. Quoted in Arthur M. Silver, "Jews in the Political Life of New York City, 1865–1897" (PhD diss., Yeshiva University, 1954), 109.

23. Quoted in Peri E. Arnold, "Immigrants to Urban Machines? The Case of Jacob Arvey and Chicago's 24th Ward," *Journal of Policy History* 25, no. 4 (2013): 472.

24. White, *In Search of History,* 20.

4. Learning for Bread and Roses

1. Quoted in Barbara Wertheimer, *We Were There: The Story of Working Women in America* (New York: Pantheon Books, 1977), 277–78.

2. Margaret Hinchey, "Thirty Days," *Life and Labor* 3, no. 9 (1913): 264–65.

3. Robert L. Reid, ed., *Battleground: The Autobiography of Margaret Haley* (Champaign: University of Illinois Press, 1982), 167–69.

4. "Jacob Loeb Pays Compliments to Teachers' Federation Heads," *Sentinel* (July 23, 1915), 3.

5. Bernard Weinstein, *The Jewish Unions in America: Pages of History and Memory,* trans. Maurice Wolfthal (New York: Jewish Labor Committee, 1957), 181, https://doi.org/10.11647/OBP.0118.

6. Ibid., 250–51.

7. Theresa Malkiel, *Diary of a Shirtwaist Striker,* 2nd ed. (New York: The Co-operative Press, 1910), 29.

8. Moses Rischin, *The Promised City: New York's Jews, 1870–1918* (Cambridge, MA: Harvard University Press, 1962), 180.

9. Abraham Bisno, "Chicago," in Charles Bernheimer, ed., *The Russian Jew in the United States: Studies of Social Conditions in New York, Philadelphia, and Chicago, with a Description of Rural Settlements* (Philadelphia; J. C. Winston, 1905), 135.

10. Morris Hillquit, *Loose Leaves from a Busy Life* (New York: McMillan, 1934), 28–29.

11. Abraham Bisno, *Union Pioneer: An Autobiographical Account of Bisno's Early Life and the Beginnings of Unionism in the Women's Garment Industry* (Madison: University of Wisconsin Press, 1967), 227.

12. See Jacob Rader Marcus, ed., *The Jewish Woman in America: A Documentary History* (Cincinnati: KTAV, 1981), 568–70, for the full text of Lemlich's speech.

13. Ibid.

14. Quoted in Nancy Schrom Dye, "Creating a Feminist Alliance: Sisterhood and Class Conflict in the New York Women's Trade Union League, 1903–1914," *Feminist Studies* 2, no. 2/3 (Fall 1975): 35.

15. Quoted in Annelise Orleck, *Common Sense and a Little Fire: Women and Working-Class Politics in the United States, 1900–1965* (Chapel Hill: University of North Carolina Press, 1995), 164, 301.

16. Quoted in Hasia R. Diner, *In the Almost Promised Land: American Jews and Blacks, 1915–1935* (Baltimore: Johns Hopkins University Press, 1992), 202.

17. *Pins and Needles,* Internet Broadway Database.

18. Quoted in Philippa Strum, "The Legacy of Labor Organizer, Mary Kenney on Louis Dembitz Brandeis, People's Attorney," *American Jewish History* 81, no. 3 (Spring 1995): 412.

19. Quoted in Allon Gal, *Brandeis of Boston* (Cambridge, MA: Harvard University Press, 1980), 64.

20. Agnes Nestor, *Woman's Labor Leader: An Autobiography* (Rockford, IL: Bellevue Books, 1954), 127, 130–31.

21. Ibid., 247.

22. Malkiel, *Diary of a Shirtwaist Striker,* 31–32.

23. Quoted in Dye, "Creating a Feminist Alliance," 28–29.

24. Quoted in Lara Vapnek, *Breadwinners: Working Women and Economic Independence, 1865–1920* (Urbana: University of Illinois Press, 2009), 140.

25. Quoted in Orleck, *Common Sense,* 72.

26. Ibid., 305.

27. Quoted in Lois Scharf, "The Great Uprising in Cleveland: When Sisterhood Failed," in *A Needle, a Bobbin, a Strike: Women Needle Workers in America,* ed. Joan M. Jensen and Sue Davidson (Philadelphia: Temple University Press, 1984), 163.

28. Nestor, *Woman's Labor Leader,* 105–9.
29. Rose Schneiderman, *Life and Labor* 2 (Sept. 1912): 288.
30. Orleck, *Common Sense,* 96.

5. Classroom Lessons

1. Quoted in Ruth Jacknow Markowitz, *My Daughter, the Teacher: Jewish Teachers in the New York City Schools* (New Brunswick, NJ: Rutgers University Press, 1993), 33.
2. Harold Riegelman, "The New Philanthropist," *Menorah Journal* 3, no. 1 (Feb. 1917): 24–30.
3. Quoted in Stephan F. Brumberg, *Going to America, Going to School: The Jewish Immigrant Public School Encounter in Turn-of-the-Century New York City* (New York: Praeger, 1986), 126.
4. Hasia R. Diner, *Erin's Daughters in America: Irish Immigrant Women in the Nineteenth Century* (Baltimore: Johns Hopkins University Press, 1983), 58–59.
5. Quoted in ibid.
6. Quoted in Claris Edwin Silcox and Galen M. Fisher, *Catholics, Jews and Protestants: A Study of Relationships in the United States and Canada* (New York: Harper and Brothers, 1934), 188.
7. E. A. Ross, *The Old World in the New: The Significance of Past and Present Immigration to the American People* (New York: Century, 1914), 41.
8. Thomas Edward Shields, *The Education of Our Girls* (New York: Benziger, 1907), 42.
9. Herbert N. Casson, "The Irish in America," *Journal of the American-Irish Historical Society* 7 (1907): 87, 90.
10. Quoted in Charles Beard, *The Rise of American Civilization,* vol. 3 (New York: Macmillan, 1942), 399–400.
11. Thomas Beer, *The Mauve Decade: American Lives at the End of the Nineteenth Century* (New York: Alfred A Knopf, 1962), 145.
12. Quoted in Janet Nolan, *Servants of the Poor* (Notre Dame, IN: University of Notre Dame Press, 2004), 92.
13. Ibid.
14. David Blaustein, *Memoirs of David Blaustein: Educator and Communal Worker* (New York: McBride, Nast, 1913), 60.
15. Sherry Gorelick, *City College and the Jewish Poor* (New Brunswick, NJ: Rutgers University Press, 1981); Stephen Steinberg, *The Ethnic Myth: Race, Ethnicity and Class in America* (New York: Atheneum, 1981).
16. J. K. Paulding, "Educational Influences: (A) New York," in Charles Bernheimer, *The Russian Jew in the United States* (Philadelphia: John C. Winston, 1905), 186.

17. Mordecai Soltes, *The Yiddish Press: An Americanizing Agency* (New York: Teachers College, Columbia University, 1950), 23.

18. *Reports of the Industrial Commission on Immigration and Education,* vol. XV (Washington, DC: GPO, 1901), 478.

19. Pauline Young, "The Reorganization of Jewish Family Life in America," *Social Forces* 8 (Dec. 1928): 243.

20. Nat Hentoff, *Boston Boy: Growing Up with Jazz and Other Rebellious Passions* (Philadelphia: Paul Dry Books, 2001), 13–14.

21. Theodore H. White, *In Search of History: A Personal Adventure* (New York: Harper & Row, 1978), 20, 30.

22. Harry Golden, *The Right Time: An Autobiography* (New York: Putnam, 1969), 30, 45–46, 49, 50, 88.

23. Michael Gold, *Jews Without Money* (New York: Liveright, 1930), 304.

24. Joseph Freeman, *An American Testament: A Narrative of Rebels and Romantics* (New York: Farrar & Rinehart, 1936), 19.

25. Ted Gostin, *Katziv Chronicles* (Los Angeles: Ted Gostin, 1991), 121.

26. Myra Kelly, *Little Citizens: The Humors of School Life* (New York: McClure, Phillips, 1904), 143.

27. I. George Dobsevage, "A List of Available Stories of Jewish Interest in English," *American Jewish Year Book,* vol. 8 (1906–1907), 137.

28. Myra Kelly, *Wards of Liberty* (New York: McClure, 1907), xii.

29. "Teachers Hear Frayne," *New York Times,* Mar. 11, 1916, 5.

30. Quoted in Irving Howe, *World of Our Fathers: The Journey of the East European Jews to America and the Life They Found and Made* (New York: Simon & Schuster, 1976), 279–80.

31. Harry Roskolenko, *When I Was Last on Cherry Street* (New York: Stein and Day, 1965), 70.

32. "Twenty-Eighth Annual Dinner of the Society," *Journal of the American-Irish Historical Society* 25 (1926): 286.

33. Quoted in Gerard N. Burrow, *The History of Yale's School of Medicine: Passing the Torch to Others* (New Haven, CT: Yale University Press, 2002), 107.

34. Heywood Broun and George Britt, *Christians Only: A Study in Prejudice* (New York: Vanguard Press, 1931), 99.

35. Claris Edwin Silcox and Galen M. Fisher, *Catholics, Jews and Protestants: A Study of Relationships in the United States and Canada* (New York: Harper and Brothers, 1934), v, 223.

36. Quoted in Rae Bielakowski, "'You Are in the World': Catholic Campus Life at Loyola University Chicago, Mundelein College, and De Paul University, 1924–1950" (PhD diss., Loyola University, 2009), 332.

37. Sheldon Kaplan, "A Jew at a Catholic College," *Ave Maria,* May 22, 1954, repr., *Catholic Digest,* July 1954, 109–12.

38. Jennifer Illuzzi and Arthur P. Urbano, "Sons of Providence: The Education and Integration of Jews at Providence College, 1917–1965," in *Rhode Island Jewish Historical Notes* 17, no. 3 (Nov. 2017): 529–57.

39. Ibid.

40. Robert J. Kaczosowski, *Fordham University School of Law: A History* (New York: Fordham University Press, 2012), 60.

41. My thanks here to Professor Suzie Pak for her notes drawn from the archives at Fordham University.

42. Quoted in Broun and Britt, *Christians Only*, 60.

43. Melvin Fagen, "The Status of Jewish Lawyers in New York City: A Preliminary Report on a Study Made by the Conference on Jewish Relations," *Jewish Social Studies* 1, no. 1 (1939): 93.

44. Paul O'Dwyer, *Counsel for the Defense: The Autobiography of Paul O'Dwyer* (New York: Simon & Schuster, 1979), 67.

45. Harold Cobin, "Democracy at St. John's," *St. John's Alumnus,* Mar. 1938, n.p.

46. Ibid.

47. Illuzzi and Urbano, "Sons of Providence," 529–57.

6. In the Face of Coughlin and Hitler, Still Standing Up for the Jews

1. "McKee's Article Written in 1915, Now Basis of Anti-Semitism Charge," *New York Times,* Oct. 17, 1933, 2.

2. Brian Hanley, "'No English Enemy . . . Ever Stooped so Low': Mike Quill, de Valera's Visit to the German Legation, and Irish-American Attitudes During World War II," *Radharc* 5, no. 7 (2004–2006): 245–60.

3. Quoted in Leonard Dinnerstein, *Anti-Semitism in America* (New York: Oxford University Press, 1994), 115.

4. Quoted in Garrison Nelson, *John William McCormack: A Political Biography* (New York: Bloomsbury Academic, 1978), 184.

5. Harry Schneiderman, "Review of the Year 5696," *American Jewish Year Book,* vol. 38 (1936–1937), 176–77.

6. Paul O'Dwyer, ed., *Beyond the Golden Door: William O'Dwyer* (Jamaica, NY: St. John's University Press, 1987), 149–52.

7. Quoted in Warren Grover, *Nazis in Newark* (New Brunswick, NJ: Transaction Publishers, 2003), 199, 236.

8. "Catholics in Fight Against Anti-Semitism," *New York Times,* June 12, 1939, 12: quoted in Mary Christine Athans, "Courtesy, Confrontation, Cooperation: Jewish-Christian/Catholic Relations in the United States," *U.S. Catholic Historian* 28, no. 2 (Spring 2010): 107–34.

9. Quoted in William E. Ellis, "Patrick Henry Callahan: A Maverick

Catholic and the Prohibition Issue," *Register of the Kentucky Historical Society* 92, no. 2 (Spring 1994): 175–99.

10. Daniel Boorstin, George Mayberry, and John Rackliffe, *Anti-Semitism: A Threat to Democracy* (Wakefield, MA: Rev. Theodore De Luca Pamphlet, 1939), 24.

11. Quoted in John Roy Carlson, *Under Cover: My Four Years in the Nazi Underworld of America* (New York: E. P. Dutton, 1943).

12. "Week by Week," *Commonweal,* Apr. 5, 1933, 620.

13. *Selected Address of Frank Murphy, Governor of Michigan, January 1, 1937, to September 30, 1938,* n.p., n.d., 69–81, https://babel.hathitrust .org/cgi/pt?id=mdp.35112104749165&seq=7.

14. Quoted in Leslie Tentler, *Seasons of Grace: A History of the Catholic Archdiocese of Detroit* (Detroit: Wayne State University Press, 1990), 336.

15. Quoted in Egal Feldman, *Catholics and Jews in Twentieth-Century America* (Urbana: University of Illinois Press, 2001), 63.

16. Quoted in Charles J. Tull, *Father Coughlin and the New Deal* (Syracuse, NY: Syracuse University Press, 1965), 91.

17. Quoted in Thomas H. O'Connor, *Boston Catholics: A History of the Church and Its People* (Boston: Northeastern University Press, 2019), 230.

18. Carlson, *Under Cover.*

19. Nat Hentoff, *Boston Boy: Growing Up with Jazz and Other Rebellious Passions* (Philadelphia: Paul Dry Books, 2001).

20. Quoted in Mary Christine Athans, *The Coughlin-Fahey Connection: Father Charles Coughlin, Father Dennis Fahey, C.S.Sp., and Religious Anti-Semitism in the United States, 1938–1954* (Maryknoll, NY: Orbis Books, 1991), 177.

21. Ibid.

22. Quoted in Moshe Gottlieb, "An American Controversy Over the Olympic Games," *American Jewish Historical Quarterly* 61, no. 3 (1972): 198.

23. Schneiderman, "Review of the Year 5696," 81–83.

24. "Rally to Defend America! Stop Hitler Now!" New-York Historical Society, broadsides, Dec. 11, 1941, https://bobcat.library.nyu.edu /permalink/f/5bhr3e/nyu_aleph001175121.

Conclusion

1. Quoted in Roger I. Abrams, "Constructing Baseball," *Cardozo Law Review* 23, no. 5 (Sept. 6, 2002): 1598, 1600.

INDEX

ABOUT THE AUTHOR

Shayne Leslie Figueroa

Hasia R. Diner is a professor emerita of American Jewish history, former chair of the Irish Studies Program, and former director of the Goldstein-Goren Center for American Jewish History at New York University. She has held Guggenheim and Fulbright fellowships and is the author of numerous books on Jewish and Irish histories in the United States, including the National Jewish Book Award–winning *We Remember with Reverence and Love*, which also earned the Saul Viener Prize for most outstanding book in American Jewish history, and the James Beard Award finalist *Hungering for America*.